"The psychotherapy culture war between prop cess-oriented approaches has gone on long enou_ in Counseling and Therapy, Peter Geiger shows us how to transcend this dichotomy. Any therapist, regardless of orientation, who seeks to be more effective will find much here to help them do so."

Derek Truscott, PhD, RPsych, professor of counselling psychology and director of counselling training, University of Alberta, Canada, author of *Becoming an Effective Psychotherapist*, co-author of *Ethics for the Practice of Psychology in Canada*

"No one has ever done this before. Peter Geiger impresses in finding intentional balance between the predominant paradigm of cognitive-behavioral therapy and historical and modern psychodynamic thought. Full of stimulating *and practical* theorizing, this book leads me to think differently and integrate my beliefs about therapy and counseling practice in a new, useful fashion. The sophisticated discussion of empathy and the place of a developmental orientation in therapy are persuasive and will make a significant difference to your client work."

Allen E. Ivey, EdD, ABPP, distinguished university professor (emeritus), University of Massachusetts, Amherst, USA, author of *Developmental Therapy,* co-author of *Developmental Counseling and Therapy*

"Thought-provoking and challenging, this book explores diverse theories of helping and distills the most critical elements of what makes a good therapist. Geiger invites readers to examine their own closely held beliefs and to consider ways in which skills can be developed throughout one's career. As one who works mostly from a 'doing' position, this book gives me a potent reminder of ways to stay connected to the feeling-sensing side of the therapeutic adventure."

Kathleen Minke, PhD, professor, School Psychology Program, University of Delaware, USA

"This is a 'must-have' book for all those interested in the challenging questions of what makes good therapy and what makes a good therapist. It is the very book I wished I had in setting out on my counselling career. Key theoretical underpinnings and therapist qualities informing clinical decision making are comprehensively contextualized and illustrated with case studies in an eloquent, narrative style."

Phillip T. Slee, PhD, professor in human development, Flinders University, Australia

"Venturing into largely unexplored territory, Peter Geiger makes explicit the reciprocity between goals and process in clinical work. This remarkable text opens up new vistas of understanding for clinicians and researchers and will be a treasured resource for years to come."

Irma Eloff, PhD, professor of educational psychology, University of Pretoria, South Africa

"In this thoughtful text, Peter Geiger invites the reader to reflect on the fundamental questions facing counselors and psychotherapists today. Whilst allowing us to remain faithful to our theoretical orientations, Geiger challenges us to question our theoretical parsing to become 'better therapists' for the sake of the clients we encounter in our daily work. This highly accessible yet theoretically incisive book is essential reading for psychotherapy trainers and trainees alike."

Maria Marchetti-Mercer, professor of psychology, University of the Witwatersrand, South Africa

"The focus is not on specific models and techniques but rather on the self of the therapist and the ability to achieve the right combination in goals and process as core factors in successful outcome. This book surely will help you become an effective therapist."

Frederick Ka Ching Yeung, PhD, principal lecturer, Department of Social Work and Social Administration, The University of Hong Kong

Geiger's practical guide to implementing evidence-based practice in psychology espouses incorporating relational methods, theories and interventions. His purposeful paradigm shift sets new standards for the education and training of psychotherapists, providing to both prospective and existing clinicians a road map for self-development and enhancing their praxis."

Gertina J. van Schalkwyk, PhD, associate professor of psychology, University of Macau

"This book has taught me much. Peter Geiger has a unique voice among teachers of counseling and therapy, invaluable for students and professors in psychology, counselor education, human services and the history of psychology theory."

Quan Chaolu, PhD, professor of psychology, Shandong Normal University, China, author of *Statistics for Psychology and Education*

"Engaging, informative, helpful and easy to understand, this book focuses on the therapist's self, clinical decision making and development. I highly recommend *Intentional Intervention* to clinicians and other helping professionals both emerging and experienced and concerned to balance goals and process in clinical work."

J. Scott Glass, PhD, chair, Department of Interdisciplinary Professions, East Carolina University, USA

INTENTIONAL INTERVENTION IN COUNSELING AND THERAPY

Intentional Intervention in Counseling and Therapy answers three questions: what heals in counseling and therapy and how? What actions in clinical decision making ensure an optimal outcome for the client? And why are some clinicians more successful than others, apparently remaining so over time? Incorporating citations across multiple disciplines, referencing authorities in both CBT and psychodynamic models, and interwoven with composite case material and session transcripts, this book unmasks the dialectic between goals and process in clinical work.

Peter Geiger is an educator, writer, and marriage and family therapist licensed in California. Between 2006 and 2013, he taught in the counseling psychology graduate program of the University of San Francisco. Geiger advises prelicensed and licensed clinicians on case conceptualization and countertransference. He is a consultant to and fellow of the Oxford Symposium in School-Based Family Counseling.

Intentional Intervention in Counseling and Therapy

Goals and process in client engagement

Peter Geiger

NEW YORK AND LONDON

First edition published 2018
by Routledge
711 Third Avenue, New York, NY 10017

and by Routledge
2 Park Square, Milton Park, Abingdon, Oxon, OX14 4RN

Routledge is an imprint of the Taylor & Francis Group, an informa business

© 2018 Peter Geiger

The right of Peter Geiger to be identified as the author of this work has been asserted by him in accordance with sections 77 and 78 of the Copyright, Designs and Patents Act 1988.

All rights reserved. No part of this book may be reprinted or reproduced or utilised in any form or by any electronic, mechanical, or other means, now known or hereafter invented, including photocopying and recording, or in any information storage or retrieval system, without permission in writing from the publishers.

Trademark notice: Product or corporate names may be trademarks or registered trademarks, and are used only for identification and explanation without intent to infringe.

Scripture quotations from The Authorized (King James) Version. Rights in the Authorized Version in the United Kingdom are vested in the Crown. Reproduced by permission of the Crown's patentee, Cambridge University Press.

Library of Congress Cataloging-in-Publication Data
Names: Geiger, Peter, 1950– author.
Title: Intentional intervention in counseling and therapy : goals and processes in client engagement / Peter Geiger.
Description: First edition. | New York : Routledge, 2017.
Identifiers: LCCN 2017002127 | ISBN 9780415789714 (hardcover : alk. paper) | ISBN 9780415789721 (pbk. : alk. paper) | ISBN 9781315202525 (e-book)
Subjects: MESH: Counseling—methods | Psychotherapy—methods | Professional-Patient Relations
Classification: LCC RC480.55 | NLM WM 55 | DDC 616.89/14—dc23
LC record available at https://lccn.loc.gov/2017002127

cover design by canizales.eu
rider and elephant illustrations by canizales.eu

ISBN: 978-0-415-78971-4 (hbk)
ISBN: 978-0-415-78972-1 (pbk)
ISBN: 978-1-315-20252-5 (ebk)

Typeset in Minion
by Apex CoVantage, LLC

Contents

Acknowledgements	ix
Preface	xi
The adroit clinician, neuroscience and the dialectic between goals and process	
Prologue	xxiii
Two theses in theory implementation • cognition and discourse in evidence, practice and outcome	

PART I
PHENOMENOLOGY OF CLINICAL DECISION MAKING   1

1 Theory   3
Observation and construction •
evolutionary aggregation and the developmental metamodel

2 Evidence   24
Physiological operationalization •
Empathy countertransference and practice-based evidence

3 Relationship   44
Mirroring and evolutionary theory •
the difference between counseling and therapy

4 Conceptualization   56
Client personality development and second-order change •
signal of the dialectic

5 Treatment   68
Pathology, adaptation, transference and transition •
the environmental call to let go

PART II
THE THERAPIST-SELF — 83

6 Synthesis — 85
Obviating the client's dilemma •
therapeutic communication •
the clinician's cardinal Archetypes

PART III
PHENOMENOLOGY OF CLINICIAN DEVELOPMENT — 115

7 Transition — 117
From good intentions to intentionality •
the beginning clinician and the Feeling-Sensing Style

8 Empathy — 125
Developing clinician emotional intelligence •
the *Einfühlung* group

9 Congruence — 145
Client negative affect and the low experiencing clinician •
neurobiology of upholding the dilemma

10 Unconditional positive regard — 162
Clinician susceptibility to client disavowal •
projective identification and the countertransference group

11 Intentionality — 173
Flow and the Good Therapist •
the final letting go of neediness

Epilogue — 185
Working hypothesis for intentional intervention •
implications for the education of clinicians

Appendix: What Is Your Preferred Style of Helping? — 189

Glossary — 195

Author Index — 201

Subject Index — 203

Acknowledgements

For Kevin

This book would not exist were it not for my father, Laci, who believed in developing the intellect and who taught me to think critically and for myself. It was my mother, Trude, who before World War II lived in Vienna not far from the Freuds, distant connections of her (then) husband, who taught me to feel and sense. My parents would be very proud of this book and of me.

This book would not exist were it not for Brian Gerrard, Emeritus Professor of the University of San Francisco, who realized I can be a good teacher and pulled strings to make it happen.

This book owes much to Michael Kahn, who died while it was being written, and is my exemplar in transference, countertransference and extension of Self.

Bill Glasser, who died shortly before I commenced writing, inspired both my teaching and thinking, and his wife Carleen has continued to provide encouragement.

The incomparable Allen Ivey, whose developmental counseling and therapy underpins this book, was the first person to read the first version of the manuscript and has been an unwavering advocate.

Judye Hess and Derek Truscott generously allowed me to bounce ideas off them.

My warm, admiring appreciation goes to Glenn Waller, Roger Hastings and Christine Padesky, each of whom was gracious enough to respond to an unsolicited email approach from me and to help me on my way.

Another Good Therapist, Tita José, circulated an early version of the manuscript among her students as a training tool.

Also proud of this book and of me is Harold Jimenez, who helped create in my life the conditions allowing it to come to fruition.

And perhaps the greatest and most fertile source of inspiration for this book has been my students. You taught me Good Education and Good Therapy. I owe you and the University of San Francisco an immense debt of gratitude.

Preface
The adroit clinician, neuroscience and the dialectic between goals and process

> Education of counselors and therapists and its outcome • academic program design and historical context • the "beautiful theory"—primacy and antagonism
>
> The phenomenon of the adroit clinician • academic, professional and personal qualities of the clinician • "therapist drift"
>
> **Dialectic between goals and process**
>
> Goals, doing and the Task Positive Brain
> Process, feeling and the Default Mode Network

"Do you know a good therapist?"

Prospective clients know the things counselors and therapists do—the techniques, processes and interventions we employ based on our knowledge and theory—are not always attended by desired results: *some* clinicians contrive to do therapy in a way leading to greater success.

This is expectable in the training environment. The learner, by definition, has not reached peak potential. Yet the differences persist beyond training. Some clinicians have full practices, some commanding high fees, and some do not. Some counselors and therapists (whether or not in private practice) seem to emanate such strength of purpose, competence and wisdom that other clinicians want to learn from them and be like them. Prospective clients want to be treated by them. *Do you know a good therapist* is a commonsense question.

Further questions are begged: *what makes a therapist "good"*? What actions does the good therapist do well, or better, what qualities does she manifest to better effect, and how are these actions and qualities coordinated to produce good outcome for the client? Our training institutions address these matters as best they may and with unease: where exactly is the dividing line between the formal academic and the personal? Knowledge of theory is clearly academic, while empathy is clearly a quality of the individual. Yet how are we to categorize the professional, nuanced deployment of empathy in furtherance of theory implementation? The cognitive and moral challenge is: to what extent are or should our academic programs be concerned with the personal attributes and development of beginning counselors and therapists as individual women and men?

In the absence of guidance from academic program directors, classroom instructors and fieldwork supervisors hesitate to intrude too far into the personal. Discussing the integration of "the developmental role of the educator with that of being the provider of support to the [trainee clinician]," Peter Hawkins and Robin Shohet, who train clinical supervisors at the Centre for Leadership and Team Development, Bath, find in the United Kingdom that "many supervisors can retreat from attempting this integration to just one of the roles,"[1] *abandoning the developmental role.*

The historical context of Hawkins' "retreat" is the lapse from pre-eminence of the psychoanalytic model, in which trainee analysts were required to undergo their own analysis, and the corresponding rise to dominance of the cognitive-behavioral model, which has reduced expectations in clinician personal development as an element in training. The consequence is apparent in many clinical fieldwork supervision groups. Discourse is inescapably confined to one of two broad types, reflecting the predominant theoretical stance of the program. If more goals-based (as defined on p. xiv), then the discourse is of adroitly choosing, timing and delivering interventions; and if more process-based, it is of adroitly feeling into a sense of what is really going on with the client. Across the theoretical spectrum the discourse in supervision groups is of beginning clinicians *displaying* adroitness, not *developing* it: the mechanisms underpinning and informing the salient personal quality of clinician adroitness—and its acquisition or augmentation—are at best insufficiently explored, at worst avoided. Fortunately the vast majority of beginning counselors and therapists do indeed expand in capacity and skill during fieldwork, and it is understandable that many of our training programs leave it there.

Yet all too often, after the fieldwork courses are completed and at graduation, essential and troubling differences remain. The less adroit beginning clinician has not managed to catch up with his more clinically successful peers. In the United States counseling psychology professors Bruce Wampold of the University of Wisconsin–Madison and Zac Imel of the University of Utah hold:

> Therapists vary in their effectiveness: some therapists consistently achieve better outcomes with their clients than do other therapists. . . . Therapists do not get better with time or experience. That is, over the course of their professional careers, on average, it appears that therapists do not improve, if by improvement we mean "achieve better outcomes."[2]

---

1 Hawkins, P. and Shohet, R. (2012). *Supervision in the Helping Professions.* Maidenhead, UK: Open University Press (McGraw-Hill), fourth edition
2 Wampold, B. E. and Imel, Z. E. (2015). What Do We Know About Psychotherapy and What Is There Left to Debate? *Accessed via* http://societyforpsychotherapy.org/what-do-we-know-about-psychotherapy-and-what-is-there-left-to-debate/

The questions persist. University of Scranton psychologist John Norcross and University of Utah psychologist Michael Lambert have sought to map the influence of clinician personal qualities on client case outcome, concluding: "the therapy relationship (in addition to the treatment method) is crucial to outcome, that it can be improved by certain therapist contributions and that it can be tailored to the individual patient."[3] The clinician's ability to manifest such "contributions" is perceived to be more a personal than a professional quality or facet of theory: via a skillful and flexible use of Self, the clinician is able to sift through all available data to pick out just the right response at just the right time, to greater clinical success.

The problem of the less adroit clinician is evident. Yet, as a field, we look the other way. There is perhaps nothing to be done. We do not wish to stigmatize our students, colleagues and friends. Or to expose our nagging doubt that, just possibly, we might have done better with this client—*or that a more adroit clinician might have succeeded*. We can rationalize away the disparities in outcomes. Not every alcoholic can be freed of his maladaptive behaviors, we perhaps tell ourselves, and not every unhappy marriage can be mended.

Other rationalizations blame the client: some clients, we hear some clinicians say, are not ready to do the work. This incomplete formulation is a deflection of responsibility. It is more accurate to say that all clients are resistant, and there is good reason for this to be so. It is the clinician's task to overcome the resistance. And now come formulations closer to the inconvenient truth: there was a set or sequence of interventions we didn't choose for this client and which, had we chosen it, might have tipped the scales. *This client needed more from us than we could deliver* is what clinicians tell ourselves when we are being honest about our failures.

The commonsense question is now reframed: *do you know a therapist who can deliver what it is the client needs and when*? Who knows what the client needs and when; or who is able to figure it out and get there while there is still time? We see here the emergence of a critical focus on case conceptualization, clinical decision making and treatment planning. We need a frame of reference for why some clients reject some perfectly good interventions and why some clinicians are able to choose a set or sequence of interventions leading to a good outcome for a difficult case. We need to understand—and be able to teach—what makes counselors and therapists "good" clinicians who rise to the clinical challenge and deliver what the client needs *even where it is not at first clear that we can*.

This book offers a definitive set of principles for understanding the phenomenon of the adroit clinician who contrives to do her interventions *intentionally*. Its thesis is offered to clinicians across all disciplines in which counseling and therapy is done, including clinical and counseling psychology, marriage and family therapy, social work and psychiatry. The principles informing intentional intervention pertain to each unique local context for and apply across the spectrum of theories in counseling and therapy.

---

3 Norcross, J. C. and Lambert, M. J. (2011). Evidence-based therapy relationships. *In* Norcross, J. C. (Ed.), *Psychotherapy Relationships that Work: Evidence-Based Responsiveness*. Oxford: Oxford University Press, second edition, p. 18

While this book necessarily comments on theory, it does not require readers to change theoretical identity, rather inviting you to look deeper within your theory.

Do you know a good therapist—and does she practice CBT? Our context is the rise to prominence in North America and elsewhere over the past four decades of the family of interventions and strategies together known as cognitive-behavioral therapy (CBT) and the concept, most often associated with it, of evidence-based practice in psychology (EBPP). Originating in the United States, CBT is a creative, active, goals-based therapy of *doing*, its protocols involving established sequences of testing, forms-filling and prescribed in-session and "homework" activities. The expression "goals-based" as used in this book describes interventions that are *directly and obviously* designed to combat the client's problem. Examples of goals-based interventions are *desensitization*, which directly tackles a phobia, and *affirmation*, which directly counters negative self-view. Table 1.1 shows an illustrative partial list of interventions categorized as "more goals-based" and "more process-based."

The characteristics of CBT allow the model to be replicated, manualized and therefore studied to a greater extent than prior clinical methods. Alongside the wide uptake of CBT, the research literature has mushroomed, finding overwhelming concrete evidence of the model's efficacy in treating an extensive cross-section of client presentations. No therapy has been demonstrated to be of so much help to so many people, and the evidential literature has convinced an entire generation of clinicians and researchers of the primacy of *doing* and *goals* in clinical work. CBT has proved highly popular with clients, clinicians, educators, insurers and public policymakers.

Defined against CBT, other forms of counseling and therapy involve fewer prescribed sequences and are characterized less by goals and *doing* and more by "process" and *feeling*. The expression "process-based" as used in this book describes interventions that combat the client's problem in a *more indirect* fashion and focusing on phenomena *underlying and paralleling* the problem. Transference

TABLE 1.1 Examples of more goals-based and more process-based interventions

Interventions in counseling and therapy	
More goals-based	**More process-based**
via altering behaviors/cognitions	via altering experience of self
psychoeducation	*active listening* (Rogers)
normalizing	*Mirroring* (Kohut)
desensitization	*interpretation* (Freud)
role-play	*Focusing* (Gendlin)
decatastrophizing	*transference work*

work, in which the focus is the relationship between client and clinician, is an example of a more process-based intervention:

CLIENT: I have problems with anger.
THERAPIST: Are you perhaps also angry with me?

The clinician has assessed the origins of the anger and believes an exploration of the relationship is a prerequisite to the client's overcoming it.

In more process-based ways of working, instead of the emphasis on *changing* maladaptive cognitions, there is an emphasis on *understanding* them, thereby developing ways for *moving beyond* the problem. Yet models of counseling and therapy are not pure, and all clinicians employ methods common to or borrowed from a variety of models: it would be strange to try to change a client's cognition if one does not also understand it; and changing the cognition is clearly the ultimate goal of seeking to understand it. Clinicians' techniques, processes and interventions, therefore, are located on a continuum, being either *more* or *less* characterized by goals and doing and, at the other pole, process and feeling.

This single observation and principle is both guiding light and point of departure to our investigation.

Many stakeholders now define and evaluate methods of counseling and therapy against CBT. This has provoked a defensive response in some clinicians not espousing it as their primary model. While CBT protocols, they concede, appear to have some efficacy, it is hard to determine whether the benefits flow from the protocols or from Norcross' therapist contributions. Then again, the antagonists continue, outcome studies often focus upon minor and short-term beneficial effects of treatment: over the medium to long-term CBT methods underperform. These salvos in what Norcross calls the "psychotherapy culture wars" between CBT loyalists and antagonists are for us further indication that the question *Do you know a good therapist* is a reasonable one: clients and clinicians alike know it to be true that some counselors and therapists (some of whom may or may not be CBT clinicians) do their techniques, processes and interventions more adroitly and attended by greater success.

But it is false to construe the culture wars as an ideological contest between competing theories of counseling and therapy. It is humans, not theories, who compete. The contest is rather one of competing clinician preferences. The universal tensions in the psychotherapy culture wars are between clinicians preferring to feel into an understanding of the client and those preferring to change the client with an active therapy of doing.

The two kinds of clinician behavioral orientation have their analogues within the discipline of neuroscience. Neuroinformatics researchers Marcus Raichle and Abraham Snyder of Washington University School of Medicine have observed that "certain areas of the brain consistently decrease activity when subjects engage in goal-directed tasks."[4] The current thinking proposes two distinct cortical networks in our brain, known as the Task Positive Brain (TPB) and the Default Mode Network (DMN). The TPB, according to Case Western Reserve University's Richard Boyatzis and colleagues, "is important for problem solving, focusing of attention, making decisions and control of action," while the DMN "plays a central role in emotional self-awareness, social cognition and ethical decision-making [and] is also strongly linked to creativity and openness to new ideas."[5] Boyatzis further speaks of "antagonism" and a "dialectical tension" between the TPB and DMN.

We know that when we are concentrating on (for example) writing an email we may not hear the doorbell. Similarly, in clinical work, when we are focusing on the client we may forget we have a cold. Very possibly we may extrapolate: when the clinician is focusing on her goals for her client, could it be she reduces her "openness to new ideas"? If so, might she miss something important—a client's subtle cue or signal? It is surely reasonable to ask not whether but *how* the ideas of Raichle, Boyatzis and their colleagues shed light on what clinicians do and on our ability to be adroit. The purpose of neuroscience research is not, of course, to correlate the clinician's increased goals-directedness with decreased process-directedness. Yet the existence of this continuum and dialectic in clinical practice and in our allegiance to clinical theory is clear.

The term *dialectic* is bequeathed us by the Athenian philosopher Plato. It implies steering a path between competing and equally valid claims: *sometimes* the best response to the angry client is a more goals-based anger management intervention; at other times the best response is to ask about his relationship with his father or discuss his response to the clinician. Adroitness, then, may be seen as the ability to know just when to choose, switch between or vary the mix of goals and process elements informing treatment. The adroit clinician *manages the dialectic between goals and process*. Table 1.2 shows an illustrative partial list of counseling and therapy models categorized as "more goals-based" and "more process-based."

TABLE 1.2 More goals-based and more process-based models of counseling and therapy

Different kinds of counseling and therapy	
More goals-based	**More process-based**
via altering behaviors/cognitions	via altering experience of self
behavioral	*psychoanalytic-psychodynamic*
cognitive	*Gestalt*
cognitive-behavioral	*person-centered*
Skinner, Beck, Ellis, Glasser, Meichenbaum, Krumboltz and others	*Freud, Perls, Rogers, Kohut, Klein, Mahler, Winnicott and others*

---

4 Raichle, M. E. and Snyder, A. Z. (2007). A default mode of brain function: A brief history of an evolving idea. *In* NeuroImage, Volume 37, pp. 1083–1090. *Accessed via* www.elsevier.com/locate/ynimg
5 Boyatzis, R. E., Rochford, K. and Jack, A. I. (2014). Antagonistic neural networks underlying differentiated leadership roles. *In* Frontiers in Human Neuroscience, 04 March 2014. *Accessed via* http://dx.doi.org/10.3389/fnhum.2014.00114

These are givens: clinicians' techniques, processes and interventions are located on a continuum, being either *more goals-based* or *more process-based*; models of counseling and therapy are not pure; and all clinicians employ methods common to or borrowed from a variety of models. The dialectical antagonism between the domains of goals and process is, with Boyatzis, equally a given. To deliver what the client needs, the clinician requires sufficient competencies in both process-based and goals-based methodologies: a lack in a particular area will make itself felt in client work.

David Burns, adjunct professor of psychiatry and behavioral sciences at Stanford University School of Medicine, writes of the discovery, prompted by concern for his patients and curiosity, that led to his *Hidden Emotion Technique*: when clients do not respond to CBT interventions it is because of "a hidden emotion or problem."[6] Burns was a biological psychiatrist and enthusiastic convert to the then-new CBT approach. His discovery, for himself and his patients, that clients experience things they do not or cannot tell us, is a perfect example of clinician adroitness. Identifying with the CBT model, and faced with a client making insufficient progress, Burns gave himself the freedom to increase use of process-based methods in *uncovering*. The resulting interpretation freed his patient from her panic attacks.

This book hopes to engage any therapist who wishes to become the best clinician she can be, *intervening intentionally* to a greater adroitness and greater success in client outcomes. If a (predominantly) process-based counselor and therapist with training in, for example, self psychology, she is aware that empathizing with client experience so as to build self-structure and thence adaptation and resilience is a process often uncomfortably dovetailed with necessary short-term clinical goals in, for example, substance and safety issues. How is she to find the sequence of clinical decisions most likely to lead to optimal outcome? The same question exercises the (predominantly) CBT clinician: she is aware that some clients have more difficulty following a prescribed sequence of interventions and are seemingly more interested in just talking. How is she to give the client what he needs while avoiding missteps?

This book, which is about *good* therapy, offers answers to these questions. Stolidly neutral in the culture wars, *Intentional Intervention* necessarily comments on CBT not because it is antagonistic to it but because CBT and the evidence-based hypothesis so thoroughly permeate the discourse. The comment of this book is that for the pioneers of CBT four decades ago the discourse was dominated by psychoanalysis and therefore the process thesis. That context allowed the pioneers to confine their teaching emphasis to goals-based techniques. But we may not assume the same mix holds good today.

Glenn Waller of the University of Sheffield, who teaches CBT and conducts research into efficacy and outcome, writes: "Even the most hardened cognitive-behavioural loyalist would have to concede that not all patients get better, even with CBT. It is important to consider the attributions that are made for these treatment failures."[7]

---

6 Burns, D. (2014). Living With the Devil We Know: We May Be Anxious, But Not to Change. *Accessed September 21st 2015 via www.psychotherapynetworker.org*
7 Waller, G. (2009). Evidence-based treatment and therapist drift. *In* Behaviour Research and Therapy, Volume 47, Issue 2, February, pp. 119–127

Waller attributes these "in so many cases" to "improper implementation" of the model because of *therapist drift*, of which "the common themes are: a failure to work Socratically; being driven by our own twisted thinking and emotions; and letting behavioural change shift off the agenda." When under pressure, Waller writes, CBT therapists may drift away from the treatment protocol into talking, in such a way as renders the therapy ineffective: clients do not get what they need.

But across the Atlantic, Jesse Owen of the University of Louisville and Mark Hilsenroth of Adelphi University commend what they term *adherence flexibility* in a study of therapist fidelity to key features in psychodynamic therapy, concluding that:

> The flexibility therapists demonstrate regarding the use of technique within a given treatment appears to be related to better outcomes across their caseload in relation to therapists who are less flexible with their interventions at the individual client level.[8]

What Waller and Owen are observing in their respective localities is the phenomenon of the dialectic. The message is mixed. In the case of the CBT clinicians studied by Waller the process (talking) emerges to supplant the goals (protocol adherence). For Waller, who studies therapists treating patients with eating disorders, a population for whom therapist drift into process may increase risk unacceptably, model adherence is key. For Owen's psychodynamic therapists the reverse is true:

> integration and an assimilative use of cognitive-behavioral techniques within a psychodynamic framework can indicate an important responsiveness that may lead to beneficial treatment process and outcomes.[9]

Different clients at different times need a different mix of process-based and goals-based interventions. The discourse in Owen's study is of *embracing* the dialectic between goals and process in counseling and therapy: psychodynamic therapists do better in "responsiveness" if they are able to assimilate CBT interventions into their work. Burns, a CBT clinician, expanded protocol to integrate psychodynamic talking. Equally understandably, and in contrast, Waller, whose own team of therapists is "probably the least drift-prone bunch around" is inclined to see adroitness in *resisting* the dialectic.

While adherence to a goals-based protocol seems a *priori* desirable, the American Psychological Association (APA), in its *Policy Statement on Evidence-Based Practice in Psychology*, appears to echo Owen in articulating an assimilative response to the dialectical tension in theory implementation by clinicians:

> The treating psychologist determines the applicability of research conclusions to a particular patient. Individual patients may require decisions and

---

[8] Owen, J. and Hilsenroth, M. J. (2014). Treatment adherence: The importance of therapist flexibility in relation to therapy outcomes. *In* Journal of Counseling Psychology, Volume 61, Issue 2, pp. 280–288
[9] *Ibid.*, p. 285

interventions not directly addressed by the available research. The application of research evidence to a given patient always involves probabilistic inferences. Therefore, ongoing monitoring of patient progress and adjustment of treatment as needed are essential to EBPP.[10]

Behind these nuanced enjoinders there is, as yet, no definitive agreement on or frame for the variables affecting model applicability and adjustment. Unless supervised by Waller, the clinician seeking adroitness is no closer to learning how to acquire it.

Intentional Intervention now fills these gaps. Our purpose is to improve client outcomes by helping less adroit beginning clinicians acquire and augment the capacity for adroit clinical decision making and become the equal of their more clinically successful peers. Examining how counselors and therapists (irrespective of theoretical orientation) make therapy either effective or ineffective gives a new lens: what determines Norcross' therapist contributions is a differentiated response, at the level of the individual clinician, to the domains of *doing* and *feeling*, goals and process, in counseling and psychotherapy. These different clinician behaviors determine whether an intervention is or is not "intentional" and thereby whether counselors and therapists can implement their interventions to greater success. The personal is key to the professional.

This book's constructive message is that good therapy can be delineated and the things good clinicians do, intervening intentionally, can be described, examined, experienced, verified, replicated and *learned* by student counselors and therapists pursuing purposeful professional self-development. Adroitness is achievable. *Intentional Intervention* is based on observable phenomena and logic, its conclusions supported by current thinking in both evolutionary science and neuroscience. Phenomenologically the practice of intentional intervention gives the client just what she needs, which is *just the right combination* of protocols and adjustments, counseling and therapy, goals and process, technique-based and relationship-based methods, theories and interventions.

Many books have been written on how to do counseling and therapy. Works by the authorities of the various theories and schools necessarily emphasize differences between models and thereby afford an incomplete perspective on the continuum of goals and process. And over the past century another theoretical thread has emerged in works looking for a unifying truth or metatheory underlying all the theories. This search is understandable. There are now, according to Derek Truscott of the University of Alberta, more than two hundred and fifty published ways of doing therapy.[11] We have to ask ourselves why.

Intentional Intervention does not add to the proliferation of theory. But it does explain why theory has proliferated: the number of combinations in goals and

---

10 American Psychological Association. *Accessed May 23rd 2015 via* www.apa.org/practice/guidelines/evidence-based-statement.aspx *drop-down tab* 'Clinical implications'
11 Truscott, D. (2010). *Becoming an Effective Psychotherapist: Adopting a Theory of Psychotherapy That's Right for You and Your Client.* Washington, DC: American Psychological Association

process needed by different clients is infinite. This book observes that all techniques, processes and interventions of counselors and therapists occur on the continuum and are either more goals-based or more process-based. *Intentional Intervention* combines this observation with the developmental model proposed by Allen Ivey of the University of Massachusetts thirty years ago in his book *Developmental Therapy* (1986). Ivey and co-authors refined and reiterated the model as *Developmental Counseling and Therapy: Promoting Wellness over the Lifespan* (2005). This book uses Ivey's developmental model and the dialectic between goals and process to illuminate clinical decision making and treatment planning—and the personal and professional development of clinicians.

Ivey introduced his developmental counseling and therapy (DCT) metamodel in the United States in the same decade in which CBT rose to dominance there. DCT requires of the clinician an additional, complex meta-level of study and assessment. These complexities limited uptake and, over the past three decades, many adroit professors and clinicians have experienced DCT as a valid, academically worthy but nonessential addition to our field's accumulated body of theory. And it is true that adroit practitioners need little help. But we also know, with Wampold, that their less adroit peers are stuck without recourse. *Intentional Intervention* now demonstrates the salience of DCT in investigating, framing and remedying the phenomenon of the maladroit practitioner.

From the perspective of raising the outcomes of less adroit clinicians to equal those of their peers, the lens provided by DCT is essential.

The reframing of counseling and psychotherapy as a dialectic between two divergent theses, goals and process (and, by extension, the two antagonistic neural networks in the clinician's brain), makes Norcross' therapist contributions as quantifiable and qualifiable as treatment protocols, giving the clinician both roadmap and gear-lever to help determine just how and just when to shift between goals and process, *doing* and *feeling*. Yet the task of acquiring adroitness—the ability to manage the dialectic so as to afford the client *just the right combination* in goals and process—is a developmental challenge for the prospective clinician. It may become apparent that the thing the client now needs from us is the thing we are not so well equipped to give. A clinician with insufficient self-preparation may implement her preferred treatment model imperfectly, as Waller notes; or her range of competency and comfort along the continuum of techniques, processes and interventions, which, with Owen, involve differing combinations of goals and process, may at times be insufficient to meet client need.

This book conclusively investigates what counseling and therapy is and how it heals. The singular verb "is" is appropriate because *counseling-and-therapy* is a unitary endeavor consisting of two distinct but inseparable clinician behaviors. At the same time we look at why clinicians are, it seems instinctively, drawn to certain theories and methods and averse to others; we will see that our ingrained preferences stem inevitably and understandably from our own developmental assets and insufficiencies as individuals and how we, each of us, respond to the inherent antagonism between our TPB and DMN. This book will advance and examine two propositions: that clinician theoretical preferences owe more to impulse than reason and that the clinician seeking greater success in meeting client need *must* respond by building capacity in the Self. Through this lens psychotherapy outcome variables and variables in therapist contributions are wholly explainable by identifiable attributes and specific capacities in the Self of the clinician—*which can be augmented in clinical training.*

This book now redefines the education of prospective counselors and therapists as a developmental endeavor that is the proper sphere of activity of the educator.

The phenomenological investigation allows a robustly utilitarian approach to theory. This book looks closely at how humans develop, grow and are healed psychologically, examining the many different things the many different clients need from the clinician so healing may occur. The investigation yields both a "theory on theory" and a new working hypothesis governing both psychosocial development and clinical practice that puts us all—counselors and therapists, their educators and their clients—on the same developmental continuum. The concept and frame of the dialectic between goals and process is applied to and tested against a range of combinations in client presentation, treatment modality and clinician training and preparedness. In each of these diverse situations the principles hold: *good* therapy gives the client just what she needs from the therapist's flexible, fluid, *intentional* management of the dialectic. The working hypothesis allows us to see that the Self of the clinician is also the clinician's primary instrument.

The risks are already clear to us, with Raichle: to the extent the therapist is engaged in a goals-directed task, she depresses activity in certain areas of the brain more suited, with Boyatzis, to emotional self-awareness, social cognition, ethical decision making, creativity and openness to new ideas. Goals depress process and, since process is integral to psychotherapy, the clinician will need to maintain a keen self-awareness of inner dialectical tension.

The concept of a dialectic—in this case that counseling and therapy is a kaleidoscopic dance between goals and process, both of which are of equal importance—is highly challenging and demands of us a particular way of thinking. But in the absence of this concept we are, collectively as a field, "flying blind." As Waller notes, echoing Owen:

> [Psycho]dynamic therapists tend to become more behavioural when faced with a complex case (defined by associated personality type), and CBT therapists tend to engage in more psychodynamic methods with such cases. These changes occur in the absence of any evidence that such pathology means that one should change therapeutic tack.[12]

---

12 Waller, G. (2009). *Op. cit.*

This book now proposes in resolution its set of principles for understanding the phenomena of adroit clinical decision making, its concept of the dialectic giving clinicians both rationale and frame for *intentionally choosing* to shift between behavioral (goals) and psychodynamic (process) methods to raise outcomes. The interface, noted by Waller, between client pathology and clinician self-preparedness is clarified. Although the concepts examined and the process of examination pose challenges, we must make the effort. When we master and harness the ambiguities we will become that adroit counselor and therapist whose techniques, processes and interventions are attended by greater success: we will have become the answer to the question, *Do you know a good therapist?*

Discussion

- *How do you understand the distinction between counseling and therapy that is "more process-based" or "more goals-based"? Do you like the terms offered? Are they, and the distinction, valid? Can you see any value in "reframing" counseling and therapy in this way?*
- *Does your academic program have a predominant theory or group of theories? To what extent are you personally drawn to these theories? Are you drawn to them because they are better and more efficacious than other theories? Or because you prefer a certain way of working with clients?*
- *In your experience as a beginning clinician, do you notice a difference among members of your cohort, class or supervision group? Are some of you "more adroit" as clinicians? Do you like the term "adroitness" or would you use a different expression? What are the factors combining to underpin the clinician's skill? What constructions do you place on your own performance as a beginning clinician?*
- *If some clinicians are indeed "more adroit" (or your preferred expression), do you have a sense of why this should be so? Is this ability or capacity a personal quality or a professional skill? Can it be taught—or developed—as a component of your academic program?*

Prologue
Two theses in theory implementation • cognition and discourse in evidence, practice and outcome

---

Outcomes and two studies • reification and adroitness • evidence-based practice in psychology

The goals thesis

A direct route to alleviating suffering

The relationship thesis

Feeling into an understanding of client experience

Dialectical tension in theory implementation • incongruity and the Socratic method • implications for clinician self-preparation

---

"... *and there is nothing new under the sun*"[1]

Having been, in the past thirty years in Northern California, successively a client, student, practitioner, adjunct professor and consultant in and of counseling and therapy, I wanted to codify all that I have learned in a book titled, simply, *Good Therapy*. It seemed to me that a Platonic Form—or Archetype—of Good Therapy exists, and I wanted to describe it for myself, my students and for anyone else interested. We know there are many different theories and schools of therapy. But, I wondered when I sat down to write, underpinning all these schools and theories, is there in the Athenian philosopher Plato's "transcendental realm of ideas" and in the Swiss psychoanalyst Carl Jung's "collective unconscious" such a thing as, simply, *good* therapy that we can recognize when it manifests in the therapy room—and irrespective of the practitioner's declared theoretical orientation?

The investigation was imposed by circumstance. Trained in self psychology, a variant in contemporary psychodynamics pioneered by Austrian American analyst Heinz Kohut, and also in family systems theory, my previous experience as a client having been with a cognitive therapist, I had been asked to teach in a graduate

---

[1] Ecclesiastes, 1:9

program with a predominantly cognitive-behavioral orientation. My students had just begun seeing clients. When we discussed their cases I was astounded by the profusion of techniques and interventions at their disposal and by their creativity and skill in choosing and using them. I also noticed that the discourse in discussing cases, clearly reflecting the students' prior training, was of adroitly choosing, timing and delivering "the right" intervention.

At times I noticed maladroitness in my students' accounts of their clinical work. A case springs immediately to mind. The client had run out of money for her child's medical needs. Instead of contacting her social worker for help, the client decided to take to the streets and "turn a couple of tricks" to earn the cash she needed. Her clinician, my student, was horrified: all her carefully chosen cognitive and behavioral interventions, informed by the goal of helping this mother turn her incoherent life around, were themselves made incoherent.

As I listened to the class discuss the case, thoughts arose in me culminating in a flash of inspiration: faced with the choice between contacting the agency social worker (who was preachy and superior and would surely judge her for running out of money) and, on the other hand, going down to the street corner to turn tricks, the client chose the path of least resistance. That she did what she did was, *for her*, within her frame of reference, a sign of resilience. She needed the money for her child, and turning tricks was a straightforward solution. I shared these thoughts with my class, who were polite but underwhelmed: they simply didn't see why I would make these comments.

These students had clearly not been trained in the same way I had to feel into an understanding of the client's real world.

This is how I became aware of profound differences, within Northern California, in the education and preparation of clinicians. Just as my psychodynamic program had not equipped me with the array of goals-directed techniques and interventions with which my students now routinely dazzled me, so their program, equally, had its gaps. The emphasis on identifying symptoms and strategies for treating them diverted the students from truly *listening* to the client and from *extending Self* to the client. I began to understand, experientially, the dialectical tension between the goals-based and process-based approaches to counseling and therapy.

The discourse of choosing the right intervention redirected attention from why a particular intervention didn't work, as well as from feeling into an understanding of underlying process. The student with the client who couldn't face her preachy social worker didn't seem to see why this phenomenon might be a relevant, even important consideration. Her job as clinician is to stop her client from doing maladaptive behaviors such as resorting to prostitution: how does it help the client for the clinician to concern herself with why such behaviors might, on that day for that client, be a manifestation of adaptiveness?

And that was the question to which I now had to find a compelling answer. It could not be a simple directive prescription to the student. Else I would have channeled San

Francisco clinical psychologist, educator and author Michael Kahn, my own supervisor. "Never lawyer the client" was Michael's catchphrase. We knew well what this meant. Before the client will interest herself in our way of looking at her situation, we must first demonstrate to her that we can understand her way of seeing things. This idea is not peculiar to self psychology—it is simply the observable reality of the clinical relationship. What my student needed was to experience this reality for herself.

Nor could I pronounce in open classroom that her client very likely finds my student to be as preachy and judgmental as the social worker. This idea is proprietary to Kohut's self psychology and psychoanalytic psychotherapy: if the client is telling her therapist she finds the social worker to be a certain way then the therapist *must* import into her case conceptualization the possibility that the client feels this way for her therapist and that feeling this way vis-à-vis significant authority figures is a prominent feature in the client's lived experience. This concept is useful because it explains the client's resistance to authority figures and—from the goals perspective, importantly—to their behavioral prescriptions. If the clinician in the case under discussion feels her good work with this client has been destroyed, the concept of the *transference* is helpful to steering the treatment to the point at which the client is now able to profit from the clinician's goals-based interventions. Seen in this light, concepts and techniques in process surely have their place, even in a program emphasizing goals.

Process was indeed being taught by my colleagues. But in our fast-paced, time-limited master's program the emphasis was on teaching theory-specific techniques and clinical "tools." The mix worked, on the whole, very well. The majority of students did not manifest the kind of maladroitness under discussion. They seemed to know instinctively that one does not lawyer the client and that it helps treatment if the clinician maintains awareness of how the client receives her messages.

The two kinds of students responded differently to me. The majority were open to exploring whether concepts from contemporary psychodynamics could assist them become more effective CBT or solutions-focused clinicians. These students were interested in my more analytical input to their cases and seemed able to integrate it into their thinking and practice. With the less adroit, less open student clinicians I had to work much harder. They felt, it seemed to me, that the methods and processes I had to teach them were *contaminating* their sense of how they wished to practice as clinicians. Thus I had stumbled into Norcross' culture wars, elsewhere described by Wampold and Imel as *The Great Psychotherapy Debate*.[2] As Norcross highlights it:

> The culture wars in psychotherapy dramatically pit the treatment method against the therapy relationship. Do treatments cure disorders or do relationships heal people? Which is the most accurate vision for practicing, researching and teaching psychotherapy?[3]

---

2 Wampold, B. E. and Imel, Z. E. (2015). *The Great Psychotherapy Debate*. New York, NY: Routledge
3 Norcross, J. C. and Lambert, M. J. (2011). Evidence-based therapy relationships. *In* Norcross, J. C. (Ed.), *Psychotherapy Relationships that Work: Evidence-Based Responsiveness*. Oxford: Oxford University Press, second edition, p. 3

This book is the distillation of my attempts to engage my less adroit students. I needed to awaken their interest in process and to reframe their experience of my teaching from contaminating their beautiful, goals-based theory to assisting them to manifest its beauty fully. In the course of this investigation I have come to understand why some counselors and therapists do their techniques, processes and interventions in a way attended by greater success and also why some clinicians feel so passionately and "dramatically" about the theory or theories we like and those we do not. The underlying reasons are the same, and they fuel the great debate and inform outcome disparities. The debate between methodology and relationship in counseling and therapy, and its lessons, are universal. Let us now observe the phenomena and assess them dispassionately.

We begin our quest for Good Therapy and to uplift the less adroit clinician with an overview of the discourse in the great psychotherapy debate. To continue using Platonic languaging, the two opposing ideas constitute "thesis" [Greek for "putting" or "placing," "position" or "argument"] and "antithesis" ["counterargument"]. On the one hand is the belief that clients are healed by and within the relationship with the therapist. The therapist's theory or method, according to this thesis, is of only incidental interest, for it is *therapists* who heal *people* and this healing occurs via an alchemy borne of interpersonal, relational elements in the therapeutic encounter. Certainly Wampold holds this view, saying: "Putting aside the debate about whether some treatments are more effective than others, it is clear that if there are differences among treatments, the differences are quite small."[4] In contrast the antithesis or opposing argument holds that the treatment modality is the primary determinant of outcome, for it is *treatments* that heal people of their *disorders*. Specific, replicable, *research-tested* treatment protocols for the specific ills of specific clients, performed in standardized ways by therapists having specific training and expertise. The personhood of the treating therapist and how it is applied in the relationship with the client is only of incidental interest.

The *relationship* thesis emphasizes *process*, specifically process in the therapeutic encounter. Process is everything that is going on psychologically in the encounter; it is, in particular, everything that is *not* being talked about overtly. To give an example: a heterosexual female client is sitting with a female clinician, talking about her problems with romantic relationships. This is the *content* of the discourse—what is being talked about. While she is speaking, the client looks at her therapist and sees (it may be) that she evidences wrinkles and other signs of aging; although the therapist's clothes are appropriately conservative, the client wonders if she can detect signs of sagging flesh underneath them; the client's eyes dart around the room, taking in further evidence. Is there a photograph of the therapist's husband or children? Does the therapist wear a wedding ring? How neat is the room? How does, the client wonders, all the while she is telling the therapist her story, the clinician herself

---

[4] Wampold, B. E. (2011) Qualities and Actions of Effective Therapists: Research Suggests that Certain Psychotherapist Characteristics Are Key to Successful Treatment. *Accessed August 21st 2016 via* www.apa.org/education/ce/effective-therapists.pdf

stack up in terms of *attractiveness* and problems/success in romantic relationships? Is she successful, is she still trying—or has she given up? Can this clinician, the client wonders, actually help her? Can she have anything useful to tell her about her problem? We see already in this brief, fantasized vignette that what is being *talked about overtly* is as the tip of the iceberg compared to the underlying cognitive-emotional process. We can infer that underlying process can cast a long shadow over what is being talked about, impacting outcome either positively or negatively. If I believe my therapist is saggy and wrinkled and has given up on trying to find a husband, then I am unlikely to put too much faith into listening to her ideas, since I am determined both to find a husband and to defy aging!

The relationship thesis is interested in the many interconnectednesses that bear upon the client's problem and contextualize it. She cannot seem to find the right man. Maybe she is over-concerned with appearance? Perhaps she has an underlying problem with intimacy? How will that manifest in the therapeutic encounter? In this approach the *considerations in process* and the belief in the *curative power of relationship* can, in the mind of the therapist, quickly eclipse considerations in goals: we have become quite carried away and almost forgotten our objectives in combatting the symptoms of anxiety and depression with which this woman came in.

Thus the relationship thesis looks beyond the content of the presenting narrative and seeks to heal the client by altering the client's experience of Self.

In contrast the *specific treatment* thesis emphasizes *content* and seeks to heal the client by *altering behaviors and cognitions*. The client is frustrated in her attempts to find a male romantic partner and wants concrete help with her feelings of frustration, loneliness and depression and to learn and try new ways of orienting herself to the search for a husband. She wants the therapist's active help in these endeavors. According to the goals-based approach, the client's depression is treated with specific techniques in cognitive-behavioral therapy, which the literature (evidence) suggests will most quickly succeed in combatting it. Concurrently the clinician will aim to teach the client new strategies to use in her partner search.

The specific treatment thesis rests upon two "reifications." A *reification* [Latin: res = "thing" and *facere* = "make"] is a complex human cognitive-emotional process, or series of such processes, which is reduced to or "made into" an abstract noun or thing, *which can then be discussed*. Reifications are everywhere and exceedingly useful. Every diagnosis is a reification. It is convenient to mental health professionals to speak of "bipolar disorder" or "a hypomanic episode." But these things do not really exist. What exists is a client who behaves and feels in a certain way and for reasons that are understandable to us if we can feel into them. When we reify—when we substitute an abstract noun or idea for authentic lived process—we necessarily look less closely at the underlying process, and we may in consequence miss something. The French political philosopher Louis Althusser cautions us to beware of "an ideology of reification that sees 'things' everywhere in human relations."[5] Reification, useful though it is in psychology to conceptualization, planning and professional communication, always imports risk of curtailment of understanding and compromised ability to choose.

The two reifications key to the specific treatment thesis are *goals* and *evidence*. Goals is a reification of *desire*—what we the stakeholders (client, clinician, environment) want to happen as a result of treatment. And in the single word, evidence, we encapsulate our complex cognitive-emotional constructions as to the specificity and efficacy of the interventions we will use to achieve the goals. It is immediately apparent that goals and evidence are so much more solid and *imminently useful* than relationship and process. The goals thesis appeals by being clear and of direct help. Who among us could argue against a goal—especially that of dissipating painful symptoms—and who would fly in the face of evidence? Surely we want to treat this woman's depression with interventions we know will work *before* we begin examining her problems with intimacy? Once we have done so, do we even need to work on intimacy? Is it not sufficient to alleviate the client's painful symptoms?

These questions, freshly visited and earnestly debated by each new class of beginning clinicians, are answerable only by the concept of intentionality as advanced in this book.

Goals and evidence are indeed indispensable. Promoting the goals thesis (and therefore, by the necessities imposed by our brain's biology, temporarily demoting process) is an everyday occurrence in counseling and therapy, often adroit, always permissible and sometimes mandatory. And it is also true that when we hold something too tightly it breaks. Reifying goals (almost) to the point of ideology is also, unfortunately, an everyday occurrence in consulting rooms, when our conceptualization of the clinical task at hand becomes too narrow and when we pursue a clinical goal too rigidly. Such was the case with my student and the client turning tricks to pay for medicine. The clinician's Task Positive Brain had become *enchanted* by the goals and turned the volume down on her Default Mode Network. Thus she failed to pick up on the client's cues and didn't notice she was going awry clinically. Her more adroit colleagues would have asked the client about the social worker's preachiness, thereby forestalling the events that took place.

When overly reifying one or both of goals and evidence, a clinician with ordinary good intentions becomes an instrument for unpredictability. To further investigate the principle of intentionality we return to our vignette: what might happen if the therapist decides to treat her romance-seeking client's depression without addressing either the hypothesis of the client's underlying problems with intimacy or the fact that the two women in this therapeutic relationship have very

---

5 Althusser, L. (Brewster, B. trans.) (1965–1969). *For Marx*. London: Allen Lane, Penguin Press, p. 230

different attitudes to personal appearance and partner-seeking? Perhaps this therapist is a first-year practicum student with a strong preference for the goals thesis and who has not been taught process-based methods. Or possibly she is a more seasoned practitioner, trained and competent in several methodologies, and, while recognizing the process issues, has nonetheless decided to focus exclusively on the presenting symptoms. Either version of our fantasized therapist in the vignette may decide—and here are the extreme reifications of goals and evidence—this case *is* about a woman whose depression *can* be relieved by specific techniques in cognitive restructuring, psychoeducation and role-play.

After several sessions the client's depression is reduced: she feels more hopeful and less frustrated and leaves therapy armed with new strategies for dating, deciding that from here her money is better spent on a facelift. Her intimacy issues are untreated and we cannot know whether her lessened depression and greater confidence will, in the medium-to-long term, make that much difference. If the facelift is attended by complications the client will feel worse off than before treatment; even if it is fully successful we should not be surprised if her intimacy issues later resurface. *Who this woman is has not changed, and the reduction in her depression achieved in treatment could very easily turn out to be temporary.* And we are here faced with our first cognitive challenge in our investigation of intentionality: do we think this outcome, the reduction in depression achieved in treatment, a "good" outcome or suboptimal? Did this client receive Good Therapy from an adroit clinician intervening intentionally? Does it make a difference to our answer if the facelift went wrong and she then hit the bottle—or if it was a resounding success and she married a millionaire?

The vignette and these projections are pure fantasy. Yet the questions arising are ones we must, in ethics, equip ourselves to answer. For they point to the constructions we place upon the *evidence-based hypothesis*. This hypothesis is not part of any theory of psychology, having been imported into psychology from medicine by (predominantly) CBT academics and researchers. The idea is simple and logical: if the clinician is up-to-date with the research evidence then she is in a position to minimize error in treatment selection. Evidence-based practice in psychology (EBPP), like its precursor, evidence-based medicine, is conceptualized as a "three-legged stool" resting on an integration of the best available research evidence, clinical judgment and expertise and client values and preferences.

In our vignette, the third leg of the stool, client values and preferences, appears at first sight to be sound. On discharge the client was happy with treatment outcome and ready to resume romantic pursuits in accordance with her values and preferences. However, as will be further demonstrated in the following chapters, client values and preferences in relation to counseling and therapy are to be mediated through clinical judgment and expertise and not reified at face value. This client could be described as "shallow." To the extent her values and preferences reflect the shallowness, is it right and does it profit her to base treatment upon them?

The second leg of the stool, the therapist's clinical judgment and expertise, also appears shaky: the better-trained version of the therapist disavowed her sense of the client's underlying intimacy issues, while the more junior clinician was not trained in uncovering and addressing them. When two legs of the stool turn out to be rotten, the primary leg, the research evidence of the efficacy of an intervention or treatment plan is, according to the tenets of the evidence-based hypothesis, insufficient to confirm the presence of EBPP, practiced according to APA guidelines.

Clinician deficiency in expertise and clinician reification in case conceptualization remove intentionality from clinical practice and void applicability of research evidence. We see, then, the problems in transferring the evidence-based hypothesis from the practice of medicine to the practice of psychology. These problems are not with the hypothesis itself, which is theoretically sound, but are entirely located within the cognitions of the treating clinician in response to client presentation.

It would be a mistake in logic to conclude that treatment has restored the client in the vignette to optimal functioning, that she is, to use the archaic psychoanalytic expression, "cured." The evidence before us is rather that she has been restored to an equilibrium by our treating her symptoms. But the client's post-treatment equilibrium is unstable, because of the presence of underlying characterological issues, just as it was before the onset of her depression (which followed the break-up of her recent relationship). The clinician practicing ethically is required to recognize these dynamics and to reflect upon the full spectrum of possibilities for outcome—short, medium and long term—of her client's treatment. Because full recognition and assessment is not necessarily possible at the outset, for reasons discussed in the following chapters, the clinician is required to remain vigilant to cues and clues yielded by the client as treatment unfolds. The clue's arrival is random:

CLIENT: I'm so grateful to you for our sessions. I feel fantastic. I'm ready to put myself out there and find my mate!
THERAPIST: That's wonderful!
CLIENT: I've decided this will be our last session. I'm saving up for a facelift.

At this point we wonder what thoughts and feelings are arising in the therapist. The client has announced impulsively that this is to be the last session and she is planning the facelift. Adroit counselors and therapists will see this as a decisive indicator that treatment is about to end prematurely, the work is not done and the apparent success will unravel. Properly decoded, such *countertransference ideation* is a particularly pertinent kind of evidence. But analysis, management and clinical use of countertransference, the salient component in clinical judgment and expertise, the crucial second leg of the EBPP stool, are not widely taught to students of counseling and therapy outside analytic programs. *What will the less adroit clinician make of what the client says*? We begin to grasp the dangers inherent in reification and encoded in the APA caution against over-reliance on probabilistic inferences.

Are we to conclude, then, that outcome is essentially a moving target? The conceptual difficulties have been harnessed by the CBT antagonists. University of Tennessee Psychiatrist David Allen is one of a number of voices insisting that research evidence is tainted by faulty cognitions in study design, saying:

> there are a nearly infinite number of factors which help to decide whether a course of a given type of psychotherapy will lead to a positive outcome, and there is simply no way to control for them all.[6]

Norcross acknowledges the concerns, asking (rhetorically), "How can we divide the indivisible complexity of psychotherapy outcome?"[7]

How the study authors design them and define and assess outcome is no secret. The issue, we are learning, is not with study design but with clinician maladroitness in *case conceptualization* and via probabilistic inferences. The *evidence* leg of the stool is perfectly sound—it is the *based* and *practice* legs that give way. But if client case conceptualization is not to be based on combatting maladaptive symptoms—on what, then, are we to base it? My student with the client who preferred prostitution over a visit to her social worker thought the case was about stopping undesired behaviors. Her Task Positive Brain's over-dominant goals-orientation prevented her from reflecting on how the client comes to be a woman of such exquisite sensitivity that she would prefer prostitution over the social worker. What if the case is more or as much about the sensitivity (or, in the vignette, the shallowness) and less (or as much) about the behaviors (or symptoms)? *Does the adroit clinician think as much in terms of treating personality as she does in terms of treating symptoms?*

In the following pages we will come to a full understanding of the developmental factors governing what we have termed clinician "adroitness" and "intervening intentionally." We will gain a sense of how the essential components of Good Therapy may be acquired and augmented in training. Without this teaching some of us may well under-serve our clients. We may mislead ourselves as to conceptualization, evidence and outcome, whether because of obstructive countertransference or because we have failed to grasp the complex hierarchy of client change. As the clinician treating the romance-seeking, shallow client in the vignette, we will, many of us, do perfectly good interventions, many or most of which will be followed by symptom reduction. But, for as long as we cannot decide if her reduced depression and enhanced ability in dating strategies is or is not a good outcome, we will be practicing unintentionally.

If the client achieves full adaptation to her life's circumstances or *second-order change* (a concept further elucidated on p. 64), it is clear treatment has been successful; if treatment does not prevent her suicide then it has clearly failed.

---

6 Allen, D. M. (2012). Why Psychotherapy Efficacy Studies Are Nearly Impossible: Scientifically-Valid Therapy Outcome Studies Are Devilishly Difficult to Design. *Accessed February 18th 2014 via* www.psychologytoday.com/blog/matter-personality/201212/why-psychotherapy-efficacy-studies-are-nearly-impossible
7 Norcross, J. C. and Lambert, M. J. (2011). *Op. cit.*, p. 11

In between there is a long and hazy continuum, including the *first-order change* afforded the romance-seeking client, as well as concepts such as "harm reduction" that imply considerable benefit but by no means a cure. Clearly we must understand the differences between these two kinds of change, first-order and second-order, and how they are brought about. Our task is to link all of these concepts into a coherent schema.

For now we may legitimately infer that goals and evidence best help the client if they are conceived and applied in a way that takes account of all those things in the big picture that in some way impinge upon their usefulness. "Conceived and applied" implies an open, two-way communication between the clinician's TPB and DMN. Burns liked to rely on his CBT protocol; but when he saw his client needed more, he allowed his DMN to guide him. Burns did not *over-rely* on his TPB. A less adroit clinician, more cut off from his DMN and therefore less *imaginative*, might have done differently and less well. So how do we find balance, make good use of the evidential literature and optimize outcomes? Can we develop a conceptual framework for the clinician to help her know when her DMN has become "too" depressed and her case conceptualization too reified and to use that knowledge to steer adroitly between goals and process?

We will apply a Socratic method to attempt to answer these questions. The Athenian philosopher Socrates was Plato's teacher and, arguably, the first cognitive therapist on record. Socrates' game, in which he mischievously delighted, was to ask a student what the student believes and then, via a series of carefully crafted questions, to expose *incongruities* in what the student is saying; eventually the student is brought by sheer force of internal logic to the point where he is obliged to recant his original statement, which he now sees is not able to be defended; he must instead look for a new formulation, a new languaging, for what he now has come to believe.

The process of testing belief against logic, thesis against antithesis, and steering a path between their competing claims is termed *dialectic* [Greek: *dia* = "through/across/apart/between" and *lego* = "pick out/read"]. The goal of dialectic is *synthesis* or "putting together" [Greek: *syn* = "with/together"]. In a synthesis *both* opposing theses turn out to be "right"—but only if they can find a way to take account of each other by picking out and putting together what fits and by eliminating or otherwise rising above the discrepancies. *It will be seen that the relationship between goals and process in counseling and psychotherapy, which either does or does not manifest over-reliance on one of them, is a dialectic.*

Humans are every day beset by conflicting theses and the need to fashion them into a synthesis in every area of our lives. A synthesis *always* demands of us more complex reasoning than did each of its underlying theses. The synthesis then becomes the new thesis—and then no doubt at some point a new antithesis arises and with it a new need for a new synthesis. A relatively simple example is the wife who is angry with her husband: should she leave him (thesis) or should she remain with him (antithesis)? The *conflict* in the dialectic causes her to *over-rely* alternately on each thesis, producing volatile behaviors attended by depression.

The synthesis most likely to be sought in therapy involves the wife developing the ability to communicate her displeasure to her husband; in this way she both "leaves" him, by asserting herself, and also can stay married to him, because she is asserting herself.

In terms of the great psychotherapy debate it is clear that, as a field, we have paid insufficient attention to the necessary dialectic in counseling and therapy between process and goals. The Socratic method focuses on identifying things that do not make complete sense, and it is here we have already begun. We have seen that a client may leave treatment apparently satisfied with its outcome but nevertheless fundamentally unchanged and very likely not equipped for stressors not only foreseeable but also foreseen by the therapist. We have, with Allen and the APA, begun to question our understanding of how outcome studies are to be used. Given the uncertainty, given Norcross' indivisible complexity of psychotherapy outcome and given the diffidence of academic programs to the phenomenon of the less adroit student, we have few bearings. But can we nonetheless feel our way, *experience* our way forward? Can we use our Socratic inquiry to construct a working hypothesis for understanding the endeavor we call, variously, either *counseling* or *psychotherapy*?

As Norcross recommends, let us: "Follow the evidence; follow what contributes to psychotherapy outcome."[8]

Our quest has purpose and urgency. Clinicians work with matters of Life and Death. Today's problem child may become tomorrow's loner gunman. Today's relapsed addict will be a drain on tomorrow's budget and may well be tomorrow's premature death. Today's revolving door client in perennial case management, today's suicide, today's chronically unhappy family are all yesterday's psychotherapy failures, and their unhappinesses serve to make their communities less secure. This being said, we do not need this book and this investigation if we think the outcomes of counseling and therapy—however we choose to assess them—are good enough and that variances or disappointments in outcome are not necessarily due to differences in clinician—our—adroitness.

Do you know a good therapist? To gain a sense of the magnitude of disparity in clinical outcome that contextualizes the question, let us summarize two studies. In 1995 Patrick Richardson and Paul Handal of Saint Louis University found that their sample:

> viewed psychotherapy or counseling as moderately effective and perceived psychotherapy/counseling to be effective for 26 to 50 percent of all cases. The perceived amount of time necessary for noticeable improvement in psychotherapy or counseling was approximately four months, and the expected necessary length of treatment was approximately eight months. Participants

---

8 *Ibid.*, p. 13

stated they were moderately willing to seek psychotherapy or counseling if they were to experience a mental problem, and reported discernible differences among the eight psychotherapy/counseling providers in terms of treatment efficacy. *Differences were also found in the relative perception of providers' personal/professional qualities and characteristics.* [PG's italics][9]

In other words, the cross-section sampled by Richardson found psychotherapy *not to be particularly effective* in 50% to 74% of cases.

In a 1993 study comparing the family therapy approaches of Georgetown University psychiatrist Murray Bowen and Californians systems theorist Jay Haley and social worker Virginia Satir, and measuring different variables, Joan Winter of the College of William and Mary found a yet more remarkable diversity in outcomes. The lowest score was Bowen—only 26.5% of client families completed treatment—and the highest, consistently over the three categories rated, was Satir: (5.1% drop-out rate, 93.7% client engagement and 88.8% completion of treatment).[10] *Do you know a good family therapist—and does she follow Satir?* The two studies confirm our sense that prospective clients of counselors and therapists have grounds to be cautious: counseling and therapy can be very well done and very effective, and it can equally be said that outcomes range widely and are therefore *uncertain*.

Wampold and Imel observe that variations in effectiveness are more between clinicians than between models. Overall, "Psychotherapy is remarkably effective," they believe, adding:

> The effects of psychotherapy are greater than the effects of many medical practices, including flu vaccines, most interventions in cardiology, and treatments for asthma, some of which are very expensive and have significant side effects. Psychotherapy is as effective as medication for most mental disorders, without the side effects. As well, psychotherapy is longer lasting than medications (i.e., lower relapse rates after treatment is discontinued) and is less resistant to additional courses of treatment.[11]

Wampold implies a greater across-the-board effectiveness than Richardson. For example, the United States Centers for Disease Control discloses that "vaccine reduces the risk of flu illness by about 50% to 60% among the overall population during seasons when most circulating flu viruses are like the vaccine viruses."[12]

---

9 Richardson, P. and Handal, P. (1995). The public's perception of psychotherapy and counseling: Differential views on the effectiveness of psychologists, psychiatrists, and other providers. *In* Journal of Contemporary Psychotherapy, Volume 25, Issue 4, Winter, pp. 367–385

10 Winter, J. E. (1993). *Selected Family Therapy Outcomes With Bowen, Haley and Satir.* Unpublished doctoral dissertation. Williamsburg, VA: The College of William and Mary (ERIC Document Reproduction Service)

11 Wampold, B. E. and Imel, Z. E. (2015). What Do We Know About Psychotherapy and What Is There Left to Debate? *Accessed via* http://societyforpsychotherapy.org/what-do-we-know-about-psychotherapy-and-what-is-there-left-to-debate/

12 *Accessed September 1st 2016 via* www.cdc.gov/flu/about/qa/vaccineeffect.htm

Yet there is a long way from "greater than" 50% to 60% effectiveness to the 88.8% completion of treatment in the case of Winter's Satirian therapists and the 97% success rate claimed for cataract operations. Wampold's "remarkably effective" still means many treatments do not succeed in giving the client what the client needs.

Norcross' and Wampold's interventions in the psychotherapy debate are our point of departure. Our goal is to help the less adroit clinician become the equal of his peers and thereby improve psychotherapy outcomes. To pursue it we must assemble a working hypothesis to link and make sense of all the questions posed. Our quest is to delineate and fully understand the nature of these certain therapist contributions that are "tailored to the individual patient" to improve the clinical relationship and treatment outcome. We will be looking to see whether and how the outcome variances in counseling and therapy are related to Richardson's clinician "personal/professional qualities and characteristics" and Norcross' "therapist contributions." We will want to form an opinion on what this may say about the qualities of clinician adroitness and intentionality and on whether Richardson's characteristics and Norcross' contributions can or cannot or should or should not be addressed in training. Following the evidence we may look again at our two studies, wondering quite why the Satirian family therapists scored so consistently highly and wondering to what extent this may be connected with the *training path and self-preparation* of therapists. As Harry Aponte and Joan Winter remark:

> Satir may be the figure in family therapy who made the development of the person of the therapist most central to her training. As she unequivocally stated: 'Our approach assumes that the therapist in his person is the chief tool for initiating change.' Her training efforts, conducted through the Satir Global Network, provided month-long residential programs for groups of therapists. . . . Designed to serve as a rebirth for the self, this process . . . [assisted] therapists in developing their own individual views and definition of self.[13]

What importance may we attach to this clue in the evidential chain? The clinicians having the most consistently good results in Winter's 1993 study were trained with a *specific emphasis on self-development*. Tita José of the University of Calgary, who supervises doctoral students, notes that student clinicians with social work training seem more adroit than students with training only in counseling psychology; she feels this is "because the training in social work encourages self-reflection."[14] We do not yet fully know what this means (or how feasible and costly this training in self-development or self-reflection may be), however we are inclined to see this correlation as an important one: our instinctual DMN has

---

13 Aponte, H. J. and Winter, J. E. (2013). The person and practice of the therapist: Treatment and training. *In* Baldwin, M. (Ed.), *The Use of Self in Therapy*. New York, NY and Hove, East Sussex: Routledge, p. 157
14 José, T. A. (2016). *Personal Communication*

already suggested to us that more self-development will likely help us better manage the antagonism between it and our TPB.

We have already begun to construct our working hypothesis. We will of necessity confine our investigation to two legs of the stool of EBPP. Since the two suspect legs of clinician contributions and client preferences are both process-based, our investigation is into process—the processes and dynamics underpinning intentional intervention. The goals-based and prior leg, that of the research evidence, is in and of itself (and with apologies to Allen) unassailable. To continue our journey we need *theory*. The expression comes from *theorein*, the ancient Greek verb meaning "look at." We need ways of looking at humans and our predicament that makes it *more possible* that we can be of more help to more people more often and more adroitly.

Since there is nothing new under the sun we must not expect, in our quest for Good Therapy and intentional intervention, to encounter novelty. Rather that we may need to *look again* at things we think we already know, in new ways and combinations of ways and making new connections.

Discussion

- *In terms of your "self-preparation," do you feel ready to serve clients in the role of counselor and therapist?*
- *How do you understand the variations in client case outcomes? Do you feel there is scope for improvement? If so, how likely is it that the path to improvement is through better understanding of the "dialectic between the goals thesis and the process thesis"?*
- *What constructions do you place on the expression "evidence-based practice in psychology"? Do you approve of using a "Socratic method" to deconstruct the "evidence-based hypothesis"? Will this help clinicians help clients?*
- *How do you understand the technical term "reification"? Why might it sometimes be very useful to "reify"? Is it true that reification by the counselor and therapist can be detrimental to client case outcome? What aspects of your client cases do you reify?*
- *In an anecdote a student clinician who was appalled by her client's behavior is presented as having a reified concept of her role as counselor and therapist: do you agree or disagree with this characterization? If you were treating this client, how would you proceed and why? If you were supervising the student in the anecdote, how would you proceed?*

Part I
Phenomenology of clinical decision making

1
Theory
Observation and construction • evolutionary aggregation and the developmental metamodel

> Theory, the clinician and "good" therapy • theory of the dialectic • theory as historically contextualized work-in-progress • theory and neuroscience
> **Metatheory of developmental counseling and therapy**
> (Dr. Allen Ivey)
> **The rider and the elephant** (Dr. Jonathan Haidt)
> Thesis, antithesis and synthesis • observable phenomena

Roads to Rome

The reification "theory" describes a constructed way of thinking about and *languaging* what has befallen the client and what it is we may seek to do about that. Through theory we find ways to understand people and conceptualize our many divergences. The first divergence concerning us is that each of us, educators and students alike, has an ingrained preference for treating the client either with an active therapy of doing, predominantly targeting symptoms, or, predominantly targeting personality, by means of feeling into an understanding of the client. We judge and draw from theory accordingly. In responding to theory we are reflexive and selective. It is therefore insufficient merely to describe or compare theory; it is necessary in addition, as Truscott urges, to consider and communicate our own personal interaction with and response to theory, including our conceptualization of how theory is brought to life and put to use in the therapy room for the benefit of our clients.[1] *And we must examine closely why we, each of us, dislike one or more theories.*

In our classrooms we teach the evolution of modern psychology theory from Austrian neurologist Sigmund Freud to the present day. The discourse is often of *progression*: older theories are dated and incomplete; newer is better, and newest is most useful to us. There is considerable truth to these ideas. Counseling and therapy is an essentially localized endeavor and, as times, context and locality change,

---

[1] Truscott, D. (2010). *Becoming an Effective Psychotherapist: Adopting a Theory of Psychotherapy that's Right for You and Your Client.* Washington, DC: American Psychological Association

so does demand for psychological services. As Bengali American philosopher Haridas Chaudhuri puts it, "Each culture and time produces its own answer to its own need."[2] Theory, then, evolves as *response to environmental challenge*.

Thus Freud, an educated, minority citizen of culturally prolific but politically fractured Central Europe, analyzed himself and took his insights into his work with his middle-class patients; his theory was a constant work-in-progress, built, dismantled, re-built, re-written, changed and refined over his long working life. George Washington University psychologist Robert Kramer traces Freud's influence through Austrian American psychoanalyst Otto Rank to University of Chicago psychologist Carl Rogers.[3] Almost fifty years junior to Freud, Rogers' observations in his work after World War II were of patients of an altogether different demographic. Each authority constantly shapes and re-shapes his theory and practice so that he can be of better use to his clients at the time and in context.

Theory on theory

Chaudhuri, whose integral philosophy teaches that "every action is succeeded by a counteraction of equal force,"[4] would not have been at all surprised by the responses in the second part of the twentieth century to Freudian theory. He would see it as entirely necessary, fitting and inevitable that the great man of cognitive theory, University of Pennsylvania psychiatrist Aaron Beck, trained in psychoanalysis, found the old to be incomplete, even misguided, and established an entirely new way of understanding emotional suffering and how we may seek to alleviate it, bequeathing us new languaging that has completely changed the discourse.

Yet we may not understand Chaudhuri's evolutionary pendulum swing to imply that the counteraction and new discourse void the preceding action. Psychoanalysis and its insights still exist. As discourse, time and context progress and evolve, the Good Therapy Archetype necessarily informs each manifestation of theory. This means that no theory is discardable and all are valuable. We may prefer Satir over Bowen. But Bowen was a great scholar and committed helper who wrote about things he saw and experienced passionately and who (correctly) believed his conceptualizations can help us. He must have had good reasons for his formulations, and if we pay attention to Bowen (though we feel more comfortable with Satir), we may learn something to assist our understanding and we may use that increment of learning to help a client. This is the discourse of theory progression and aggregation: Beck builds on and adds to Freud.

Such is the ideal synthesis. Yet there are problems in teaching and learning theory. The discourse of theory progression and synthetic aggregation yields easily to the discourse of supersession. It is apparent that the insights of the newest or newer theory or theories are most informed and most relevant to the times. Humans, as we shall go on further to explore, gravitate to certainty and lean toward extrapolation.

---

2 Chaudhuri, H. (1977–1989). *The Evolution of Integral Consciousness*. Wheaton, IL: Quest Books, paperback reprint: ISBN 0-8356-0494-2
3 Kramer, R. (1995). The birth of client-centered therapy: Carl Rogers, Otto Rank, and 'The Beyond'. *In* Journal of Humanistic Psychology, Volume 35, pp. 54–110
4 Chaudhuri, H. (1977–1989). *Op. cit.*

The process thesis also has its antagonists. In academic programs highlighting or emphasizing change tasks in therapies of doing, some of us will inevitably over-rely on half the story, that of treating symptoms: CBT *replaces* psychodynamic theory.

For Truscott, our theory antagonism, our liking or disliking for one or more theories, begs investigation. I may dislike a theory for a number of reasons. I do not fully understand it or do not myself possess or have not developed the skills to use it effectively. That theory and I are not a "fit." Perhaps the theory comes with unsettling memories: a clinician once used it on me, and it didn't feel comfortable or didn't work. Or perhaps its authorities write in technical languaging that is simply too difficult for me to read. Perhaps the theory comes with unpalatable ideas and associations pertaining to human nature, which my belief system rejects. *And I may also reject a theory because it requires more of me in either goals or process than I am in a position to give the client.*

Now we can begin to understand the origins of the polarization of cognition in the psychotherapy debate. Our theory partisanship is reflexive and *defensive* and comes from a position—this has to be the correct analysis of the countertransference—of fear and alienation. More crucially, our theory partisanship is not *useful*. Is it not rather more useful to the client if I ask myself the question: *what is it I do not see about this theory that the theory's authorities do see and how does it come about that they are able to use the method effectively and I am not?*

For surely the only "good" theory, the only theory of any interest, is the one we can use *now* to help *this* client. If, conversely, we are not right now succeeding in helping this client, perhaps we should broaden our scope and look past our fear and outside our comfort zone to master an alternate, ancillary theoretical stance that will improve our work? Surely we must, in ethics, do this, lest our theory partisanship become an obstructive countertransference. Once we add these ideas to our working hypothesis, the inescapable conclusion is that it is no longer good enough for us to say, "That theory is not for me." The risk of missing something of vital importance to our work with a client—even one client—is simply too great. Rather we must, with Truscott, "continuously revise and expand [our] personal theory by assimilating the rationale, goals and change tasks from other theories."[5]

The codification of new theory always involves new *languaging* describing what has befallen the client and what it is we may seek to do about that. New languaging always results from and confers new insights and may be striking. But often what is being talked about or emphasized in the new way is not, in and of itself, new. Thus, when we teach that Rogers postulated his three (as I call them) "essential therapist qualities" of *congruence*, *unconditional positive regard* and *empathy*, how do we intend our students to understand the significance of what they hear? In seeking to highlight Rogers' contribution to theory are we implying that therapists before his codification did not exhibit such qualities and therefore their work was necessarily inferior to Rogers'? Or do we believe that these earlier therapists did exhibit, must have exhibited the "Rogerian" qualities, perhaps languaging or positioning them differently in their theoretical writings, and that it is Rogers' positioning,

---

5 Truscott, D. (2010). *Op. cit.*, p. 172

emphasizing and languaging we feel has a clearer voice for us today, which is why we like to teach it? The question and distinction are significant in good education, the elimination of theory partisanship and to the pursuit of our quest.

Good theory

I am indebted to British psychiatrist Jeannette Josse for the construct of Good Therapy.[6] We were talking about *school-based family counseling and therapy* (SBFC&T), a then relatively unpublicized metamodel predicated upon the goal of school success. Jeannette asked me what the clinician does that makes it SBFC&T, as opposed to, say, school counseling, family therapy or school social work. I described these things and she said, "Oh. Good therapists have always done that." Indeed. University of San Francisco professor emeritus Brian Gerrard tells me he first made the formulation "school-based family counseling" in 1983 upon the launch of a new program in San Francisco Bay Area schools; the new program, he says, deserved new languaging.[7] The new languaging has, over time, afforded new theoretical insights, which is the great evolutionary benefit conferred by new reification; yet although the languaging is new the practitioners and proponents of SBFC&T, including University of British Columbia emeritus professor John Friesen, trace the model's lineage to Viennese physician-psychotherapist Alfred Adler.[8]

The things school-based family clinicians do predate the formulation.

Similarly, while Rogers codified, languaged and wrote extensively about congruence, unconditional positive regard and empathy, these essential therapist qualities existed at all times before Rogers and *independently of his theorizing*. Freud, in order to help his patients with Good Therapy, must have practiced and manifested these essential therapist qualities in his way: according to his last surviving patient, Margarethe Lutz, he was, in 1936, "fatherly, friendly, full of understanding. A friend. [*PG's translation of:* "väterlich, freundlich, verständnisvoll. Ein Freund."][9] And, as we shall see in the following chapter, Freud did indeed language these things and constellate them into his theoretical writings in his own way.

And so we can begin to look at our accumulated body of theory in a somewhat different fashion, perhaps making it easier for us to follow Truscott and Norcross in rising above the culture wars and the discourse of supersession. For theory is built in increments, each increment augmenting what has gone before. Each

---

6 Josse, J. (2004). *Personal Communication*
7 Gerrard, B. A. (2008). School-based family counseling: Overview, trends and recommendations for future research. *In* International Journal for School-Based Family Counseling, Volume 1/1. Accessed via www.schoolbasedfamilycounseling.com
8 Friesen, J. (2003). *In* Geiger, P. B., Carter, M. J. and Gerrard, B. A. (Eds.) (2005). *Proceedings of the 2003 Oxford Symposium in School-Based Family Counseling*. San Francisco, CA: Institute for School-Based Family Counseling
9 Lutz, M. (2009). *Interview* with Christine Dohler, SüddeutscheZeitung-Magazin, 13

authority draws from the Archetype of Good Therapy, which synthesizes goals and process, to build on pre-existing theory and seeks to describe and teach us those things he or she sees and which seem to her or to him to be either useful or important or both. Each successive theorist seeks to *redirect and refine our focus* and, in so doing, builds new *languaging*. As much as the new languaging may help our understanding, neither the new way of looking at the situation, nor the new theory nor the newly redirected and refined focus mean that the actions or intent behind or described by the languaging are new or that, importantly for our purposes in this argument, the new languaging, focus and theory are, necessarily for us, new shortcuts to or guarantors of Good Therapy. Or that we should view the old languaging of preceding theorists as "wrong." Should we not rather view each contribution to our aggregated theory as an auxiliary perspective or thesis, promising additional pertinent, potentially valuable information that we may be able to use to broaden our understanding and our clinical skills *now with this client*?

A particular *individual* theory is a response to its time. Our *aggregated* theory exists so that we can extract from it what is useful, applicable and *perennial*. San Francisco therapist and feminist Sarah Soul, educated in a predominantly goals-based academic program, believes: "There are some things in psychology for which the only adequate explanation is [psycho]analytic."[10] If Soul is correct then we need to look at our theory and its developmental trajectory in new ways. Presaging Norcross, Wampold and Truscott, Michigan State University's Adrian Blow and colleagues seek to delineate the relationship between therapist and theory. As Blow puts it:[11]

> We believe that effective clinical models are an indispensable part of good therapy—not because a particular model contains unique healing power, but because models provide the vehicle through which many common factors are potentiated. We further believe that models work through—and therefore largely as well as—the therapist. Models are words on paper, and as such are not 'effective' in and of themselves; rather, models help therapists be effective. Similarly, therapists help models *appear* effective. Models either come alive or die through the therapist. [*PG's italics*]

Blow's 2007 discussion of therapist "common factors" is thus a reiteration of Rogers' more parsimonious 1957 theorizing:

> One of [the theory's] implications is that the techniques of the various therapies are relatively unimportant except to the extent that they serve as channels for fulfilling one of the conditions [I have enumerated].[12]

---

10 Soul, S. (2016). *Personal Communication*
11 Blow, A. J., Sprenkle, D. H. and Davis, S. D. (2007). Is who delivers the treatment more important than the treatment itself? The role of the therapist in common factors. *In* Journal of Marital and Family Therapy, Volume 33, Issue 3, July, pp. 298–317
12 Rogers, C. R. (1957). The necessary and sufficient conditions of therapeutic personality change. *In* Journal of Consulting Psychology, Volume 21, pp. 95–103, http://dx.doi.org/10.1037/h0045357. Now in the public domain

8 • Phenomenology of clinical decision making

As with Norcross, the discourse implicit in both Rogers and Blow is that all theories necessarily are composites governed by the perennial dialectic between goals (techniques and priorities of the various theories) as organized more by our Task Positive Brain and process (channels for fulfilling the therapeutic preconditions, common factors or contributions) as experienced more in our Default Mode Network.

The rider and the elephant

Philosopher and psychologist Jonathan Haidt of New York University has examined ancient and modern conceptualizations for the human mind and its processing. He creates his own, *the rider and the elephant*, explaining: "Modern theories about rational choice and information processing don't adequately explain weakness of the will. The older metaphors about controlling animals work beautifully."[13] Haidt follows neuropsychologist Michael Gazzaniga, who studied so-called split-brain patients, in referring to the language centers on the left side of the brain as the "interpreter module, whose job it is to give a running commentary on whatever the self is doing, even though the interpreter module has no access to the real causes or motives of the self's behavior."[14] This *confabulation*, Haidt argues repeatedly, is what the rider does to convince himself he is in control of the elephant. The rider, of course, has his analogue in the TPB, the elephant in the DMN. They *can* work very well together [Figure 1.1]. Yet the rider's knowledge sits uneasily atop the elephant's wisdom. Sometimes the elephant simply does whatever it is she wants to do. Then it is up to the rider to spin a narrative around what she is doing [Figure 1.2]. Thus we begin to feel our way toward a deeper understanding of the drivers of antagonism in the great debate. Haidt would dismiss all our confabulations: our elephant chooses our theory for us, and our rider simply tries to make it look good. Since our rider is confabulating, the more theory partisan our behavior, the more shrill our voice in the culture wars, the more out of balance is our mind—and our clinical work.

Figure 1.1 Harmony

---

13 Haidt, J. (2006). *The Happiness Hypothesis*. New York, NY: Basic Books, p. 4
14 *Ibid.*, p. 8

Theory • 9

Figure 1.2 Confabulation

By way of example I write about myself. I can understand the technical languaging of self psychology, in which I am trained, while I find the constructs of the object relations theorists to be cumbersome and their writings correspondingly difficult to parse. Though I do not doubt their insights and contributions to theory, I seldom quote from them. I vividly recall wanting to marry my mother and can therefore see why Freud held the Oedipal conflict to be central; but I can equally well see why Rank insisted on the significance of separation anxiety in the pre-Oedipal stage. More than one thing can be central, and the wish to avoid separation is cognate to the wish to belong with. My personality and manner is naturally *feeling-sensing*, so I instinctively default to the Rogerian style of working. What I will later in this chapter propose as the *Feeling-Sensing Style* is, as we shall go on to examine, heavily reliant on the qualities and characteristics of the DMN that underpin and inform the Rogerian prerequisites; my TPB and *Doing Style*—where the clinician makes best use of the panoply of techniques and protocols in CBT, which afford a direct route to problem solving and symptom reduction—mostly (and not always adroitly) defers to the elephant. I am a process-preferring clinician.

But the quest upon which we have embarked forces me to conclude that in order to maintain good outcomes for my clients I must not consign my Doing Style permanently to a position of deference: if I over-rely on my Feeling-Sensing Style I abandon the dialectic and imperil the client. Yes, we can all be Good Therapists. Yes, we can, with Blow, still have our preferred theory or theories, and we can do so in a way that, with Chaudhuri, allows for plurality and synthesis. And we can still be, as clinicians, either more Doing or more Feeling-Sensing. The difference, now, is that we can be more cognizant of the outcome implications and more mindful of how our personal skills and deficits can lead us *not to notice* when the client needs more from us in our non-preferred Style. *Good Therapy, again, is when the client is given exactly what she needs.*

Humanistic psychology: toward a unifying metatheory

Freud is said to be the founder of the "first force" in psychology, psychoanalysis, while Rogers is credited with being an early proponent of humanistic psychology, the "third force." Again, the emergence of the subsequent literature, emphasis and languaging does not allow us to conclude that Freud was not humanistic. Rather it *helps us see* those attitudes in Freud that were, patently, humanistic, such as his response, in 1935 by letter written in English,[15] to the mother of a gay man: "Homosexuality is assuredly no advantage, but it is nothing to be ashamed of, no vice, no degradation. It cannot be classified as an illness."

Humanistic psychology usefully helps us view human beings and the human psyche as *inherently inclined to growth or development*. Like a tree enjoying the right environmental conditions, if our environment is benign, we have within us everything it takes to reach our full potential. This *developmental* hypothesis provides a fundamental underpinning to concepts of psychological healing and behavioral remediation and the acquisition of coping strategies and skills toward improved lived experience. As we shall see, it is fundamental to Good Therapy and to using interventions adroitly and intentionally.

The developmental hypothesis makes sense to us because we can see the evidence all around us. We know there is an element of *predictability* to human behavior and experience. You get out what you put in. People who are loved are lovable. People who are abused become abusers. Those who are often encouraged often succeed and are seldom too dispirited when they do not. Those who are often criticized go on to experience difficulties in, as Nancy Schlossberg of the University of Maryland has reformulated Freud's teleological definition of mental health, the ability to "Love, Work and Play."[16] It makes sense, then, that the more the clinician believes, humanistically, in the client's capacity to grow, develop and adapt to put the problem behind her, the more the client is likely to profit from treatment. This belief of the therapist in the client, which we shall later examine more closely under Rogers' rubric of unconditional positive regard, we shall find to be a dynamic, positive force and a *precondition for healing*. This humanistic attitude is an essentially *hopeful* philosophy and countertransferential stance, and we are inclined, instinctively, to adopt it into our working hypothesis.

The developmental schema

In their impressive codification *Developmental Counseling and Therapy*,[17] Allen Ivey and his co-authors have expanded the developmental hypothesis into an overarching metatheoretical umbrella. The DCT metamodel has helped me, as described in the third part of this book, awaken my students' interest in rising above

---

15 Freud, S. (1935). *Anonymous* (Letter to an American Mother). *In* Freud, E. (Ed.) (1960), *The Letters of Sigmund Freud*. London: Hogarth Press, pp. 423–424
16 Schlossberg, N. K. (1984). *Counseling Adults in Transition: Linking Practice With Theory*. New York, NY: Springer
17 Ivey, A. E., Ivey, M. B., Myers, J. E. and Sweeney, T. J. (2005). *Developmental Counseling and Therapy: Promoting Wellness Over the Lifespan*. Boston, MA: Lahaska Press, Houghton Mifflin

theory debate to focus on the common threads in doing Good Therapy. Building on the work of Swiss psychologist Jean Piaget, Ivey proposes that our cognitive-emotional functioning, processing, communication and consciousness occur at all times in one or more of four *Styles*—"Sensorimotor" and "Concrete" (corresponding approximately to Piaget's "preoperational" and "concrete operational" stages) and "Formal" and "Dialectic-Systemic" (building on Piaget's "formal operational" stage). Humans develop competencies in the four Styles as best we may in the particular circumstances attending our development and in ways that are sequential, incremental and augmentative and that, moreover, occur *over the lifespan* and *as a logical response to environmental challenge*. Each of DCT's four Styles of cognitive-emotional functioning and communication exists on its own continuum and may be qualified or subdivided, for example, into "early" and "late" stages.

Our way of speaking and behaving is the product of our developmental achievement across each of the four Styles. In general, or in relation to a given issue, we exhibit one or more "preferred" Styles of processing and we may subordinate or avoid one or more Styles. The schema allows clinicians an expanded understanding of the interface of emotion and cognition and an expanded accuracy in assessing abilities and deficits in client functioning. We can identify *developmental blocks*, which Ivey describes as "cognitive/emotional styles or modalities that block the client from functioning relative to a particular issue."[18] DCT assessment allows the clinician to tailor interventions in two ways: *matching* the client's Style helps the client tell her story in her way; while subsequent *mismatching* or *Style-shifting* can be planned to improve functioning by augmenting the client's capabilities in a subordinate or avoided Style.

The DCT schema may be summarized as follows:

Sensorimotor

In the Sensorimotor Style *emotions* predominate, and the person "is" the emotion—to the extent the client may not even be able to tell her story coherently.

Client development mediated in the Sensorimotor

Sensorimotor interventions and psychotherapeutic techniques emphasize uncovering and allowing the emergence of underlying feelings; methods include Freud's free association, Perls' Gestalt Therapy and Gendlin's Focusing.

"Style-shifting" the client to the Sensorimotor

Because of the *primacy of the Sensorimotor* this is one of the most important *Style-shifts*. Typical are therapist transactions of: "And how did that make you feel?" and (better) *reflection of feeling* as in: "Your mother criticized you and you felt . . . is it . . . unlovable . . . ?" Other methods for concentrating

---

(Copyright 2005 [All quotes and figures reproduced by permission of Taylor and Francis Group, LLC, a division of Informa plc])
18 Ibid., p. 110

on the message of the Sensorimotor are found in Gestalt's *intensifying the feeling* and in visualization and other techniques for going inside the body.

Concrete

In the Concrete Style facts, figures and factual narratives predominate in the person's communications, sometimes excessively; often affect is hardly in evidence—for example, the client may recount her story and talk about having felt sad without appearing touched by any sadness as she discusses events; in the wider culture things largely get done in the Concrete Style, and Ivey notes that many client presentations are predominantly Concrete.

Client development mediated in the Concrete

Concrete interventions and psychotherapeutic techniques are correlated to the problem solving approaches in counseling and psychotherapy and in particular the cognitive-behavioral approaches that emphasize *doing* and *homework*.

Style-shifting the client to the Concrete

Clients often tell their story in late Concrete/early Formal fashion using reification. Details of what actually happens or happened are obscured, and this limits the therapist's ability empathically to feel into the client's situation, thereby also limiting assessment and hypothesis-building; in these cases the therapist will say something like: "Can you give me an example . . . ?" or "You describe your mother as being very manipulative and I'd like to know what this manipulativeness looks like in practice: can you tell me about when this happened last . . . ?" The clinician often follows with prompts of: ". . . and what happened then, what did she say?" The Style-shift to the Concrete is often a precursor to the Style-shift to the Sensorimotor: ". . . and then she said she was very disappointed in you and then you felt . . . is it . . . unlovable?"

Formal

In the Formal Style the person increasingly makes use of observation of *patterns* in events and behavior, draws *inferences* from the patterns and talks about these inferences; Ivey hypothesizes that the development of empathy occurs along with development in the Formal Style of cognitive-emotional functioning, and he says this Style is predominant in most counselors and therapists.

Client development mediated in the Formal

Formal interventions and psychotherapeutic techniques are based on *interpretations* and *thinking*. All approaches use the Formal Style in various ways. The idea is that the client is confronted with *what is really going on and why* and is able to decide to change behavior accordingly. Crucial to psychotherapeutic success in this Style is the *process* of how the patterns and inferences are discussed between clinician and client and whether the client is sufficiently developed in the "higher Styles" (Formal and Dialectic-Systemic) to be able to change behavior when confronted with an interpretation.

Style-shifting the client to the Formal

A predominantly Concrete client may be encouraged to Style-shift into Formal pattern thinking by discussing a series of events with him in the Concrete Style and then adding *if . . . then . . .* markers, for example: ". . . so *if* you tell your wife you have been thinking about her project *then* she will feel very appreciative of you . . ." often following with a further prompt: ". . . and hasn't the same sequence happened on a number of occasions now?" The *if . . . then . . .* markers and further prompting is best done with a *tone of discovery and curiosity* in relation to the client's experience and not with a tone of (the Formal therapist) cleverly revealing these things (to the Concrete client).

Dialectic-Systemic

The Dialectic-Systemic Style is defined by the person's ability to "*think outside the box*" and, functioning from an "anthropologist's" or "ethnographer's" *big picture* or *systemic* perspective of *curiosity*, see "patterns of patterns" in her or his lived experience and relationships.

Client development mediated in the Dialectic-Systemic

Dialectic-Systemic interventions and psychotherapeutic techniques are based on inviting the client to consider and develop her story having regard to context and interconnectedness; the Dialectic-Systemic is correlated with systems theory and therapies such as feminist therapy and multicultural counseling and therapy—and school-based family counseling and therapy.

Style-shifting the client to the Dialectic-Systemic

Clients having complex, multifaceted issues including trauma and oppression can best find resolution in the Dialectic-Systemic; Style-shifting to the Dialectic-Systemic may occur from any Style; typical therapist encouragers are: "You have all these different things going on, pulling you in all these different directions: how do you make sense of it, how do you put it all together for yourself?" and "Given the difficulties your mother encountered both in her early life and when she became a mother, it wasn't so easy for her to give you the care you needed—yet where does this leave you now in terms of how you feel about her?"

In DCT the developmental goal is optimal or sufficient adaptation to prevailing environmental circumstances: it may be that we were not much challenged by our environment to develop competencies in, say, our Dialectic-Systemic Style; yet, if we are also symptom-free, Ivey sees us as being exactly where we need to be. The developmental goal of *sufficient adaptation* is thus *specific to person, time and context* and is moreover equally applicable to any point in the lifespan. Ivey formulates the goal thus:

> **What is desirable for human development is a balance between the ability to enter into a full expression of feelings, as represented by Sensorimotor experience, and the ability to become more concrete and analytical as the situation changes.**[19]

The comprehensive DCT schema gives us a developmental lens through which we can better assess both ourselves and our clients and accurately correlate our interventions to the client's level of development and environmental challenge. A salient aspect has already been flagged: *does the client have sufficient developmental capacity in the higher Styles to make sense of patterns and use them to change?* Our treatment plan and the adroit timing of interventions such as interpretation, psychoeducation and some goals-based techniques and protocols must depend on our assessment of the client from within the DCT schema. This is of profound significance. *Every clinician implementing an intervention the client then fails to adopt has failed to prepare the client for the intervention by laying the developmental groundwork.* DCT reveals why the intervention did not succeed and also helps the clinician pinpoint the developmental next steps in the treatment plan for this client, so the failed intervention may be reiterated successfully.

As Ivey describes it elsewhere,[20] we practice intentionally when we choose and apply our interventions at all times knowing why we are doing these things and what the potential or likely results of our doing these things will be in terms of fostering necessary developmental acceleration and/or remediation. Intentionality, then, imports some level of *predictability* to the work.

DCT theory relies on the *primacy of the Sensorimotor*: our emotional process—our feelings—are mediated via our other three Styles into cognitions, which we then weave into a *self-narrative* of memory and experience.[21] The links with narrative therapy and cognitive theory are very clear—as are the links with theories emphasizing early childhood experience and therapy approaches that rely on *process* and *Mirroring* (with upper-case M, further described in Chapters 2 and 3), for example, person-centered therapy and self psychology. It is in our ongoing, everyday task of mediating our Sensorimotor via our Concrete, Formal and Dialectic-Systemic Styles of cognitive-emotional processing that we may encounter difficulties. It may be we are not capable of, adaptively, giving "full expression" to our Sensorimotor experience; our feelings are more disturbing than we dare acknowledge, given our present, limited cognitive processing (meaning-making) capacity in (one or more of) the other three Styles. Because we cannot

---

19 *Ibid.*, p. 110
20 Ivey, A. E. and Ivey, M. B. (2003–2007). *Intentional Interviewing and Counseling: Facilitating Client Development in a Multicultural Society.* Pacific Grove, CA: Thomson/Brooks/Cole, pp. 16–17
21 Ivey, A. E., Ivey, M. B., Myers, J. E. and Sweeney, T. J. (2005). *Op. cit.*, pp. 22–23

adaptively process our experience we will resort to keeping our feelings from consciousness and full expression via one or more defense mechanisms that compromise, at times severely, our meaning-making, thinking, behavior and ability to respond. We are therefore unable to rise to the prevailing environmental challenge and we may become symptomatic, which compounds our stress. The road to more adaptive functioning, then, lies in augmenting our capability specifically in the cognitive-emotional Style or Styles in which our further development will permit or restore adaptive meaning-making and full processing of underlying Sensorimotor experience.

Ivey's schema is key to unlocking the mystery of the variability of client response to clinician intervention. This is a prodigious claim that we will wish to test in action before fully confirming it into our working hypothesis. It is a claim that has the potential to change everything: if we can accept as logical Ivey's reasons for understanding the variability in—and even *predictability of*—client response to certain interventions then this will, surely, very greatly facilitate more precise, more intentional treatment planning. And better outcomes. Moreover, to the extent the success of such interventions depends less on the "rightness" of one side in the culture wars and more on assessment of *the developmental preparedness of the client for the specific intervention at the time the specific intervention is made*, Ivey may help us lift the veil and see beyond the antagonistic theses.

We can very easily test this part of the working hypothesis: my student with the client with the preachy social worker can decide to work on the developmental issue of the client's sensitivity to being judged inferior and determine whether doing so paves the way for the client's adoption of less risky and more assertive behaviors. If my student finds this is indeed so, then she will conclude that process-based, developmental work offers an indirect but sure approach to clinical goals that cannot be reached by more direct methods.

Ivey further theorizes that our character structure or "Personality Style" is also our primary defense mechanism, inevitably leading each of us to what Brandeis University's George Kelly described as "one's personal construction of life."[22] In ensuring that we do not express and process a part of our experience fully, our Personality Style defenses serve a useful purpose in adaptation—the best we can do at the time. If or when they become overwhelmed, perhaps in response to a renewed "environmental insult," we manifest symptoms and behaviors that may require clinical attention.[23] We are therefore to consider the symptoms and behaviors that have brought the client to therapy as *manifestations of personality*. Ivey's schema predates and presages the return in the new, Fifth Edition of the American

---

22 Kelly, G. A. (1991). *The Psychology of Personal Constructs, Volume Two: Clinical Diagnosis and Psychotherapy*. London, UK and New York, NY: Routledge, p. 193
23 Ivey, A. E., Ivey, M. B., Myers, J. E. and Sweeney, T. J. (2005). *Op. cit.*, pp. 287 *et seq.*

Psychiatric Association's *Diagnostic and Statistical Manual of Mental Disorders* to what New York-based psychiatrists Bret Stetka and Christoph Correll describe as "a more unified and dimensional view of personality, character, temperament, and mental illness."[24]

> ***Key to Ivey's schema is our understanding that the client's adaptation is informed by her personality and that if we wish to help her change her adaptation we must look to help her grow her personality.***

As therapists we are therefore at all times engaged in the treatment and developmental remediation of personality. Cornell University's John Clarkin, who works with New York City's Personality Studies Institute agrees, saying:

> while symptom reduction is important, it is the interpersonal issues that should be the major long term focus in therapy. The heart of the matter in personality disorders is the patient's conception of self and others. The ultimate goal of treatment should be interpersonal functioning that allows for pleasure, interdependence, and intimacy in relationships.[25]

As we proceed in our quest we reflect on the implications in case conceptualization and in relation to the dialectic between goals and process: *how the client relates* is the process element behind the presenting problem. Our fantasized client in the vignette, who wondered whether her therapist was best placed to help her find a romantic partner, was inclined to feel critical of the therapist's appearance and dismissive of her capabilities; if her response to the men who show interest in her is cast in similar maladaptive mold—as Kelly and Ivey, with Freud and also Beck and now Clarkin, advise it must be, then we can begin to see the true nature of the obstacles to her success in romance.

As discussed, the DCT therapist mediates or remediates the client's development by first meeting or joining the client in the client's preferred or dominant Style of cognitive-emotional processing and then Style-shifting the client as appropriate. Clinical decisions are informed by the therapist's developmental case hypothesis and intentional treatment plan flowing therefrom. We present almost infinite variations and gradations in the manifestation of our preferred or predominant Style in different domains or endeavors. A simplified example given by Ivey is of a heterosexual male client who experiences his wife as "frigid." The DCT assessment is that the client brings insufficient empathy and pattern recognition—held to be functions of the Formal Style[26]—to transactions in the marital relationship.

---

24 Stetka, B. S. and Correll, C. U. (2013). A Guide to DSM-5. *Accessed September 21st 2014 via* www.medscape.com/viewarticle/803884

25 Clarkin, J. F. (2012). An integrated approach to psychotherapy techniques for patients with personality disorder. *In* Journal of Personality Disorders, Volume 26, Issue 1, February, pp. 43–62

26 Ivey, A. E., Ivey, M. B., Myers, J. E. and Sweeney, T. J. (2005). *Op. cit.*, p. 32

Although the client evidently has sufficient ability in his Formal Style to meet environmental demands in the context of his workplace, when at home with his wife, he reverts to a more Concrete manner in communicating his desires to her, to which she responds with rejection. Accordingly the therapist's assessment and case hypothesis require him to augment and expand the client's abilities in the Formal Style specifically to improve functioning in the marital context. When discussing the presenting problem the therapist "meets" his client in the client's preferred, Concrete discourse and then Style-shifts the client into the Formal, using *if . . . then . . .* markers.[27]

DCT follows the Platonic–Piagetian model of cognitive development in seeing the Sensorimotor as the "foundation layer" with the Concrete, Formal and Dialectic-Systemic stacked in successive, overlaying tiers, hence the "stack diagram." [Figure 1.3] Thus when the therapist decides to shift the client away from the client's predominant Style to another Style in which development is required, Ivey terms it *vertical development* ("ascending" or "descending" the stack). Expansion of client capability within one of the Styles is termed *horizontal development*. For a client lacking in Sensorimotor ability and having unexpressed, disavowed or otherwise unprocessed, un-felt feelings the therapist will envisage descending Style-shifting to the Sensorimotor and subsequent horizontal development within the Sensorimotor. Careful assessment is required: feelings waiting to be released can be felt, owned and integrated only to the extent the client has sufficient developmental assets in the higher Styles with which to process the feelings. For some clients, those having a profound reservoir of unprocessed feeling and in whom insufficient "ability to become more . . . analytical as the situation changes" is a significant factor in the feelings remaining unprocessed, it is necessary to balance Style-shifts (from, say, the Concrete) into the Sensorimotor with ascending vertical development into the Formal and "early" Dialectic-Systemic.

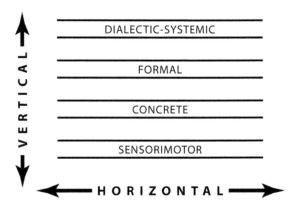

Figure 1.3 DCT developmental schema: "stack diagram"

---

27 *Ibid.*, p. 31

Thus vertical and horizontal development are matters involving some complexity, requiring of the therapist an adroitness in knowing when and how to shift and redirect focus. Where feelings are repressed the clinician's task is to help the client "[enter] into a full expression of feelings as represented by Sensorimotor experience" and, as this occurs, to process the newly felt feelings in the other three Styles so the client may incorporate them into her self-narrative together with the associated, adaptive revisions in her meaning-making (cognitive restructuring). In terms of horizontal development, "more complete development in each consciousness Style is what is sought,"[28] says Ivey. *The more we, each of us, expand our capacities in each of our Styles, the better we become equipped to handle environmental challenge.* More is better. In terms of vertical development, "higher is not necessarily better."[29] Ivey here diverges from Plato in not seeing Dialectic-Systemic thinking as the developmental goal. In the DCT schema, development is a means to adaptation and not a spiritual end in itself. The developmental goal is defined as *adequacy* across all four Styles for adaptation to the challenges at hand. Yet as we have seen the higher Styles of Formal and Dialectic-Systemic have an important function in our adaptation as it is in these Styles we begin to understand (Formal) and then fully resolve (Dialectic-Systemic) our more complex issues.

As treatment progresses, the client's developmental augmentation both vertically and horizontally across all four Styles obviates the need for defensive structures—and permits feelings safely and adaptively to be felt, processed and communicated. In delineating DCT developmental sequences of emotional release and subsequent cognitive processing Ivey describes the work historically referred to by the term *depth psychology*.

Neuroscience

To further our Socratic inquiry we have enlisted the support of neuroscience. Cross-referencing another academic discipline is at best a risky undertaking and points strongly to Haidt's rider's desire to confabulate. Yet these considerations continue to appear helpful and perhaps we can remain mindful of the risks. Recent discoveries by University of Arizona professor of psychiatry, psychology and neuroscience Richard Lane and colleagues have revitalized and confirmed our body of theory. The DCT schema is supported by positron emission topography (PET) scans, which allow mapping of "structures on the medial surface of the frontal lobe that participate in (i) background feelings, (ii) attention to feelings and (iii) reflective awareness of feelings."[30] It makes an enormous amount of sense that the DCT concept of vertical development, with its hypothesis that our emotions are mediated within cognitive processes that differ from each other in Style,

---

28 *Ibid.*, p. 25
29 *Ibid.*, p. 140
30 Lane, R. D. (2008). Neural substrates of implicit and explicit emotional processes: A unifying framework for psychosomatic medicine. *In* Psychosomatic Medicine, Volume 70, pp. 214–231, p. 221, Figure 2

should be associated with the firing of neurons *in different parts of the brain*. Lane goes on to observe:

> Reflective awareness, or metacognition, requires the creation of a representation of experience, and this representation will affect how future emotional information is interpreted and experienced. The acquisition of reflective awareness is a key goal of treatment in patients with more primitive personality organizations.[31]

Far from replacing or modernizing our theory, neuroscience rather can be seen as confirming and strengthening its historical base in phenomenological observation. The evolutionary concept of phylogenesis confirms the existence of differentiated levels of unconscious processing, including both psychosomatic mechanisms and the primitive emotional drives that led Freud to hypothesize the *id* and Haidt his elephant. As Lane puts it:

> Primary emotion is the phylogenetically older behavioral and physiological expression of an emotional response. Primary emotion occurs automatically and without the necessity of conscious processing.[32]

But neuroscience does not confirm the stack diagram. The "Ivey Instrument,"[33] reproduced in the Appendix, is an educational tool used to assess the disposition of the beginning clinician to prefer either goals-based or process-based methodologies. In it the four DCT Styles are shown in an altogether different "wheel diagram" (p. 193). This discloses that the Sensorimotor and the Dialectic-Systemic share a boundary. With Plato and Piaget, Ivey discusses vertically ascending levels of higher mental formal operations: the Dialectic-Systemic, therefore, is developed and accessed *through the Formal*. But the wheel diagram discloses that the Dialectic-Systemic *is equally accessible from the Sensorimotor*. This is of some significance.

We all know people who have had little in the way of conventional schooling—the domain of the Concrete and Formal or, as I here propose, the *Doing Style*—but who nevertheless strike us as being full of an innate wisdom; these people, some of whom are described as being "of few words," often astonish others with pronouncements, evaluations and decisions that somehow go to the heart of the matter and, as a result, feel completely "right" to observers. In other words, the person is possessed of a formidable Dialectic-Systemic ability. Similarly we have encountered elders with compromised cognitive abilities who from time to time astonish and delight us with comments—it may be in response to a television show or overheard conversation—of prodigious insight. These people, I propose, are relying on the *Feeling-Sensing Style*, which encompasses the Sensorimotor

---

31 *Ibid.*, p. 222
32 *Ibid.*, p. 220
33 Ivey, A. E., Ivey, M. B., Myers, J. E. and Sweeney, T. J. (2005). *Op. cit.*, Appendix 5

and Dialectic-Systemic; moreover they have developed in the Dialectic-Systemic by *accessing it through their Sensorimotor*. The Dialectic-Systemic is therefore more than a higher cognitive mental process springing out of Piagetian formal operations. Like Freud's *Sichhineinversetzen* (discussed in Chapter 2), the Dialectic-Systemic involves a physiological process of inner sensing: it belongs to the elephant and the DMN and can occur, with Lane, in the absence of conscious processing.

This proposal brings DCT theory into alignment with current thinking concerning the Task Positive Brain and the Default Mode Network. While both neural networks are conduits for all four DCT Styles, Ivey today correlates the DMN with the Sensorimotor and Dialectic-Systemic, saying they are "important"[34] in this network. Correlating the DMN with the Feeling-Sensing Style and the TPB with the Doing Style is helpful and useful to us in shedding light in several areas. It explains, for example, how it comes about that a developmentally consonant version of the Dialectic-Systemic Style is also manifested in children possessing only rudimentary Formal competencies.[35]

And the correlation further illuminates our understanding of the Self of the clinician. The proposed modification to the DCT schema accords with the phenomenology of counseling and therapy. I will use the expression "Doing Style" to denote clinician behaviors in which Ivey's Concrete and Formal Styles are predominant and working together, which include thought-driven action as required for implementation of goals-based technique; and I will use the expression "Feeling-Sensing Style" to correspond with clinician behaviors informed by the Sensorimotor and Dialectic-Systemic Styles, such as manifesting the essential personal qualities of the therapist and noticing the client's subtle cues and clues. I offer these new terms in the hope they will assist us in our quest to understand the variables in clinical outcomes.

Can theories talk? Discovering common ground

Our aim, in summary, should not be to determine which theory or theories are best (or most to our liking) and then disregard and disavow all other schools and authorities. Our aim rather should be to use all the accumulated wisdom of all our authorities and theorists to gain an ever clearer understanding of the reality behind the construct—the reality in human life and in the human psyche and brain. Such an understanding will help us "translate" from one theory to another and better understand—and use and illuminate—each.

What, for instance, is the difference between the "maladaptive cognition" of cognitive theory and the "introject" of the analysts? The answer is: *form*. The languaging of cognitive theory makes the client the agent of the cognition while the

---

34 Ivey, A. E., *Personal Communication*
35 Ivey, A. E., Ivey, M. B., Myers, J. E. and Sweeney, T. J. (2005). *Op. cit.* (cf. p. 118)

languaging of psychoanalytic theory emphasizes that the cognitions came from someone else via projection/introjection.

What is the relationship between building, in the client, "coping skills"—a technical languaging of cognitive-behavioral practice—and the self psychological term "self-structure"? The answer is: *close*. The coping skills have to be built on the foundation of the developed/developing self of the client.

Do the Gestaltists really mean it when they dismiss the concept of transference? The answer is: *not really*. While the Gestaltists do not use transference as a primary concept they certainly address it if a *Gestalt* involving the client's attitude to the therapist rises to prominence.

Where theories or theoreticians *apparently* contradict each other we need to respond, as to any environmental challenge, by *developing*. We must become *more Dialectic-Systemic* in our ability to "pick out" and "put together"[36] the encoded messages in the patterns of patterns in the available evidence: there is, waiting for our discovery, a reason for the apparent discrepancy between the theories and it will profit us and our client if we go look for it.

More Dialectic-Systemic

Ivey variously describes our Dialectic-Systemic Style as defined by our ability to *think outside the box* and consider ourselves and our relationships and our functioning *fully in context*, from a multitude of perspectives and informed by a multiplicity of viewpoints. Key attitudes in our Dialectic-Systemic are *curiosity* and an anthropologist's or ethnographer's *big picture* perspective. Our quest to shed light on both the culture wars and disparities in psychotherapy outcomes is an interest stirred in us by our Dialectic-Systemic as well as an environmental challenge spurring us to further development in this Style.

For we are all theorists. The authorities gave us our theory, I believe, not as Moses gave his Laws but as a work-in-progress. Freud, Rogers, Beck, Kohut, Klein, Ainsworth, Glasser, each developed her or his theory over the period of a long working life, in many instances incorporating radical changes—most recently Glasser even changing the name of his method from *reality therapy* to *choice theory*. Were these authorities all still practicing and writing today, the adjustments and the new insights would continue. Freud and Beck would catch up with each other and embrace. We must therefore continue their work and Ivey's and further develop our body of theory. We may do this not only in the established manner, drawing inferences from observable phenomena and logic, but also drawing from the many advances in neuroinformatics research, which both confirm our established theory and, by helping inform clinical choice (as examined in Chapter 9), further strengthen and expand it.

Intentionality, then, which requires us at all times to keep in mind the likely consequences of our interventions, is not only a construct of Ivey's Dialectic-Systemic

---

36 *Ibid.*, pp. 415–416

thinking but, further, requires *us* to think Dialectic-Systemically—in the way we draw from theory in order better to see the client's situation, form our case hypothesis, build our treatment plan, implement our interventions and import a degree of predictability into our work. We need to know and to be accountable for why we are choosing and tailoring the mix of interventions in a particular way for a particular client and how we expect our approach will help and over what timeframe. The crucial thing to keep in mind, always, is: *how can I make my response to theory useful to my work with this client?*

A final word about theory. *We must not confuse and conflate theory with therapy.* A theory is a "way of looking at" or "lens." A therapy is a way of helping. A theoretical lens is the product of an evolutionary force or counterforce *and therefore cannot, ever, be complete* in the sense that we need look no further to help all our clients. Therapy, the Platonic Form or Archetype, in order to be complete—and with the T capitalized—requires the practitioner to manage the dialectic between goals and process and draw as necessary from both process-based and goals-based methods, theories and interventions. CBT *plus* talking. Freud *plus* Beck. The pioneers of CBT rightly expected great things from their new lens but cannot have intended the suppression of process and psychodynamic tools. Adroit goals-preferring clinicians, with Burns, know this instinctively. Their less adroit peers can be helped to embrace both goals and process; or, in the case of less adroit process-preferring clinicians, both process and goals.

Summary

In our preliminary excursion into theory we have been invited to look at humans as developmental beings and to look at theory with an eye to inclusion and synthesis. Our theory is a work-in-progress—and so are we. We have already noted, with Aponte and Winter, that therapist self-development is a salient issue. And we suspect our preferences—behaviors, cognitions and confabulations—in the culture wars or great debate [Figure 1.4] correlate with and stem from our developmental assets and deficits. The implication is that from time to time we therapists are ourselves called upon to *develop*—for example, our quest looks to be inviting us to become more Dialectic-Systemic.

Figure 1.4 The great debate

And this is already happening in that it begins to seem more understandable and ordinary and less mysterious that CBT should be experienced, by earnest and well-meaning people, as, variously, a very effective and a not very effective model. For one thing, a process-preferring clinician with an under-developed Doing Style and a disinclination to implement "rigid" protocols might for those reasons seek to cast doubt on CBT. Then again, as Waller finds, treatment is not so effective when clinicians using the model manifest maladroitness. Ability to manage the dialectic between goals and process—which is located not only within the therapy but also within the clinician's Self in her antagonistic TPB and DMN—looks to be an essential component in both the evidence-based hypothesis and the proper implementation of not only CBT but any model.

In the following pages we will further examine the hallmarks of Good Therapy and the obstacles to it. Perhaps, as imagined earlier, we are too attached to the process thesis and apt to lose sight of the presenting problem and goals? We may *think* we are fully implementing our preferred models and appropriately drawing from our theories. We may feel secure in our ability to manage both our own feeling responses and the goals-process dialectic; yet we may be insufficiently developed in our Dialectic-Systemic to pick out and process the patterns of patterns in all the evidence. Whichever developmental hindrance applies, until we rise above it, we may not (however hard we try) be able to use our models optimally for client outcome.

Psychotherapy, then, is a developmental endeavor. The task of the counselor and therapist is to help the client rise above the challenges that have brought forth her symptoms. Let us continue to follow the evidence and examine how this is accomplished.

Discussion

- *Does client work benefit if the clinician is "more Dialectic-Systemic"?*
- *How do you understand the concepts of "theory on theory" and "theory as work-in-progress" and "we are all theorists"?*
- *How do you understand the role played by neuroscience in relation to theories of psychological development, psychopathology and counseling and psychotherapy?*
- *How do you understand the DCT "metatheory"? Do you believe theories can "talk" and that Freud was "humanistic"?*
- *Does the schema of the four DCT "Styles" of cognitive-emotional functioning strike you as either true or useful? Ivey says that most therapists are predominantly Formal: do you agree? Do you feel the proposed extensions in terminology—"Doing Style" and "Feeling-Sensing Style"—have value? How does your preferred theory of counseling and therapy relate to Doing and to Feeling-Sensing?*

2
Evidence
Physiological operationalization • Empathy countertransference and practice-based evidence

> Countertransference and the adroit clinician • the physiology of Empathy • transference • the therapeutic prerequisites as primary manifestations of the Therapist-Self
>
> The case of Kevin • the case of Ghislaine
>
> "Operationalization" • Empathy and Mirroring • clinical evidence and projective identification • the clinician's specific developmental attainment

Kevin, 49, self-refers, apparently in crisis. Using a standard protocol to assess for suicide the clinician decides Kevin need not be hospitalized. Yet at the end of the session the clinician's mind is troubled. The client "ticks" just one "box." Kevin is a single white male over 40, a group considered at higher risk for suicide. The other puzzling thing is that his presenting problem seems so—the clinician is almost embarrassed to think—trivial; surely there is more to Kevin's distress than the things he talked about in session? Kevin does not return for follow-up. Six months later (now in treatment with a different therapist), he kills himself.

Norcross, Wampold, Rogers and Blow have flagged the common factors that come not from the theory but from the therapist. They point to the dialectic between goals (theory) and process (therapist contributions) in counseling and therapy. Just as the only theory worth employing is the one we can use now to help *this* client, what if the evidence most meriting the close attention of the therapist is the therapist's own countertransference? As Virginia Satir and French American social work professor Michelle Baldwin have noted:

> The therapist's ability to check on his own internal manifestations is one of the most important therapeutic tools he has. If his internal experience of an interview is different from all other data he is observing and he is fairly sure his reaction is not related to something going on in his

personal life, then the most effective way to proceed is on the basis of that internal data.[1]

Satir's enjoinders are, clearly, an analogue to the APA guidelines in relation to clinical judgment and expertise and the avoidance of probabilistic inferences.

Nowhere can these enjoinders be more necessary than in the endeavor of assessing for suicidality. The client in the vignette ticked just one box. Because it was "just" one box—Kevin had no plan or means for committing suicide and had not previously attempted suicide—the first clinician judged it safe to refrain from hospitalizing him, and this decision proved technically correct in the short term, since Kevin was six months' distance from killing himself. But the clinician was left with a very uncomfortable "internal manifestation" and thoughts of: *what if this single ticked box were, somehow, the one that mattered*?

The dialectic between goals and process pits a protocol based on aggregated data from assessments for suicide performed at other times by other therapists on other clients against *this* therapist's countertransference with *this* client. Was Kevin's going on to kill himself six months later something that could have been forestalled? Had he been hospitalized that day, would everything have turned out differently? This tragedy reinforces our commitment to look for Good Therapy and improved outcomes and points us to examine, with Satir and Baldwin, whether and when the evidence meriting the most weight is in the therapist's countertransference. Let us therefore look at what this expression means.

Countertransference is defined for our purposes as "*all and any thoughts, feelings, responses and reactions, conscious, pre-conscious or unconscious, of the clinical professional in relation to or when sitting with the client.*" In supervision or case consultation, there are multiple sources of countertransference: as well as that in the treating therapist, there will be countertransference in the supervisor or consultant and in the supervision/consultation group members. It is well and widely understood that countertransference can be *obstructive*: a female clinician, it may be, has just been through a messy divorce; unconscious of her motivations to replay her own incomplete *Gestalten* she may not realize she is projecting her attitudes onto her client who, it happens, also has marital difficulties. More subtle manifestations of obstructive countertransference exist within the phenomenon of clinician maladroitness.

Obstructive countertransference is antagonistic to Good Therapy. But when countertransference is accurately analyzed and skillfully utilized it becomes a significant factor in therapeutic healing. For Satir was describing—and Kevin's clinician was experiencing—the phenomenon of *projective identification*, which San Francisco analyst Thomas Ogden considers to be "the basic unit of study of the therapeutic interaction."[2] In the mechanism of projective identification, thoughts

---

1 Satir, V. and Baldwin, M. (1983). *Satir Step by Step: A Guide to Creating Change in Families*. Palo Alto, CA: Science and Behavior Books, p. 233
2 Ogden, T. (1979). On projective identification. *In* International Journal of Psycho-Analysis, Volume 60, pp. 357–73, p. 366

and feelings arise in the therapist that are in fact not "related to something going on in [the therapist's] personal life" but that are nonverbal communications from the client, unconsciously projected. Similarly, in supervision or consultation, thoughts and feelings about the case arise in the consultant (or group) that are unconsciously projected nonverbal communications from the treating therapist; such communications may originate from within the client, having been introjected by the therapist. Without this theoretical rationale the only way to describe the phenomenon is by using nonacademic concepts such as "intuition."

Process

Which is why, in the vignette, the first clinician's countertransference was significant. *Something told him that Kevin really might kill himself.* What if, sometime before the end of the session, he had made the switch from goals to process and said:

> You know, Kevin, I could just let you go home. Or I could hospitalize you. Using standard assessment tools I rate the probability of your killing yourself as low enough to allow me just to let you go home. But there's a voice inside me saying this is bigger than I think and that, although you have checked out pretty well in the past fifty minutes and are feeling calm right now, you really might kill yourself because of this problem. Not now, not this weekend—and not even this month—but what if the problem doesn't go away? And I need you to help me out: I feel there is something about your problem that I am not fully understanding? What is it about the situation that is so really, really bad and that I haven't quite been able to grasp? I feel there is something I have missed. Can you tell it to me again?

If the first clinician had said something like this, what kind of impact would this have had on Kevin?

To answer this question we must step back, temporarily, from the goal of assessing Kevin's suicidality and review his process. To this end we must give our Default Mode Network free rein, *feeling and sensing* our way into an understanding. Kevin has been struggling with a problem. His first response is to try handle it himself. Sometimes he may (for example) go for a run or to an aerobics class from which he may return feeling better. In such ways he puts off seeking help. But the (with Ivey) Personality Style defenses are breaking down, and each subsequent assault of the terrible feelings is worse. Kevin gives up chasing endorphins through exercise and decides to see a therapist. The fifty-minute interview is with an empathic, caring, interested clinician. The Mirroring Kevin receives in the interview (the term "Mirroring" to be defined later in this chapter) is comforting and relieving and he feels more composed. The fifty minutes with the therapist has had a similar effect to doing aerobics or going on a run. Yet, as Kevin experiences it, the interview with the clinician ends on a note of uncertainty if not emptiness. The clinician has been comforting but has contributed no insight to Kevin's presenting issue. Kevin leaves with the polite lie that he will return next week and continue the therapy. What is it that he needed from the clinician but was not able to ask for and did not receive? And what would have been different if the clinician had conducted the session in the manner just proposed? What is communicated to Kevin by the clinician's self-disclosure, if it occurs, of the "voice inside . . . saying this is bigger" and "I need you to help me out?"

Let's imagine we are Kevin. We have been struggling with our problem and getting nowhere. And now our therapist is telling us . . . why, it's like he's in the struggle too, right there with us! We can see the effort he is making. He's saying, yes, it *is* difficult to make sense of these things. No, it's *not* clear-cut. In saying these things, he is not minimizing our distress; rather he is saying we have a good reason for our distress and he is personally invested in helping us get to the bottom of it. Yes, in terms of having solved our presenting problem, we are no better off at the end of the session, but we have found a friend, an ally! When we hear the clinician affirm that our issue is indeed hard to pin down we hear also the subtext that, between the two of us, we will find a way to pin it down! Which brings hope: we now feel like it could be worthwhile to pursue further discussion with this clinician. *The goal of the first session is that there be a second.* Would not our fantasized intervention have begun a deepening of the therapeutic conversation and would this not have improved Kevin's chances of, as Ivey would conceptualize it, acquiring the developmental skills to move beyond his terrible dilemma?

Here in this case the *clue*, the evidence that mattered most, was to be found not in reifying the protocols for assessing suicidality but, with Satir, in the countertransference of the treating therapist. We see now why Ogden is at pains to underline the saliency of projective identification. The client was not saying in words but was unconsciously projecting the ideation that his problem was worse than he had been able or willing to articulate and that he really might kill himself because of it; and the clinician introjected these ideas. Had the clinician accurately analyzed his countertransference and skillfully found a way to reopen the conversation in the manner suggested he would have been in a position to demonstrate to the client his very considerable empathic attunement—and thereby *reach* this hard-to-reach client and begin to uncover the hidden problem.

Empathy

Kevin, a highly capable and articulate man, was nevertheless unable in fifty minutes to convey his problem in words. DCT helps us understand the dynamics thwarting communication. We become symptomatic when we fail to balance entering into a full expression of feelings, as represented by Sensorimotor experience, and the ability to become more concrete and analytical as the situation changes. By definition we are avoiding our Sensorimotor and failing to process feelings adequately in our Concrete, Formal and Dialectic-Systemic. It therefore makes sense that the client can talk for an hour about his problem and still not succeed in communicating exactly what the problem is. The therapist is therefore required to gain a *felt sense* of the problem.

And here we must look more closely at what we mean when we use the word *empathy*. Curiously, it is a neologism. British American psychologist Edward Titchener, whom, with Ivey, we would describe as a highly Sensorimotor individual, coined the word "empathy" in an attempt at a direct translation of the German word *Einfühlung* (meaning "feeling-into") in a set of philosophic lectures describing phenomena in Sensorimotor experiencing.[3] To add to our curiosity it seems possible we have a discrepancy in theory since Ivey, as we have seen (p. 12), considers empathy to be something we develop along with our Formal Style. We wonder . . . do the expressions "empathy" and "*Einfühlung*" in fact have a range of meanings along a continuum between their everyday use and their usage, developed over time, as technical expressions in academic psychology? Is Titchener's original attempt at translation—in his context of art or performance appreciation—meaningful to us? Is Rogers' empathy the same as Titchener's? We must look to German, the first language of psychology, for answers.

Munich psychologist and social scientist Doris Bischof-Köhler confirms that what I will from now on call "everyday" empathy (lower-case "e") is indeed a Sensorimotor phenomenon mediated through specific developmental attainment in pattern recognition—the ability to recognize and distinguish between Self and other.[4] The apparent discrepancy in theory is therefore easily resolved, it being pattern recognition and ability to distinguish between Self and other that, according to Ivey, develop along with the Formal Style. But what I will from hereon call psychotherapeutic Empathy (upper-case "E"), the intentional Empathy of the therapist, is clearly of a different order. Viennese social worker and journalist Niko Katsivelaris illuminates the distinction using, differentially, each of *Empathie* (a retranslation back into German of the Titchenerian "empathy"), *Einfühlung* and its analogue *Einfühlungsvermögen* [*vermögen* = "be in a position to/be capable of"]. Discussing and citing Rogers extensively Katsivelaris presents us with this startling passage:

> The goal of person-centered psychotherapy, in which interviewing techniques—in particular the technique of active listening—arise from operationalizations of empathy, is thus the optimization of the human being—his best possible 'direction'—through feeling-into [client experience]. [*PG's translation of*: "Das Ziel der Personzentrierten Psychotherapie, das Ziel ihrer Techniken der Gesprächsführung—insbesondere des Aktiven Zuhörens—als Operationalisierungen von Empathie ist also die Optimierung des Menschen—seine bestmögliche 'Führung'—durch Einfühlung."][5]

Einfühlung [= "feeling into"] is a process having both directionality and duration, whereas (lower-case) empathy/*Empathie* [Greek = "in-feeling"] is, for Katsivelaris, a state having neither. For the nonclinician, *Empathie* is reached through an *Einfühlung* that is not "operationalized." For the clinician, through continued, intentional *Einfühlung* and ongoing operationalization, the process is transformed into psychotherapeutic (upper-case) Empathy/*Einfühlung*. The

---

3 Titchener, E. B. (1909). *Lectures on the Experimental Psychology of the Thought-Processes.* New York, NY: The Macmillan Company
4 Bischof-Köhler, D. (2009). Empathie, Mitgefühl und Grausamkeit und wie sie zusammenhangen (Empathy, compassion and cruelty and how they connect). *In* Psychotherapie, 14 Jahrg. Bd. 14, Heft 1, pp. 52–57
5 Katsivelaris, N. (2012). Normalisierung mit Gefühl? Empathie in der Sozialen Arbeit (Normalising with feeling? Empathy in social work). *In* soziales_kapital wissenschaftliches journal österreichischer fachhochschul-studiengänge soziale arbeit, Nr. 8. *Accessed January 2014 via* www.soziales-kapital.at/

compound *Einfühlungsvermögen* confirms that an essential feature of the clinician behavior is agentive doing.

Einfühlung and *Einfühlungsvermögen* were phenomena in experiencing and interpersonal understanding explored at the end of the nineteenth century most notably and controversially by the German philosopher Theodor Lipps, of whom, according to Berlin psychiatrist Christiane Montag and her colleagues, "Sigmund Freud was a knowledgeable admirer." Lipps, says psychotherapist Anastasia Patrikiou, who practices in Athens and London,

> made the leap from understanding Einfühlung as a concept fundamental to the aesthetic encounter, to one which he thought formed the primary mechanism for recognizing others as creatures with a mind. German philosophers explained that our aesthetic appreciation of objects were based on psychological processes evoked through our senses. Lipps understood Einfühlung as a phenomenon of "inner imitation" in which the mind mirrors the mental activities or experiences of another person as we observe their bodily activities or facial expressions. In his thinking he anticipated recent neuroscientific findings around mirror neurons as mechanism of basic empathy.[6]

For Lipps, according to Montag, another's "perceived movements and affective expressions are 'instinctively' and simultaneously mirrored by kinesthetic 'strivings' and experience of corresponding feelings in the observer."[7]

The physiology of empathy

Einfühlung is further discussed by Berkeley psychologist and family therapist Judye Hess. While Lipps' kinesthetic strivings are pre-conscious—not operationalized—Hess and co-author Ross Cohen describe a purposeful process of psychotherapeutic *Einfühlung*: the clinician "intentionally lets her boundaries become a bit more permeable with a view to letting in and soaking up just a little bit of each one of the family members."[8] The therapist extends and operationalizes Self for the client's benefit. *Einfühlungsvermögen* is, then, the entire wealth of the faculties and emotional intelligence possessed by the therapist purposefully, dynamically and *physiologically* applied to feeling into an understanding of the client. It is, in other words, the primary manifestation of the Therapist-Self (a construct further explored in the second part of this book).

Psychotherapeutic Empathy or *Einfühlung* is *a dynamic process in countertransference*. Feeling-into an understanding of the client and her situation is a

---

6 Patrikiou, A. (2014). Empathy and earned security: Reciprocal influences, ruptures and shifts in the psychotherapeutic process. *In* Odgers, A. (Ed.), *From Broken Attachments to Earned Security: The Role of Empathy in Therapeutic Change*. London: Karnac Books, pp. 107–126
7 Montag, C., Gallinat, J. and Heinz, A. (2008). Theodor Lipps and the concept of empathy: 1851–1914. *In* American Journal of Psychiatry, Volume 165, p. 10, October
8 Hess, J. and Cohen, R. (2008). *Core-Focused Family Therapy: Moving from Chaos to Clarity*. Ravensdale, WA: Idyll Arbor, p. 15

reciprocal, interactional, physiological, intersubjective sequence *that occurs over time*. We can therefore agree with Katsivelaris' understanding of Rogerian Empathy. *Einfühlungsvermögen* is what makes the listening "active." Rogers' tapes and writings well illustrate the process, his theory rests upon it and without it there simply is no therapy. Ivey agrees, saying both "*Our first task as professional helpers is to understand how the client makes sense of the world [Ivey's italics]*"[9] and "The process of developmental assessment is best conducted with [E]mpathic understanding as the primary goal."[10]

It further appears that Freud experienced the process of trying to understand the patient in the same way. Middlesex University's Werner Prall discusses in his doctoral thesis Freud's usages of *Einfühlung* and *Sichhineinversetzung* [*PG's translation*—"displacing oneself into the other"]:

> *Sichhineinversetzung*, putting oneself into the other, is here used synonymously to *versuchen zu verstehen*, trying to understand. This use of expression is repeated on the following page: "Das Sichhineinversetzen, Verstehenwollen ist. . . ." ["Displacing oneself into the other is wanting to understand." *PG's translation*][11]

Freud, then, like Rogers, operationalized Self in wanting to understand the client. While acknowledging "the predominantly objectivist stance of Freud who pursued an ideal of the analyst as scientist," Prall's conclusion is that a "hermeneutic Freud" existed along with the "epistemological Freud," which "raise[s] the question . . . to what extent he intended this scientific ideal to be translated into clinical practice." Empathy, Prall says, was for Freud a necessary precondition:

> Freud's conception of empathy as putting oneself into the place of another is intrinsically linked to the wish to understand the other. The intention to understand is not described as prior to the mental movement of *Sichhineinversetzen*, it does not motivate or 'set off' the empathic move; instead, the two processes are presented as happening simultaneously, as being two aspects of the same movement. It is not by coincidence that Freud uses the metaphor of *Sichhineinversetzen*, a term implying physical movement, for his discussion of empathy, nor that his first use of the term empathy concerns the understanding of physical movement. Empathy, as it is here linked with the notion of imitation, *is* a physiological process.[12]

---

9 Ivey, A. E., Ivey, M. B., Myers, J. E. and Sweeney, T. J. (2005). *Developmental Counseling and Therapy: Promoting Wellness Over the Lifespan*. Boston, MA: Lahaska Press, Houghton Mifflin (Copyright 2005 [All quotes and figures reproduced by permission of Taylor and Francis Group, LLC, a division of Informa plc]), p. 22
10 *Ibid.*, p. 101
11 Prall, W. (2000). *Understanding the Patient: The Hermeneutics of Psychotherapy*. PhD thesis. London: Middlesex University, p. 13
12 *Ibid.*, p. 15

An ordinary human behavior is in a purposeful way changed by the therapist to extraordinary effect and becomes a force for therapeutic healing and development. For the adroit, emotionally intelligent clinician, Empathy comes naturally, even unthinkingly, as a physiological process. For the rest of us these operationalizations of Self are behaviors we must in different measure acquire, augment and practice in the context of our professional training. This is sensitive territory and we begin to understand, with our Dialectic-Systemic processing, adept at picking out patterns of patterns, why some of our training institutions are shy to address this intersection of the personal and the professional.

The following case vignette well illustrates the dynamics of *Einfühlung*. I had been seeing Ghislaine for two years. At eighty-three she was terminally ill and in hospice. One day she told me about her abortion, an event she had never before mentioned and which had taken place fifty-four years previously. I listened and responded in the sorts of ways many therapists—many *male* therapists—might. My countertransference was shock. Not so much that Ghislaine had had an abortion but that she had, at the time, been engaged and that she had not told her fiancé about the pregnancy. My countertransference was distinctly *chauvinistic*—a phenomenon of some significance in projective identification since Ghislaine was a Caribbean gentlewoman of the generation that had not bothered to educate its womenfolk because "women get married."

The following week Ghislaine told me again about the abortion, going through the story a second time and supplying additional details. At the time she had the pregnancy test she was already struggling with conflicted feelings in her relationship. She was coming to the realization that her fiancé was alcoholic and that the marriage would not take place. Since she had not been to college and had learned no trade or profession, her prospects for supporting herself were poor enough; as an unmarried mother they were, she concluded, hopeless. How could she possibly manage in the only position open to her—if, as an unmarried mother, she were even accepted for the position—of ... *a secretary*? I listened very intently and ... *I got it*. Ghislaine had been a woman with few resources on the verge of breaking off her engagement. Her *dilemma* was acute. She chose abortion over single motherhood.

Empathizing: confirming not condoning

Her choice, horrible as it was for her, followed Ghislaine's personal logic and *made sense*. Given how hard it would be to make it as a secretary, given that she had been bred not to earn her living independently but rather to be pretty and amusing, bred, in fact, for the lighthearted lifestyle she had hitherto enjoyed with her fiancé, I found it entirely understandable that she had felt she had no alternative. It was thus I was able, finally, to *empathize* with my client. "You had to do it," I said, with congruence, "You saw no other way, you had no choice. I absolutely get that." By the manner of her exhaling as she said a fervent, "Thank you," I knew that this single transaction was the culmination of Ghislaine's therapy. She died not long after.

My ability in *Sichhineinversetzen* to feel myself into Ghislaine's dilemma allowed me to empathize with her decision to have the abortion. *It is essential to our discourse to be aware that empathizing is not to be confused with condoning.* I was able to enter Ghislaine's frame of reference of fifty-four years before and experience her situation as she did then and with the resources then available to her. Her dilemma and her decision made sense as she had experienced it and as she retold her story. Ghislaine wasn't asking me to *agree* with her decision or to *evaluate* it as "right" or even as (patronizingly) "right for Ghislaine at the time." She was not interested in my condoning the decision. Her interest—her profound need—lay in taking me back to revisit her former Self and to witness her former Self in process.

Mirroring

At the time of these sessions Ghislaine was terminally ill and struggling with *Integrity vs Despair*—the eighth and final stage of the psychosocial life cycle posited by developmental psychologists Erik and Joan Erikson[13] when they were working at the University of California, Berkeley. To maintain Integrity she urgently needed to know that her responses to events were *Mirrorable*: in other words, she could be this person and have these feelings and make these decisions and—in spite of the fact that these decisions had terrible consequences—her making them did not exclude her from the human race and her decisions were *human* decisions, understandable to another human being. Yes indeed, a woman can do desperate things, with which she will have to live forever afterwards and which will ever cause her pain. For Ghislaine's diagnosis was somatoform pain disorder. This deeply feeling, highly Sensorimotor, highly intelligent woman had struggled mightily for decades and, unable to condone her own undisclosed and un-Mirrored actions, had unconsciously meted out to herself her own punishment within her own body.

When discussing the psychotherapeutic use of Mirroring, I like to capitalize the word, to distinguish the therapist's intentional, developmental response to his intersubjective experience of the client from other therapist actions (conscious or otherwise) also variously described as mirroring, such as adopting the body position or vocal tone of the client. I prefer University of Illinois professor Thomas Schwandt's definition of *intersubjective*: "an understanding is intersubjective when it is accessible to two or more minds (subjectivities)."[14] The Archetype of Mirroring is, according to English pediatrician and object relations theorist Donald Winnicott, the reflection of the baby's Self in the mother's face: "what the baby sees is himself or herself. In other words the mother is looking at the baby and *what she looks like is related to what she sees there*. [*Winnicott's emphasis*]"[15] The definitions and languaging are very different—but these things are surely two sides of the same coin. Each subject in the intersubjective Mirror can project elements of the Self into the mutuality of the experiencing, thereby altering it for both. Thus our parents love us—and they also *evaluate* us; and when they do so they bring in their

---

13 Erikson, E. H. and Erikson, J. M. (1998). *The Life Cycle Completed*. New York, NY: W. W. Norton
14 Schwandt, T. A. (2006). Inter-subjective understanding. *In* Jupp, V. (Ed.), *The SAGE Dictionary of Social Research Methods*. Accessed via http://dx.doi.org/10.4135/9780857020116
15 Winnicott, D. W. (1971). *Playing and Reality*. New York, NY: Basic Books, pp. 111–112

own hopes, prejudices, weaknesses and distortions—in other words, their level of developmental attainment. As Los Angeles analyst Roger Hastings comments:

> a 'view' or a mental attitude [M]irrored toward us by a needed other can have a penetrative effect because its reflection immediately becomes, at least briefly, a part of how we see ourselves. Adequate psychological boundaries are made or lost right here.[16]

It is these "deficits"[17] in parental Mirroring, as Kahn, following Kohut, describes them, that lead persons in later life, as Hastings goes on to say, to "struggle in understanding how and where their own feelings originate." Clients in this situation require developmentally appropriate and remedial Mirroring from the psychotherapist so as to build what Kahn and Kohut term *self-structure*.[18] When I am accurately and empathically, intersubjectively Mirrored by someone who manifests congruence (further discussed later in this chapter) and who therefore projects into the Empathic encounter only the unconditional positive regard of the Therapist-Self, I can truly know my own feelings and experience . . . who I am. As British psychotherapist and author Paul Renn states, "More narrowly, the [M]irror transference requires the therapist to [M]irror the patient's exhibitionistic display and thus to *confirm* it. [*PG's italics*]"[19] And it is upon this bedrock of self confirmation and true self-knowledge that the possibilities for change are grounded. As Australian psychologist Ronald Lee and colleagues point out, this vital Kohutian Mirroring is, most emphatically, not a "technique:"

> we accept that if [M]irroring is mistakenly thought of as a technique and not as *the experience of the patient* it may well lead to an addictive need for further [M]irroring. [*PG's italics*][20]

Improper attempts in Mirroring, then, whether by the parent or the therapist, lead to a false, "addictive" self. To Mirror properly we have to *discover* the thing about the client we are Mirroring, as I did with Ghislaine and, with and in the moment of that discovering, make an intersubjective connection. Mirroring, then, is congruent self-disclosure of therapist countertransference, following and occurring as a result of Empathic attunement, which affirms and confirms

---

16 Hastings, C. R. (2013). Something Happens: Mirroring in Intersubjective Connection. Institute of Contemporary Psychoanalysis. Accessed February 9th 2014 via http://icpla.edu/wp-content/uploads/2013/08/Something-Happens-Mirroring-In-Intersubjective-Connection-FINAL.pdf
17 Kahn, M. (1994). *In lecture*
18 Kahn, M. (1991). *Between Therapist and Client: The New Relationship*. New York, NY: W. H. Freeman and Company, pp. 105–106
19 Renn, P. (2007). Summary and Comment from a Relational Psychoanalytical Perspective on *The Mirror Transference in the Psychoanalytic Psychotherapy of Alcoholism: A Case Report* by Gustafson, J. (1976), *In* Yalisove, D. L. (Ed.) (1997). *Essential Papers on Addiction*. New York, NY: New York University Press; uploaded to www.counselling-directory.org.uk/counselloradvice9632.html June 13th 2007
20 Lee, R. R., Rountree, A. and McMahon, C. (2008–2010). *Five Kohutian Postulates: Psychotherapy Theory From an Empathic Perspective*. Plymouth: Jason Aronson, p. 70

34 • Phenomenology of clinical decision making

client experience—and, crucially, which process in confirmation and affirmation *becomes client experience intersubjectively shared with the therapist.*

Our theory on theory suggests that this Kohutian Mirroring, which, with Renn, confirms client experience and therefore self, is and has always been present in Good Therapy, whether before or after Kohut and irrespective of the therapist's declared orientation. As discussed in relation to Ghislaine, the therapist is never required to condone but rather, as noted by Chicago professor of psychiatry Michael Basch, to know:

> that the greatest gratification a patient can have is to be properly understood. It is the fear of not being understood that makes the patient mobilize wishes for indulgences [*such as condoning*] that are not truly gratifying. [*PG's insertion*][21]

It is the reciprocal, intersubjective process of *being understood*, as experienced by the client under the therapist's *Mirroring*, that helps the client build the self-structure (Kohut) that allows for the developmental gain (Ivey) that will in turn allow the person to leave the dilemma behind. Again, the therapist is not required to condone; what the therapist is required to do is to *understand* and *Mirror* the client, thereby confirming self.

There are many ways to Mirror. With Ghislaine I used a more explicit way, summarizing her experience, reflecting her feelings and telling her, congruently, I absolutely get it, I am there with her in that situation experiencing the situation and the choices as she experienced them and through her eyes and with her feelings. But many Good Therapists are able to convey these things in sufficient measure to the client nonverbally or less explicitly or differently. Philadelphia psychologist Judith Beck, Aaron Beck's daughter, demonstrates such *affective Mirroring* in a videotaped interview. Beck, who is concerned to dismantle "automatic thoughts" including "picture thoughts,"[22] of course never tells her client verbally that these cognitions are understandable: she doesn't have to, *since her understanding is evident in her affect*. The essential task of Mirroring is performed so long as the client feels, with Basch, fully gotten, fully understood—and fully received into humanity.

Transference

Transference is defined for our purposes as *"all and any thoughts, feelings, responses and reactions, conscious, pre-conscious or unconscious, of the client in relation to or when sitting with the clinical professional."* The client will at all times have a plethora

---

21 Basch, M. F. (1986). How does analysis cure? An appreciation. *In* Psychoanalytic Inquiry, Volume 6, pp. 403–428
22 Beck, J. S., with Carlson, J. and Kjos, D. (Eds.) (1999). *Brief Therapy Inside Out: Cognitive Therapy of Depression* (DVD). Phoenix, AZ: Zeig, Tucker and Theisen

of such responses to the therapy and to the therapist, who, as Rogers and Blow, with Norcross and Wampold, have shown us, is the vehicle for the therapeutic process. These responses are mediated by the client's Personality Style, which, with Ivey, we see as her way of defending against too painful experience. Which experience we now understand, with Hastings and Kohut, was too painful at least in part because of inadequate parental Mirroring. *It is impossible therefore to conceive of any discussion taking place between therapist and client in relation to the presenting problem without the intrusion of dynamics in the relationship.* Kahn held that when the client tells the therapist he was angry today at work with his boss, then it is very likely also to mean he is feeling some anger in relation to the therapist right now, *in the transference.* Kahn requires the therapist then "decode the transference" thus:

THERAPIST: Your boss really got under your skin today, didn't she. I can really feel that. You have, I sense, had quite a struggle today with irritation and anger. And ... it wouldn't surprise me in the least if some of that anger were also directed at me: it makes a lot of sense to me that you, right now, have some complaints and irritation directed at me....

This therapist transaction is termed a "transference interpretation" or "transference invitation"[23] and any consequent discussion of the client's experience of the therapist is termed "transference work." In self psychology theory, transference work is the crucible for personality change via the mechanism of *corrective emotional experience* further described in the following pages.

Congruence

According to our working hypothesis, therapist contributions to outcome are made when the clinician extends Self to the client by operationalizing countertransference. These clinician behaviors require certain competencies in the Feeling-Sensing Style, among them the essential Dialectic-Systemic quality of curiosity. In the context of the therapeutic frame her curiosity allows the clinician to suspend her own prejudices and—free from the burden of condoning—to feel into, even *sink into* the client's personal world and private logic. As discussed, this is an intentional, reciprocal, interactional, physiological, intersubjective process, *occurring over time*. Each of our authorities in theory describes therapeutic communication in terms involving movement and duration. *Einfühlung* cannot be immediate and, fortunately, even clients like Kevin do not require that the clinician quickly uncover the hidden problem. What is required is that the counselor and therapist at all times maintain her *congruence*. Rogers writes thus:

> The first element could be called **genuineness, realness, or congruence**. The more the therapist is himself or herself in the relationship, putting up no professional front or personal facade, the greater is the likelihood that the

---

[23] Kahn, M. (1991). *Op. cit.*, pp. 60–62

client will change and grow in a constructive manner. This means that the therapist is openly being the feelings and attitudes that are flowing within at the moment. Thus, there is a close matching, or congruence, between what is being experienced at the gut level, what is present in awareness, and what is expressed to the client. [*Rogers' bold italics*][24]

This means, for example, the clinician does not tell the client he completely gets her predicament when he is, in fact, still struggling to understand. In fact, if the therapist is indeed struggling to understand, the struggle is potentially valuable countertransference and very possibly an important clue to the client's experience and frame of reference. At such times—and as discussed in relation to Kevin—the Good Therapist maintains congruence and brings the discussion into the transference by saying something like: "You know, [client], something is eluding me and I don't feel I completely get what you're telling me. . . ." The therapist practicing (with Ivey) intentionally will expect one of a limited number of things to occur after such a transaction: the client might supply missing information, much as Ghislaine did the second time we discussed her abortion; or the client might take up the transference baton and run with it—perhaps *this* is her underlying, real problem, perhaps her entire experience is that no one, ever, completely feels into and gets what she is telling the person.

In setting out the general principles of his theory, Rogers previews Basch's maxim that the greatest gratification a patient can have is to be properly understood. Rogers' fifth "necessary and sufficient condition for therapeutic personality change" is that: "The therapist experiences an empathic understanding of the client's internal frame of reference and endeavors to communicate this experience to the client."[25] We are again to understand therefore that what is, ultimately, healing for the client is not *hearing* the therapist say, "I get it," but rather *the experience by the client of the therapist's authenticity in the intersubjective encounter* as the therapist arrives at the point of getting it. For it is, as Lee points out, the client's experiencing the therapist's authenticity that, lest there be any remaining doubt, is what makes Mirroring "proper." It is the crucible for the necessary developmental expansion of the client's Self.

For Rogers, congruence is the "first element" in the manifestation of the Therapist-Self, followed, in his hierarchy, by unconditional positive regard and only then by Empathy. While the therapist is congruent, the client on the other hand is, by definition, "in a state of incongruence, being vulnerable or anxious."[26] *Incongruence* is therefore, in the more parsimonious Rogerian languaging, the description of someone not able to find "balance between the ability to enter into a full

---

24 Rogers, C. R. (1980). *A Way of Being*. Boston, MA: Houghton Mifflin, pp. 115–116
25 Rogers, C. R. (1957). The necessary and sufficient conditions of therapeutic personality change. *In* Journal of Consulting Psychology, Volume 21, pp. 95–103, http://dx.doi.org/10.1037/h0045357. Now in the public domain
26 *Ibid.*

expression of feelings, as represented by Sensorimotor experience and the ability to become more concrete and analytical as the situation changes." Congruence, then, is, for Rogers, the developmental goal of the person—which also means the therapist—and we shall return to examine its significance in relation to the preparation of clinicians.

We now have three developmental mental health goals: the teleological Freudian-Schlossbergian Love, Work and Play; Ivey's balance between full Sensorimotor expression and adaptive processing; and Rogers' elegantly parsimonious reification of congruence. We see that each authority illuminates a different component in the complex sequential processes of living with sufficient adaptation to the environment: if we are able to enter into a full expression of feelings, as represented by Sensorimotor experience, balanced with the ability to become more concrete and analytical as the situation changes, we will then be congruent and will be well-placed for adequacy in our life's tasks of Loving, Working and Playing.

Unconditional positive regard

"What if," a student once asked me, "my client is a child molester? I have two daughters and the idea of child molestation fills me with absolute horror. How could I empathize with such an individual—how could I maintain unconditional positive regard? If I am to be congruent I would recoil from such a client." This is a hard question and when it was posed to me in one of my early classes I don't believe my answer did it, or the questioner, justice. I will attempt a better formulation here, beginning with the disclaimer that I have not myself been in such a position.

It is clear that, if a therapist's obstructive countertransference is such that he abandons the struggle to understand the client, healing of the kind we have been discussing cannot occur. So why, how and under what circumstances might a therapist who is a concerned father of two daughters try to understand a client who is someone who did or would or could molest a child? I begin my answer with theory. Our humanistic and developmental theory tells us that humans are designed to grow into beings who can Love, Work and Play, adaptively and cooperatively, within society. Since the child molester's strivings in the direction of Love are coercive, maladaptive and anathema to society, they must stem from a developmental deficiency that, we can further hypothesize, had its origins in deficits in parental Mirroring—and quite possibly in the experience of being molested or otherwise inappropriately exposed to sexuality when a child. We may become curious, wondering in our Dialectic-Systemic quite how the person came to be this way—and we may even find within us some compassion for this client with so disastrously compromised a faculty for Love. Just as Mirroring is not condoning, so unconditional positive regard does not mean that we regard the client's behaviors unconditionally as positive; it is rather that this regard is for the client as a fellow human being, another person struggling to develop adaptively, whose Self has become shipwrecked, terribly, on the rocks of a developmental insufficiency.

And we are, in fact, permitted one condition for our positive regard and our working hypothesis. Rogers enumerates a sixth necessary and sufficient condition for therapeutic personality change, that: "The communication to the client of the therapist's empathic understanding and unconditional positive regard is to a minimal degree achieved."[27] The client has to be to a minimal degree *engaged* in the therapeutic process. The child molester client of my student's fantasy must show some sign of becoming interested in the therapist's help in developing a better adaptation, one less painful and destructive to Self and other and correspondingly more acceptable to the environment.

This difficult topic brings a further observation: the therapeutic frame requires the clinician to embody and emanate the therapeutic preconditions from and within the Therapist-Self *only for fifty minutes at a time*. Perhaps my student was worried that becoming a therapist and practicing unconditional positive regard might involve him in suspending core aspects of his Self as a man, husband and father. That worry is eminently understandable—and evaporates once the beginning counselor and therapist realizes that the Therapist-Self is an augmentation to and not a replacement of who he is. Clinicians often talk about how the therapeutic relationship is a *different kind of relationship*; and one facet of this is that the therapist is able to nurture, for fifty minutes at a stretch, as a client someone with whom she could not in any way envisage an everyday kind of fellowship.

Good Therapy is, with Ivey, essentially about helping the client develop the capacity in the parts of the Self she or he must augment in order to meet the current environmental challenge; while, according to Rogers and Basch, the context for therapy is the client's struggle for understanding and the therapist's struggle to provide and communicate that understanding. Good Therapy, then, is most emphatically not about providing answers; as Satir declares:

> I am not trying to solve a specific problem such as should they get a divorce or should they have a baby. I am working to help people find a different kind of coping process. I do not see myself as wise enough to know what is the best thing for a person to do. Should the wife ask her mother-in-law to leave? Should she demand that she leave? Should the wife leave her husband if the mother-in-law doesn't leave? These kinds of questions are not mine to answer. My task is to help each person with his or her own coping so that he or she can decide to do the things that work for him or her.[28]

The therapist's unconditional positive regard, then, lies essentially in a position of deep respect for the client as *agent*. There is an understandable, human reason for the client's predicament, actions and omissions. By definition the client is doing her best—and the therapist can help her develop the capacity, via an expanded, augmented Self, to make more adaptive, agentive behavioral choices. The clinician's respect for the client-as-agent acknowledges also that she has done a great deal of thinking before coming to therapy.

---

27 *Ibid.*
28 Satir, V. and Baldwin, M. (1983). *Op. cit.*, p. 186

Her disavowal (a concept elucidated in Chapter 4) notwithstanding, the alcoholic *already knows* in her Dialectic-Systemic that her level of drinking is affecting her quality of life; the wife, in Satir's example, already knows her problem is that no-one listens to her. Very likely each of these clients has received a great deal of advice from well-meaning friends, co-workers or family members to the effect that the one stop drinking and the other speak up for herself. The therapist, on the other hand, is curious rather than prescriptive: how is it that these clients cannot bring themselves to do the things they know they could or should do and therefore must disavow the evidence of their own Dialectic-Systemic and of their family and friends?

Nondefensiveness

We have wondered whether the outcome for Kevin would have been different if the therapist in that first session had self-disclosed his process and extended Self, saying, "Help me out, Kevin. What is it you are trying to tell me that I am not getting? I feel like I don't fully understand or appreciate the extent of this problem so . . . can you tell me again? Or—can you tell me another way, can you tell me if you feel I really get what you're going through?" What would Kevin's reaction have been if his therapist had asked him to talk about his experience of their conversation? What if, having not expected this, he became angry? If the therapist, in choosing (unusually, even for a self psychologist) to shift into transference work in the first session, is also practicing intentionally, then one of the expectable, predictable responses is certainly anger. San Francisco clinical psychologist Brant Cortright, writing with Kahn and Hess, follows Kohut in emphasizing *nondefensiveness*, saying:

> We define non-defensiveness as being open, truly open, to receiving and ingesting feedback. The ability to take in feedback is essential in this psychotherapy business, because being a therapist is an ongoing lesson in humility.[29]

If the client reacts with anger to the transference interpretation, then the Good Therapist, intervening intentionally, plans to elucidate the anger, saying: "You are angry with me, Kevin. You have been talking to me for an hour and now it turns out that I don't understand you any more than you understand yourself—have I got that right?"

And then, operationalizing *Einfühlungsvermögen*, the clinician will empathize with the feelings *underlying* the anger in a Style-shift to the Sensorimotor:

> You must feel so lost, bewildered and frightened, having come to me for help and now what I have said has made you doubt whether I can help you. I feel your fear and your doubt. You should know that I am committed to

---

29 Cortright, B., Kahn, M. and Hess, J. (2004). Speaking from the heart: Integral T-Groups as a tool for training transpersonal psychotherapists. *In* The Journal of Transpersonal Psychology, Volume 35, Issue 2, pp. 127–142

helping you find the answer—and, while you are in this place of fear, hurt, doubt and anger, I will stand with you and help you shoulder those painful feelings.

And then, perhaps, Kevin cries, perhaps for a long time. And then, in the continuation of the therapeutic conversation, it turns out that Kevin has for most of his life been pursued by a sense of not being fully understandable, not being fully seen. And this was the expectable alternative client response to the transference interpretation: that the client jumps straight to, "Yes, I don't really feel you get it. I don't ever feel anyone gets it and I'm not even sure I get it myself." And now we are in a position to begin the real work.

Let us try again to imagine how Kevin feels. His therapist has *gone out of his way* in self-disclosing an earnest struggle to understand him and to help him feel his feelings and understand himself; furthermore the therapist has fully allowed Kevin his anger—and is more present to Kevin after the anger than before. These things—which have created *intimacy*—have *never before happened in these ways* in any of Kevin's relationships. Kevin's "corrective emotional experience in the transference" has begun, with Kahn following Kohut.[30] Kevin now has less reason to be angry: why wouldn't he begin to hope he *can* make a breakthrough with *this* therapist? And, as intimacy and his self-development continue in therapy, would not the new hope drive out any thoughts of ending his life?

Kohut delineated and languaged the *self disorders* in the 1970s. His concept of clinician extension of Self to afford the client *corrective emotional experience* is a critical healing factor in client presentations in which personality is key. The accelerating incidence of self disorders makes it clear that such "Kohutian" competencies are required by counselors and therapists of all orientations and whether primarily preferring goals or process ways of working. San Diego State University professor Jean Twenge chronicles "an epidemic of narcissism":

> We know that narcissism has increased over time among individuals based on several datasets. College students now endorse more narcissistic traits than college students did in the 1980s and 1990s; in one large sample the change seemed to be accelerating after 2002.[31]

Chaudhuri would expect a culture witnessing increased incidence of self disorders to bring forth the answer to the need. And indeed we see this in the new focus on personality in the DSM-V, and in voices such as Ivey's, Kelly's and Clarkin's. Kohutian theory is enjoying new iterations in analogues such as the *transference focused psychotherapy* (TFP) of the Personality Disorders Institute of the Weill Medical College of Cornell University and in Lee's Empathink Association based

---

30 Kahn, M. (1991). *Op. cit.*, pp. 91–93
31 Twenge, J. M. (2009). *The Narcissism Epidemic: Living in the Age of Entitlement*. New York, NY: Simon and Schuster

in Victoria, Australia. If good case conceptualization is, as our working hypothesis tells us, to treat personality along with (and, if mandated by the dialectic, before) symptoms, then Kohutian process methods indeed turn out to be an indispensable component in the armamentarium of the adroit CBT practitioner.

And clinician nondefensiveness, an indispensable component of transference work, becomes the fourth essential therapist quality, after the three posited by Rogers. And then there is curiosity, another attribute of the Dialectic-Systemic: now we have five. The Good Therapist manages her countertransference and, with Ogden, uses it as her primary therapeutic tool in feeling herself into an *intersubjective* understanding of the client, her Therapist-Self embodying, emanating, practicing and modeling *congruence, unconditional positive regard, Empathy, nondefensiveness* and *curiosity*. And it is this understanding and the communication of it between the subjects that unlocks the way forward and makes developmental gain possible, including via corrective experiencing for clients manifesting the self disorders, in ways we shall further examine.

Practice-based evidence

Mediated within the clinician's Task Positive Brain and Default Mode Network, the dialectic in counseling and therapy between goals and process governs all clinical decision making. The dialectical tension between the opposing theses is found in every aspect of the work, existing also in the evidence of the protocol or literature (goals), as against the evidence of our countertransference sensorium (process). Competency in managing the dialectic is the "clinical expertise" component of evidence-based practice in psychology. It is what gives the client what the client needs and when. Its presence allows Kevin's first therapist to make a difference.

While Kevin is a fantasized composite, his legacy to us is to illustrate how absolutely important it is for the clinician to manage the dialectic. Understanding how the clinician can do all the right things and yet not give the client what the client needs means understanding the complex relationship between research conclusions, clinician training and practice and clinical outcomes. A significant rubric is provided by East Carolina University psychiatrist Sy Atezaz Saeed, who designs algorithms for evidence-based psychopharmacotherapy. As Saeed notes:

> Evidence-based practice enhances the overall care delivery system by providing treatments that are proven to be effective, by using systematic outcome management components and then feeding this information back to the system to enhance training in the areas consistently shown to be areas where outcomes appear to be lagging behind the defined thresholds. [Figure 2.1] illustrates the vicious cycle relationship between clinical care, outcome management and training.[32]

---

32 Saeed, S. A. (2005). Evidence-based psychopharmacotherapy: Medication guidelines and algorithms. *In* Stout, C. E and Hayes, R. A. (Eds.), *The Evidence-Based Practice: Methods, Models, and Tools for Mental Health Professionals*. Hoboken, NJ: John Wiley & Sons, p. 85 ff

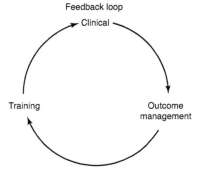

Figure 2.1 Vicious cycle: vulnerability of feedback from outcome to training

Source: Saeed, 2005, reprinted with permission from John Wiley & Sons.

Saeed, with Waller, is concerned with the quality of feedback return from clinical outcomes to practicing clinicians, elsewhere referred to as *accountability*. Waller's idea is to break the vicious cycle by assuring a two-way flow of communication: from outcomes back to practicing clinicians and from practicing clinicians back to training programs.

In another study, citing both therapist drift from protocol and how "clinicians' own cognitions, emotions and other characteristics might interfere with the use of such [protocols]," Hannah Turner of the British National Health Service and colleagues including Waller hypothesize that the phenomenon is not limited to the treatment of eating disorders. Turner concludes:

> future research . . . will determine whether these findings relating to CBT for the eating disorders apply to other disorders and therapies. . . . A more objectively driven pattern of feedback to supervisees . . . might help to increase the likelihood of evidence-based interventions being delivered in routine clinical settings.[33]

Clinicians, then, are apt to aspire to evidence-based interventions, but whether they can contrive to deliver them is another matter. We seek Good Therapy and an understanding of why, in what manner, when and for how long each of the opposing theses holds (temporarily) the key to optimizing outcome for the client. Our purpose is to improve and refine our understanding and practice of evidence-based methodology. Not every CBT clinician is as adroit in contrivance as Burns—and the same can be said also of clinicians who are not CBT clinicians.

---

33 Turner, H., Tatham, M., Lant, M., Mountford, V. A. and Waller, G. (2014). Clinicians concerns about delivering cognitive-behavioural therapy for eating disorders. *In* Behaviour Research and Therapy, Volume 57, pp. 38–42 [All quotes reprinted with permission from Elsevier]

We have come full circle. But our conclusion goes further than Turner's: our working hypothesis now looks to require all clinicians to receive training in Kohutian methods (or analogues) sufficient to permit them to manage the dialectic, practicing from within their preferred model. How this may be done within a program primarily espousing CBT is shown in the third part of this book.

Process vs goals

And now the false dichotomy in the culture wars and great debate is entirely laid bare. No one will ever prove or disprove either the thesis of "therapists heal people" or of "treatments heal disorders." For both are of necessity happening at the same time, as Blow and Norcross remind us. Our quest is not to decide the culture wars in one side's favor but rather, by following what contributes to outcomes, to understand and manage the dialectic between goals and process in counseling and therapy.

We note that the dialectic between the dual pathways of treatment *is in the service of the goals and is itself a process*. The Good Therapist is therefore, we can again infer, required to accrue capacities in the process-sensitive "Feeling-Sensing Style" of the Self that allow her to perform the essential therapist task of managing the dialectic.

Discussion

- *How do you understand the concept of projective identification?*
- *Do you agree with Ogden that projective identification is "the basic unit of study of the therapeutic interaction?" What can he possibly mean by this?*
- *How do you reconcile it when your Feeling-Sensing Style, with an "internal manifestation," tells you one thing and your Doing Style, perhaps via a supervisor's instruction, tells you another?*
- *The therapeutic encounter between "Kevin" and his clinician is here presented in idealized form. Kevin was depressed and the immediate clinical goal was to avert suicide. The therapeutic encounter between "Ghislaine" and her clinician is similarly presented. Ghislaine was dying and the clinical goal was the Eriksonian "eighth stage" task of the triumph of Integrity over Despair. Could these goals have been reached more efficiently and more adroitly than here portrayed?*
- *How do you experience empathy? Is it, as suggested in this chapter, something "physiological"? How do you understand the clinician's "operationalization" of Empathy?*

3

Relationship

Mirroring and evolutionary theory • the difference between counseling and therapy

---

Clinician extension of self • Mirroring and intersubjectivity • proper and improper Mirroring • vulnerability of the clinician • client's dilemma

The case of Joty

Accountability and the goals–process decision tree
Indivisible co-occurrence of counseling and therapy

Confirmation of client self: the developmental basis for the goals thesis

---

> *"It is a central tenet in the practice of psychotherapy that the relationship between patient and therapist is the primary tool used for change."*[1]

Psychotherapy, then, is a developmental endeavor performed across two distinct, inseparable domains, the domain of *process* and the domain of *goals*, the necessary dialectic between which the therapist manages by operationalizing countertransference so as to extend Self. The clinician's own developmental assets and deficiencies will predispose us to favor one domain over the other. But if we can nonetheless contrive to draw sufficiently from each domain we can indeed be the solution to Turner's question: *are evidence-based interventions in fact being delivered in routine clinical settings*?

Turner's hypothesis corroborates ours: standing in the way of correct implementation of the evidence-based model are *the personal developmental issues of the clinician* such as (in the study cited) anxiety over client response to aspects of the manualized treatment plan.[2] Some practitioners fall short in Norcross' therapist contributions and Wampold's contextual factors and in the necessary and

---

[1] Edwards, J. K. and Bess, J. M. (1998). Developing effectiveness in the therapeutic use of self. *In* Clinical Social Work Journal, Volume 26, Issue 1, Spring, pp. 89–105
[2] Turner, H., Tatham, M., Lant, M., Mountford, V. A. and Waller, G. (2014). Clinicians concerns about delivering cognitive-behavioural therapy for eating disorders. *In* Behaviour Research and Therapy, Volume 57, pp. 38–42 [All quotes reprinted with permission from Elsevier]

significant countertransferential operationalizations of the Therapist-Self. Some, less adroit, less emotionally intelligent clinicians insufficiently mobilize their Dialectic-Systemic to look beyond the presenting discourse so as to be able to import into treatment the APA-mandated "decisions and interventions not directly addressed by the available research"; and they are perhaps, such as some clinicians studied by Turner (and supervised by José), insufficiently self-reflective—another attribute of the Dialectic-Systemic—as regards their failures in full implementation of protocols (and in case conceptualization).

Drift from the dialectic

These deficiencies are equally accessible to each clinician, whether we incline more to goals-based or process-based methods of counseling and therapy. Our models are, with Blow, the vehicle for potentiating Good Therapy, which necessarily requires skills in both goals and process for successful implementation. "Therapist drift" is, we now see, reframed: it is a deviation not necessarily (though it may be) from narrow model attributes in either goals or process but rather, more fundamentally, from the Archetype and from the dialectic.

In the Therapist-Self, *process* correlates with *Feeling-Sensing Style* correlates with *Sensorimotor plus Dialectic-Systemic* and the clinician's Default Mode Network, while *goals* correlates with *Doing Style* correlates with *Concrete plus Formal* and the clinician's Task Positive Brain. As Ivey advises, "higher is not better," and if we are underweight in one or more Styles, it is more likely we will find difficulty meeting certain clinical challenges. Managing the dialectic has a different appearance in each client case. Therapists, then, are required, with the APA, *to know, judge* and *decide* when it is more and when it is less beneficial to make clinical decisions from within or from outside our preferred default model, the ways of practicing in which we are most comfortable and least anxious. In this way the clinical relationship is like any other: we are apt to become pressured when someone asks something from us that we are not so well equipped to give.

Our DCT assessment of the less adroit clinician has already disclosed an overreliance on the Doing Style: reification in case conceptualization is the behavior of a clinician relying too much on Concrete processing and early Formal reasoning. In the Feeling-Sensing Style the less emotionally intelligent clinician's Sensorimotor is unsupported by adequate development in the Dialectic-Systemic. Clients respond to how clinicians are. The implications for the education and preparation of beginning counselors and therapists are perfectly clear: *this is a developmental endeavor and such development of the student is the proper sphere of activity of the educator and training institution.*

As our quest for Good Therapy advances we necessarily continue the focus on the two process legs of the stool of evidence-based practice in psychology: clinician contributions and expertise and client values and preferences. We have observed that, for some clinicians in a predominantly cognitive-behavioral and solutions-focused academic program, the environmental call to development is to advance in the Feeling-Sensing Style of the Dialectic-Systemic and Sensorimotor. But what of clinicians working predominantly within the relationship thesis in, for example, an academic program oriented to self psychology: is their environmental call to development to advance in the Doing Style? Speaking for myself, this is patently true. And I too needed to advance in the Feeling-Sensing Style. That process-preferring clinicians have no need of better outcomes, that students of process-based methods evidence no maladroitness in theory implementation and no need to advance in the Feeling-Sensing Style along with the Doing Style is not a credible proposition. All our evidence points unmistakably in the same direction. In terms of horizontal development, "more," repeats Ivey, "is better."[3] This is particularly the case if we are preparing to become a therapist. To understand fully the requirements for development of the Therapist-Self, we continue to examine the phenomenology of the clinical encounter and what it is therapists do.

Psychotherapy and process

In the first stage of psychotherapy, while goals, urgency and risk are specific to each case, the process is the same: the therapist works to arrive at an understanding of the client and to create for the client an intersubjective experience of feeling understood. Our arrival here constitutes the first pivotal point in treatment (the second being the full unfolding of the client's dilemma, further discussed in Chapter 5). This place of therapeutic communication is a potent juncture where, as Hastings comments, "adequate psychological boundaries are made or lost," depending on the properness of the intersubjective connection in the Mirror. In other words, dependent upon the Self, congruence and countertransference management of the therapist.

To test our hypothesizing we should be on the lookout for instances in which, when therapist and client arrive, via the therapist's proper Mirroring, at an intersubjective experiencing, the client evidences a constructive internal shift. We must gather our own data on when, again in Hastings words, *something happens*. Something giving the client "more room" psychologically, more self-structure, more self-understanding, more tolerance and more choice—all of which then re-present themselves as manifestations feeding back into the clinician's countertransference. The client is free, now, to choose to take a developmental step that has hitherto eluded her, and how wonderful that feels both to her and to her clinician.

"Personal/professional qualities and characteristics"

We are feeling our way into an appreciation of what Norcross, Richardson, Blow and others interested in understanding outcome mean by therapist contributions and common factors. We are inclined to place prominently in our working hypothesis the formulation that differences in therapist behavior and client outcome are due to

---

3 Ivey, A. E., Ivey, M. B., Myers, J. E. and Sweeney, T. J. (2005). *Developmental Counseling and Therapy: Promoting Wellness Over the Lifespan*. Boston, MA: Lahaska Press, Houghton Mifflin (Copyright 2005 [All quotes and figures reproduced by permission of Taylor and Francis Group, LLC, a division of Informa plc]), p. 261

differences in therapist use of Self in client engagement. It turns out that Mirroring may be properly done, affording the client developmental gain—or not. When Mirroring is properly done, the experience of having self "confirmed," the Winnicottian experience of "seeing himself in the [therapist's] eyes," the experience of connecting with the therapist's experience of him and then drawing, deriving something from that, somehow changes the client's experience of himself. A metaphorical inner combination lock releases... and the client has thereby become "bigger," more congruent and more able to meet environmental challenge. Just like that. In the domain of goals and from our Doing Style, we may or may not have, in the same session, used a technique in psychoeducation or in role-play, and we may or may not have set the client "homework" according to a protocol. But what we have as Good Therapists done is, with Freud, "put ourselves inside the client," experienced his perspective on our joining him and conferred something of our perspective to his experiencing.

We have data suggesting that the therapist, in Katsivelaris' languaging, *operationalizes* Self in a manner that *allows something to happen in the client* in, as Hastings describes it, "the moment of magic."[4] We have seen something of the magic: it is the kind that can persuade a client like Kevin that he has real hope if he returns to continue the work with this clinician. We will go on to examine other instances. And no doubt each of us has further data, having experienced such moments of magic in our own work, whether as client or clinician. Yet even as we feel our way here to this pivotal point in our quest, our understanding proves elusive and we are reduced to expressions such as "something happens" and "moment of magic." While for some of us these expressions may be sufficient to maintain enthusiasm for our working hypothesis and its validity, others among us require further explanation and corroboration.

Evolution

Here Massachusetts psychologist Malcolm Slavin and colleagues have come to our aid. Seeking better to explain and understand the intersubjective component in human development and in psychotherapy Slavin affords us a compelling, sophisticated hypothesis in evolutionary psychology, most recently distilled into a paper discussing a topic of some relevance to our quest: "Aspects of the treatment relationship in which the analyst's needs inevitably clash with those of the patient."[5] Slavin proposes that the evolutionary forces that contributed to the human infant's needing a prolonged period of dependency have put our species some distance away from the natural way primates adapt to the phenomenological world. To compensate for what we have lost, we have had to develop other ways

---

4 Hastings, C. R. (2013). Something Happens: Mirroring in Intersubjective Connection. Institute of Contemporary Psychoanalysis. *Accessed February 9th 2014 via* http://icpla.edu/wp-content/uploads/2013/08/Something-Happens-Mirroring-In-Intersubjective-Connection-FINAL.pdf, p. 49
5 Slavin, M. O. (2012). Lullaby on the dark side: Existential anxiety, making meaning and the dialectics of self and other. *In* Aron, L. and Harris, A. (Eds.), *Relational Psychoanalysis, Volume 4: Expansion of Theory*. New York, NY and Hove, East Sussex: Routledge, pp. pp. 391–413

of constructing reality. Malcolm Slavin and Massachusetts psychoanalyst Daniel Kriegman have elsewhere put it thus:[6]

> As a species we have 'sacrificed' certain kinds of hard-wired, innate knowledge about ourselves and the world. In exchange we developed the capacity to construct a map of the self and the object world based on our ongoing experience of ourselves, the world's response to us and the complex interplay that results as these phenomena become intertwined with each other as well as our reactions to them.... We are 'hard-wired' with a program that permits (and requires) us to learn much about ourselves and the world through interactional patterns.

Other people's intersubjective influencing is indispensable to our meaning-making. Slavin's argument resonates with Ivey's conceptualization of the higher Styles and with how it comes about that humans have needed to develop in them in the ways we have; this idea at the same time provides bedrock for Jung's theory of the collective unconscious and the transpersonal dimension. Hastings' response to Slavin is enthusiastic; the evolutionary hypothesis, he writes, helps:

> connect [M]irroring experiences with attachment processes and the many existential motivations which make the need for human connection so distinctive. It is ... as though the thread of connection runs between the [M]irroring situation through the intersubjective motives to evolutionary strategies. It describes the human need to constantly construct forms of living through family, work, myth and ritual that are meaningfully connected to others. When is meaning made? Perhaps only when we can 'feel' the connection.[7]

And this necessity for the therapist to *feel* in extending Self is why our work is not so easy—and why, as discussed earlier, the process in *Einfühlung* necessarily occurs *over time*. "Connecting," says Hastings,[8] "requires that we be vulnerable to the other with our entire 'insides,' that we open to what we would feel if *we* were the one in the first-person." The Therapist-Self, then, is required to operationalize not only Empathy but also *vulnerability*. The pivotal place of intersubjective understanding is properly reached at a measured, purposeful pace. It is not something to be rushed into.

The "therapist's dilemma"

If we accept into our working hypothesis the notion that the "magic moment" in psychotherapy is when the client "feels the connection" and can respond to the intersubjective experience by evolving or developing, then we must also accept that this proposal must inform our idea of "client-centeredness." In the intersubjective

---

6 Slavin, M. O. and Kriegman, D. H. (1992). *The Adaptive Design of the Human Psyche: Psychoanalysis, Evolutionary Biology and the Therapeutic Process*. New York, NY: Guilford Press, p. 138
7 Hastings, C. R. (2013). *Op. cit.*, pp. 19–20
8 *Ibid.*, p. 7

connection aspects of the therapist's experience and subjectivity become fused into the client's. This creates a dilemma for the therapist. What if, a student asks me, my client has a deeply religious persuasion and does not want her daughter to marry outside their faith? What if I see the connectednesses between all faiths and the client's experience seems, to me, more primitive? How can I be perfectly client-centered and avoid introducing my spiritual biases into the treatment? The question is a good one—and it is answered by following the evidence presented by the developmental model. The client is experiencing, with Ivey, an environmental challenge. It could be—and perhaps will be, but, with Satir, we cannot know this ahead of the event—that the fantasized client's eventual response to the challenge will indeed be to develop a more Dialectic-Systemic perspective on faith, similar to the therapist's. Should we be alarmed if this indeed turns out to be the outcome? If this does turn out to be the outcome, should we feel guilty because we have "tampered" with the client's belief system? Or is there a way of getting the client and her daughter on the same page that obviates the therapist's dilemma? It is a cornerstone of the teachings of the narrative school that therapist and client "co-construct" a new reality or self-narrative for the client—can such co-construction also satisfy our precepts as to client-centeredness?

We already know the answer. It is yes. Provided that the therapist can start out by feeling his way into an understanding of the client's dilemma and, with Ivey, Mirror the client's more Concrete experience as a woman of faith. A therapist stance of "persuading" or "teaching" or "coaching" or "counseling" serves only to convince the client to hold more tightly to her construction of the problem and place of stuckness. Her evolution, her development is *the client's own*, and it must be done her way:

CLIENT: My faith is everything to me and always has been. In our culture from even before a child can talk she knows she is surrounded by her faith and that her family have always been and always will be followers of the faith. All the things I have ever done and ever learned are illuminated only against the one backdrop of our beliefs and customs.

THERAPIST: I am, I think, beginning to understand. If your daughter were to marry this man who does not have this shared experience, context, beliefs and customs, it would turn your whole world upside down; it would negate everything you have ever done and everything your parents have ever brought you up to do and everything you have brought your daughter up to do and to value. It feels to me . . . like it would sort of *cancel out* all that you and your family stand for and have always stood for. Which includes all the great sacrifices you all have made over the years.

CLIENT: Yes, it would be devastating. . . . [*cries*]

CLIENT: I'm very glad you understand me. I was afraid you wouldn't. My daughter doesn't, of course, understand me and even some of my friends and relatives, people in our community who share our faith, seem to feel that I am being very old-fashioned and that I should move with the times.

THERAPIST: I do understand you. Moving with the times is perhaps for other people. For people like you and your family it feels vital to hold to what you know. You do not know what it might lead to if you do not.

CLIENT: Yes. . . . [*cries*]

CLIENT: We needed to leave our country and come here. I didn't want to. I knew these things would happen.

THERAPIST: You knew these things would happen?

CLIENT: Yes. I had no choice. . . . [*cries*]

THERAPIST: You had no choice but to leave your country with your husband and you knew—is it—that these things would happen, that changing your country would change your family? You have been living with this hard knowledge all these years while your daughter has been growing up? You have been carrying a great burden.

CLIENT: Yes. And all of the time I was wondering . . . could I live with that, if my daughter marries someone not of our faith. . . . [*cries*]

THERAPIST: You have done all this wondering . . . almost, it seems to me, like you have been *preparing yourself to, if you have to, persuade yourself*—is that it, have I got that right?

CLIENT: Yes. And I *can't persuade myself* to allow it. I don't want to! [*cries*]

THERAPIST: Is it . . . is it that a part of yourself thinks you should allow it or you must allow it? Is that what you are saying?

CLIENT: I see how the world is. Things change. . . .

THERAPIST: *If only they didn't change!*

CLIENT: [*sighs*]

In this fantasized interview, the client knows the therapist most probably has some ideas about the inevitability of change. Her daughter has the same ideas, with which she has forcibly bombarded the client. The mother comes to therapy with a conflict of many years' gestation. Her need, with Renn, is to confirm Self intersubjectively and to find out exactly what it is that, after all these years of worrying about this issue, she, now the moment of decision has arrived, will make of it. The fact the therapist *has felt himself into her wish for changelessness* has confirmed it, in the way the daughter's opposition and well-meaning friends' counsel could not. The therapist has, congruently, looked at it her way—and his so doing has now made internal space for her and given her courage to look at it from her Dialectic-Systemic perspective of *the inevitability of change*. And it is a small step from here, we see, to the discussion, which the client herself will begin as her Dialectic-Systemic prompts her to seek the synthesis, of the common truths underlying faiths.

But it need not go like this. We could see mother and daughter conjointly and facilitate their communication and DCT development. Perhaps, after communication is restored, the daughter decides against marrying her boyfriend and that the old ways are simply too valuable to drop. This is *their* process and their faith, not ours. Whatever the family chooses, we will have had a part in making that choice possible.

We can conclude, then, that we can have it both ways, indeed this is expected of us: we can be both entirely client-centered and congruent—true to what we know. We note, with our Dialectic-Systemic and with Chaudhuri, that we have resolved our therapist's dilemma in the same way the client has resolved hers, via a *synthesis of opposites*.

The difference between psychotherapy and counseling

Our fantasized client, whom we will call Joty, has a *thesis* to the effect that her life is and always has been contextualized in and upon her faith. The *antithesis* is that things change, particularly when one is compelled to move oneself and one's family into a new country and context. We saw very clearly in the fantasized dialogue—and we have met the same thing often in our own lived experience—that Joty will have one response to us if we pressurize or "lawyer" her with "facts" and "inevitabilities" and quite another response if we listen without pressurizing. If we *tell* Joty that she cannot resist evolutionary change, we will find that she redoubles her efforts in resistance. If, on the other hand, we empathize with her painful reluctance to let go we may well discover she will find it in her Self to do so. There is a profound difference to be seen between, on the one hand, the provision of information or advice to someone who needs it and, on the other, a developmental endeavor in which we work to help the client find information or advice within her Self *via an expansion of Self*. There can be no clearer distinguishing between the root meanings of the two expressions "counseling" and "psychotherapy." *Counseling* derives from the Latin *consilium* meaning, variously, "advice," "counsel," "consultation"; while *psychotherapy* derives from the Greek *psyche* ("soul," "breath of life") and *therapeia* ("healing," "ministering to").

Though counseling and psychotherapy are *in essence* completely different sets of behaviors, upon close examination it is apparent that they are very rarely, if ever, performed in "pure" form: a certain amount of overlap or admixture is inevitable. For example a psychoeducation (more counseling, because information and advice-giving) intervention may be done therapeutically with both explicit and implicit Mirroring. We can imagine a manualized sequence in CBT methodology (more counseling because administered) performed, variously, with minimal clinician self-engagement or with a steady emanation from the clinician of all the Rogerian and Kohutian qualities. In the real world of the consulting room, Ivey's purposeful circumlocution "counseling and therapy" describes the unitary synthesis of elements in unstable proportion and subject to a dialectic.

What happens if we do not teach these differences to our students? In the case of those more adroit prospective clinicians who are naturally emotionally intelligent, warm, empathic and Mirroring, their default behaviors will import psychotherapy and psychotherapeutic gain into administering even the driest goals-based protocol or clinical "tool." But in the case of those students who are perhaps drawn to *Doing* models and interventions precisely because they seem, on the face of it, to require less of the clinician in terms of engagement with and extending Self to the client, it will be seen that it is absolutely vital both to teach these differences and to facilitate developmental augmentation of the Therapist-Self.

Process *and* goals

And our Dialectic-Systemic, which is so much quicker than our Formal, has spotted the correlations even before we can write or read the words: the domain of counseling (teaching, "fixing," advice-giving) is informed by the domain of goals, the domain of psychotherapy ("ministering to the soul") by the domain of process. The more the clinician does counseling (goals) with a client who needs psychotherapy (process) the less likely it is that treatment will be effective; the more the clinician does psychotherapy (process) with a client who needs counseling (goals) the less likely it is that treatment will be effective. The more the clinical experience is intersubjective, the more *therapeutic* it is; the more, however, the practitioner is concerned with "fixing" the client's problem, the more she or he is interested in doing so without full *Sichhineinversetzen* into the client's experience and with less by way of extension of Self to the client, the less "proper" Mirroring the client will receive and the less will be her opportunity, with Kohut, to build self-structure and develop out of her self disorder: the client will experience a lesser level of connectedness with her therapist and a correspondingly lesser level of, with Ivey, developmental gain. And whatever the clinician's methodology of allegiance the less likely is it that this treatment will count amongst those with more successful outcomes.

Goals and goals-based methods are fundamental and intrinsic to counseling and therapy. Goals is why we are here. The *client-specific content* of the goals varies. The process element in the goals is invariable: in DCT the goal expressed as a reification of process is sufficient adaptation; for Rogers it is congruence and with Schlossberg it is Love, Work and Play. It is also, surely, true to say that the two theses in this dialectic *need* each other. There can be no concerns for process unless there are also concerns for goals. And there can be no focus on goals without a corresponding focus to process. We begin, then, to understand the confusion in the terminology. Psychotherapy and counseling *must inevitably co-occur*. They are not the same but they are inextricably plaited together in the therapy room.

Accountability and the goals-process decision tree

Accountability is a recent construct formulated in response to the concern that evidence-based interventions are not being delivered by some clinicians. According to North Carolina State University professor of counselor education Stanley Baker,

> Counseling practitioners who evaluate their local interventions can use the findings to improve their practices and to be accountable to their stakeholders. This accountability process involves action research as opposed to outcome research. Action research focuses on generating local rather than generalized knowledge (as is the case with outcome research).[9]

---

9 Baker, S. B. (2012). A New View of Evidence-Based Practice. *Opinion Post. Accessed October 30th 2016 via* http://ct.counseling.org/2012/12/a-new-view-of-evidence-based-practice/

Baker's idea is analogue to Turner's and Saeed's. "Action research" in this context incorporates Satir's emphasis on the clinician's internal manifestations: therapy, we recall, is an essentially localized endeavor between client and clinician. An accountable clinician, therefore, is able to give an account of her clinical actions in managing the dialectic between goals and process, *as it pertains now to this client.*

In the case of the alcoholic client with a history of relapse, the developmental, accountable treatment plan is to keep him safe while equipping him with tools to stay sober while also developing his personality as required to allow him to make good use of the sobriety tools. The investigation of relapse triggers is a goals-informed treatment necessity and we may be inclined to categorize the relapse prevention worksheet as a "more goals-based" intervention. Yet it is, inevitably, also vehicle for the psychodynamic element, its questions serving to stimulate client process and uncover underlying feeling, paving the way for client and therapist to look together at the cognitions informing the relapse impulse and at their early origins. *The dialectic between goals and process is therefore intrinsic to the worksheet tool.*

Augmentation of the process component in treatment allows for the working through of any incomplete *Gestalten* in issues of abandonment, betrayal or shame and which may impede the goal of sobriety—and (with Waller) which may impede completion of the worksheet. This work is hard, the dialectic finely balanced and, in the hypothetical example given, the alcoholic client needs the clinician to have mastery in both goals-based and process-based methods. If the clinician, believing in the curative effect of the analytical working through, *over-relies* on process, the stress on the client of the revival of the ancient feelings could trigger the feared relapse; if, in the (possibly process-preferring) clinician's judgment, a relapse is not improbable, this is a countertransferential signal to shift the balance back now in favor of the goals-based component by (for instance) reiterating the intervention of the worksheet to strengthen the client's Doing Style resolve to take appropriate action in the face of the cognitive-emotional triggers.

The example helps us better understand Waller's therapist drift. The *apparently* goals-informed protocols necessarily stimulate process and therefore *talking*. And we see more clearly how goals and process are a kaleidoscopic co-occurrence: it is not possible to disentangle or to "measure" goals and process elements in treatment. What is possible—and mandatory—is to understand and respond to signals that one of the elements has become too dominant or is insufficient and that the client is not, right now, receiving what she needs. In knowing and deciding when the dialectic demands either more process or more goals, there are two points of reference. The first is the client's response: is she disengaged or disengaging; or has she (however weakly or imperceptibly) projected her response into the clinician's countertransference, providing a cue or clue that the trajectory of treatment contains an insufficiency in either process or goals? The second point of reference is the clinician's cognitions in relation to the most recently pursued interventions: was the clinician resisting (in the example) either the worksheet or the talking? Mastery of the two points of reference, client response and clinician cognition, confers intentionality, as further explored in Part III of this book.

Summary

So we begin to understand that this thing we have called "therapy" or, perhaps, "counseling" (according to our own preference) is, in reality, both. The composite endeavor stemming from the operationalization of the Therapist-Self is, rather, ***counseling-and-therapy***. The part of the endeavor that is psychotherapy is differentiated by its location in the Feeling-Sensing Style and *is indeed* describable as the clinician working to understand and extend Self to the client and *is indeed* reducible to "therapist contributions" including the evidence of our own countertransference and the evolutionary magic of the intersubjective connection we establish. The part of the endeavor that is counseling is differentiated by its location in the Doing Style and does indeed require of the therapist, as the evidence-based hypothesis suggests, much specific learning, activity, judgment and wisdom. And accountability. Both parts of the endeavor require extensive and particular training, experience and knowledge.

And we can further see how important it is to the outcome of our work that we know who we are. Are we more counselor, yet working therapeutically by using Mirroring intersubjectively? Or are we more therapist, yet with sufficient access to techniques and strategies from the Doing Style toolbox? Can we be more inclined to one but still manifest both as and when required? Either way we must heed Truscott: it is simply no longer good enough to say we are disinclined to draw from this or that theory or method and will practice exclusively from our default zone of maximum comfort.

And if Hastings is right and doing therapy well requires us to operationalize our vulnerability in extending Self, then we can also begin to see not only how the clinician may fall short but also the weighty implications for the proper preparation of the clinician to do the work. Bringing our vulnerable Self to the encounter is surely something we are, all of us, scared to do, and, if the ability to do so is indeed a necessary component of Good Therapy, then we each one of us risk therapist drift. And what if the clinician is too vulnerable in his vulnerability? Again we recall the part of our working hypothesis that suggests the way clinicians practice correlates with our predilections and prejudices and the balance in assets and liabilities within our Therapist-Self.

Discussion

- *Do you feel, or want to be, more a counselor or more a therapist?*
- *Do you prefer to think of yourself as a "counselor" or a "therapist"? How do you respond to the suggestion that you are, in fact, a "counselor-and-therapist"? Is the distinction here advanced between counseling and psychotherapy useful?*

- *How do you experience your vulnerability? How do you feel about using it in the professional context, extending your vulnerability into the therapeutic encounter in the service of the client?*
- *Do you find Slavin's evolutionary hypothesis helpful? How does "proper" Mirroring (here defined as psychotherapy) help advance specific clinical goals and counseling interventions?*
- *Do you sometimes experience the "therapist's dilemma" here outlined? Do you agree with how it was handled by Joty's clinician?*

4
Conceptualization
Client personality development and second-order change • signal of the dialectic

---

Case conceptualization and the developmental model • disavowal and the client's story • first-order change and second-order change • intersubjectivity

Operationalizing and extending Self
Engagement of the hard-to-reach client

Treating symptoms or developing personality • duty to follow the client's lead and duty to look beyond

The case of Chantal

"Happy people are happy in relationship; unhappy people are unhappy in the context of relationship."[1]

Los Angeles psychiatrist and theoretician William Glasser defines our happiness as a function of how we relate. Humans are designed to relate to and communicate with each other; when we are floundering in these essential tasks of living, we become discouraged; and when our discouragement reaches a critical point, we enter therapy. It is also, as Kohut, Kahn, Ivey, Hastings and Slavin severally teach us, in and through suboptimal relationship that psychotherapy clients have become unhappy and incongruent. As Cortright puts it: "after decades of disavowal, most people are very out of touch with their feelings,"[2] and it follows logically that many, if not most incoming clients are somewhat like Kevin, with a story and a presenting problem that do not, quite, add up and are not so easy to communicate and understand. How exactly are the client's problems and the client's relationships connected? Like Kevin, many clients *reify* or Concretize their presenting problem, tending to frame their discourse around *things and situations* rather than *feelings-in-relationship*.

---

[1] Glasser, W. and Glasser, C. (2005). Treating Mental Health as a Public Health Problem. *Presentation* to the Oxford Symposium in School-Based Family Counseling, Brasenose College, Oxford, Monday August 8th
[2] Cortright, B., Kahn, M. and Hess, J. (2004). Speaking from the heart: Integral T-Groups as a tool for training transpersonal psychotherapists. *In* The Journal of Transpersonal Psychology, Volume 35, Issue 2, pp. 127–142

Thus Kevin's presenting problem, so puzzling to the first therapist, was that he had moved out of his rented apartment and bought a house—and come swiftly to feel terrible about his "mistake." While everyone can regret a mistake, the self-deception is to pretend that what we regret is the *thing* we messed up and not the *relationship failures* implied by our messing it up. To illustrate the principle further let us now personalize the fantasized client in Satir's quote (p. 38), who comes to therapy asking if she should leave her husband. Her name is Chantal, and her problem is her husband allows his mother to rule the roost. Kevin talked for an hour, Concretely and Formally, about why he *ought to have known* not to give up his lease in the first place; and Chantal comes looking for answers to the Concrete question of *what should she do*. Kevin did not discuss relationship and Chantal's similarly late Concrete/early Formal discourse mostly circumvents feelings—particularly about how her husband allows his mother to upset her.

The defenses in Personality Style, as Ivey conceptualizes it, are failing and the painful feelings are breaking through; the clients seek a return to the familiar and comfortable state of disavowal and come to therapy hoping the clinician will supply the necessary psychological reinforcements to enable such return. Joty would have liked to turn the clock back for herself and her daughter. Chantal is wanting to return to her preferred self-narrative of being untroubled as a wife and mother, and Kevin wants to return to his previous sense of being a smart guy on top of life's important decisions and who always makes good choices.

Disavowal

All clients are looking to escape their encroaching feelings by turning the clock back to disavowal even though in their Dialectic-Systemic, as we have earlier theorized, they know, as Joty knew, that the clock cannot be turned back. But when we cannot see the way forward we cannot *let go* of the (perfectly factual and developmentally sound) idea that we were, when our previous defenses were working, in reasonable shape. And, as we shall go on to examine, the concept of "letting go" is key in transition theory and will become an important aid to our case conceptualization.

In British psychoanalyst James Strachey's *Standard Edition of the Complete Psychological Works of Sigmund Freud*, "disavowal" is the translation into English of *Verleugnen*, the word used by Freud to describe the little boy's response to his startling discovery that the little girl does not have a penis.[3] Hard to translate into English, which has no exact equivalent, *Verleugnen* literally means: "making a liar of oneself." Basch is widely credited with reviving and updating Freud's insight to confirm the ubiquity of this defense mechanism that is neither, on the one hand, repression nor, on the other, denial. Expressed metaphorically, disavowal is a refusal to notice the lines between the dots. Expressed in a Concrete example, *Verleugnen*

---

3 Freud, S. (Strachey, J. B., Freud, A., Strachey, A. and Tyson, A., Eds.) (1956–1974). *The Standard Edition of the Complete Psychological Works of Sigmund Freud*. London: Hogarth Press

58 • Phenomenology of clinical decision making

is when a wife chooses to believe that her chronically absent husband really is working late at the office. As Basch describes it, disavowal refers to instances:

> where the [perception] has not been eliminated but only its significance for the observer has been distorted, rationalized or misinterpreted in the interest of preventing anxiety.[4]

In Cortright's simpler languaging, "in disavowal, we pretend that something or someone does not affect us as much as they really do."[5] Clearly disavowal is an analogue to incongruence—and therefore a key component in the client's presentation. This is how Chantal has been accustomed to disguise her relationship unhappinesses into "being perfectly content if mother-in-law stays away," and this is how Kevin used to disguise his, with his sense of being the man whose intelligence ensures he always comes out ahead. *We see that when our Sensorimotor might hurt us we are apt to take refuge in the Concrete and the Formal and in reification.* In these ways, and as we saw in Kevin's first session, the client's presenting narrative is inevitably in some way understated. [Figure 4.1].

Figure 4.1 Disavowal

---

4 Basch, M. F. (1983). The perception of reality and the disavowal of meaning. *In* Annual of Psychoanalysis, Volume 11, pp. 25–53
5 Cortright, B., Kahn, M. and Hess, J. (2004). *Op. cit.*

Good case conceptualization incorporates both goals (the implications of the client's presenting narrative) and process (how the client's orientation to self-in-relationship is the inevitable precursor of the problem and goals). We see again, with Ivey, Clarkin, Lee and Glasser, that, behind the content of the presenting narrative, which might be about *things*, what we are also treating is the client's *personal style of relating and responding*. Underlying this is the psychic pain and arising out of the pain are the painful behaviors bringing the client to the consulting room. Haidt would no doubt see client disavowal in terms of the rider urgently confabulating away the evidence of her DMN. The dialectic resurfaces in terms of the client's orientation to her goals and disavowal of her process.

Looking beyond the presenting problem

Thus my student's case (p. xxiv) was about the prostitution behaviors *and* the client's sensitivity to being looked down upon; Kevin's was about the mistake *and* about why it's so important *for him* not to make a mistake; and Chantal's is about her impossible mother-in-law *and* how it comes about that Chantal is, as Ivey would have it, insufficiently developed in one or more DCT Styles to rise above the environmental challenge mother-in-law poses.

Yet although we know there is more, we cannot *look beyond* the presenting problem and narrative until we have looked *at* them. We meet, respond and relate to the client exactly where she is. As further elucidated in the third part of this book, our intentional plan is to begin in the goals discourse and assess the client's response, thereby generating further data to inform our case conceptualization. If the presenting problem overlays, with Burns, a deeper, underlying issue, this will become clear as the therapeutic conversation progresses. With a more complete conceptualization of who and what it is we are treating we are more prepared to respond to the dialectic with the particular mix of goals and process needed by *this* client.

As we journey with the client into her inquiry, our duty completely to understand her is, as we saw with Joty, quite simply inescapable. As Rogers describes it:

> being [E]mpathic is to perceive the internal frame of reference of another with accuracy and with the emotional components and meanings which pertain thereto ... it means to sense the hurt or the pleasure of another as he senses it and to perceive the causes thereof as he perceives them.[6]

"To sense the hurt or pleasure of another" is (lower-case, everyday) empathy. To do all these other things constitutes Katsivelaris' "operationalization." How each counselor and therapist does, performs, manifests or emanates *Einfühlung* to arrive at an intersubjective understanding of the client and how we each experience the process

---

6 Rogers, C. R. (1980). *A Way of Being*. Boston, MA: Houghton Mifflin, p. 140

and seek to describe it in metaphor is specific to the individual clinician. I find it helps me to conceive, kinesthetically, of "under-standing" as *standing under* the client and I like to hyphenate the word to remind me of its physiological component.

Einfühlung is a process toward engagement. Because of the client's disavowal and understatements and because people use language differently, the therapist cannot take it for granted that her attributions to even everyday words and expressions match the quality of the client's actual experience. Particularly when expressions are reified and evaluative. The Good Therapist therefore will, as described by Chicago psychotherapist and psychology professor Barbara Brodley, take pains to "check, test or verify the accuracy of his or her subjective empathic understanding"[7] and at times might interrupt the client—breaking a cardinal rule of active listening—in order to ask *questions necessary to understanding*, as in the sequence:

CHANTAL: As I have said, my mother-in-law is very *overbearing*. . . .

THERAPIST: [*interrupting*] What do you mean by "overbearing"?

CHANTAL: It's all about her, and her son, and her grandson and I just can't stand hearing it all. . . .

THERAPIST: [*interrupting*] Hearing her say what? Tell me about an incident you are thinking of, Chantal; I would like to experience it as you experienced it. What were the circumstances, how did it start and what exactly did she say and do?

CHANTAL: Last week we were together in the kitchen, just the two of us, fixing lunch for the boys . . . [*continues without interruption*]

The elements of client disavowal, incongruence and reification are evident in this brief, fantasized dialogue. Chantal is inclined to complain about patterns ("overbearing" mother-in-law) from her early Formal Style and in a reified, impressionistic, *evaluating* manner. "Overbearing" = "bad." To be able effectively to help his client the therapist needs to feel into what is going on, and to do this he needs to be able to, as I term it, "run the tapes" of at least one interactional scene between Chantal and her mother-in-law. This is accomplished by the interruptions, which, as discussed (p. 12), constitute an initial DCT Style-shift from Formal to Concrete.

Acute observers of transference and countertransference will notice also that in this fantasized vignette the therapist, with his intrusive interrupting, risks becoming as overbearing as the mother-in-law! And this is where we again see the crossover in counseling and therapy from the focus on *content* to the focus on *process* and intersubjectivity in the clinical relationship. In terms of *case conceptualization* is

---

7 Brodley, B. T. (1992–1996). Empathic understanding and feelings in client-centered therapy. *In* The Person-Centered Journal, Volume 3, Issue 1, *and citing*
  Brodley, B. T. (1985). Criteria for making empathic understanding responses in client-centered therapy. *In* Renaissance, Volume 2, Issue 1, pp. 1–3. *And* Rogers, C. R. (1986). Reflection of feelings. *In* Person-Centered Review, Volume 1, pp. 375–377

this about a woman with a difficult mother-in-law, or is this about a woman whose way of being-in-the-world, whose way of being-in-relation—whose Personality Style—might tend to bring out in others the overbearing part of the personality that resides, somewhere, in all of us? Certainly our fantasized client, Chantal, has brought out the overbearing part of the therapist's personality, and the therapist needs carefully to analyze his countertransference before proceeding.

For our DCT model suggests Chantal's issues with mother-in-law are not so much about the mother-in-law (however irritating this good woman is) as they are about Chantal's not having the developmental foundation to rise to the challenge mother-in-law presents. DCT thereby points to a deeper underlying problem in Chantal's manner of negotiating relationships, based on her Personality Style. Pursuing such thoughts, our fantasized therapist becomes indeed curious. Is Chantal's husband—were her father, mother—also overbearing? Or is there a role reversal in the marital relationship and is it Chantal who "overbears" her husband? Is Chantal, in fact, a woman of strong opinions, and is her conflict or dilemma around *wanting to impose her ideas on others*? But is she then prevented from actively telling people what she wants them to do by one of her most firmly held ideas, that a woman, especially a youngish woman, *mustn't be seen to be assertive*? Caution in conceptualization extends to treatment: our countertransferential ideation *at least suggests* that administering (for example) assertiveness training to Chantal to strengthen her in negotiations with mother-in-law may fail. As already noted, it is safest to assume the client has already wondered about becoming more assertive and has rejected the notion because of, with Burns, *a hidden emotion or problem*.

Yet in her presentation Chantal does seem to be making the problem about her mother-in-law. And when we "run the tapes," she does appear to lack assertiveness. So we pursue our goals-based strategy and invite Chantal to role-play "remonstrating with mother-in-law." But she leans back in her chair and seems to be feigning enthusiasm for the role-play gambit. And now we have arrived at an inflection point in clinical decision making. *Chantal is showing us very clearly that she will not take the role-play home from the therapy room.* We know, from our theory of the dialectic, this means we must now switch from goals to process. Before we make the shift—and to see how DCT bears on the dialectic between goals and process in counseling and therapy—let us also now make a developmental assessment of our client.

Chantal is predominantly Concrete in the way she tells her story. Her affect is range-bound, and the clinician cannot feel much in the way of pain (or other emotion) emanating from her. Except perhaps irritation: her voice is somewhat charged only when discussing mother-in-law's rudenesses. When she talks about patterns of behavior and feelings she "talks about" them with at least as much Concrete as Formal, holding herself stiffly. Thus her Formal and Sensorimotor expression are gripped and held in a narrow range by being Concretized. Conversations begun by the clinician around how other people—perhaps her husband?—see the problem go nowhere. Chantal seems as passive in these conversations as she does in the role-play. It is clear, then, that she is stuck in the Concrete Style. She does not enter into a full expression of feelings. Nor does she become more analytical as the situation changes. *Her limits in the Sensorimotor and in the Formal preclude the intervention of assertiveness training*. British social psychologist Michael Argyle wrote: "[One] problem with the concept of assertiveness is that it is both complex and situation-specific . . . Behaviors that are assertive in one circumstance may not be so in another."[8] In DCT terms, Chantal does not have the developmental assets in emotional intelligence to manage the dialectic identified by Argyle between passivity and rudeness. *She cannot therefore make use of the role-play intervention—and to implement it now is therefore maladroit.*

We have further evidence supporting our decision to shift to process in the clinician's projective identification countertransference. Yes, the mother-in-law likely is very difficult—and it could very well be that Chantal, who is unpracticed in remonstrating, would benefit from some role-play exercises in how best to handle conversations with her, *but what if a deeper fear prevents Chantal from profiting from such an intervention?* The existence of such a deeper, darker fear, perhaps around being rejected for speaking her mind, may lie behind the closed-off Sensorimotor and the under-developed Formal. Which is why Chantal has a dilemma. Other persons may greatly annoy her and—since the avenue of assertively remonstrating is not open to her—she is powerless in terms of changing her exposure to such annoyance. It is therefore inevitable, inescapable that her therapist too will annoy her. As by the maladroitly timed role-play.

Since Chantal's response to annoyance in relationship is indirect, she may cancel a session, arrive late or otherwise act out. If her Personality Style has more "borderline" elements than we realized, she may leave treatment and seek another therapist. It is therefore imperative that the clinician pre-empt any such behavior by giving Chantal the hope, as previously suggested in relation to Kevin, of entering a new world, experiencing a *different dimension* in relationship. The therapist, Chantal will observe, can be just as annoying—and overbearing—as anyone else; and yet . . . he is trying to communicate, kindly, to her that he understands the effects of his annoyingness and overbearingness; *and no-one else has ever done this*! In fact, thinking about it, the fact the therapist understands the effects of his behavior seems to go a long way to lessening these effects, making them more tolerable! The therapist Mirrors and confirms Chantal's experience of annoyance in the therapeutic relationship and so she stays—and becomes interested and engaged in doing transference work, in discussing her relationship with the therapist.

Kahn follows other self psychologists in discussing the client's *corrective emotional experience in the transference* and the building of *self-structure* as a direct, intended consequence of experiencing the therapist's Mirroring.[9] The client simply becomes "bigger." The family system remains challenging. But now, with a bigger Self, where previously there was no way out from a clash of interests or wills—other than into Bowenian uproar or internalizing anger and disavowal—there are, suddenly, expanded options. Because the client has now built self-structure and

---

8 Argyle, M. (1981). *Social Situations*. Cambridge: Cambridge University Press, p. 50
9 Kahn, M. (1991). *Between Therapist and Client: The New Relationship*. New York, NY: W. H. Freeman and Company, p. 102

become bigger, her disavowal is necessarily, as Cortright terms it, "eroded."[10] The feelings of shame, previously too painful to experience fully and therefore tenaciously and at vast cost defended against, have now been experienced with the therapist and ... have lost much or all of their power. For it turns out that Chantal believed, maladaptively, that she would be utterly rejected if ever she allowed herself to be fully congruent in her anger—for this was the sense she got from her mother when very young and which inevitably and under-standably led to her developing the precise defensive structures she did.

When all Chantal's previously defended-against Sensorimotor experience is fully allowed and processed into a new self-narrative of expanded awareness—in DCT terminology after horizontal development in both the Sensorimotor and the Formal—and with some excursions into the Dialectic-Systemic—then mother-in-law becomes who she really is, the annoying mother-in-law of an adult woman and no longer a transference proxy for the fragile mother of the vulnerable little girl who could not tolerate her little girl's anger. With her libidinal energies freed and with expanded functioning across Ivey's four Styles, Chantal is now in a position to choose (with Glasser) from a range of more adaptive behaviors; or, in the languaging of another theory and because mother-in-law, who has her own problems, is genuinely annoying, to learn and adopt appropriate "coping skills." With increased self-esteem—the intersubjective byproduct in Kohut's theory of the therapist's congruent Mirroring—Chantal is able to find ways of communicating to mother-in-law with congruence and, demonstrating to mother-in-law that daughter-in-law is changed, is able to force a corresponding change upon the family system.

And, if at this point she feels she needs it, Chantal will herself ask the clinician for more role-play exercises in remonstration.

Change

We have located the difference between adroitness and maladroitness in case conceptualization and clinical decision making: it is the difference between Chantal leaning back in her seat in passive rejection of the role-play intervention and Chantal eagerly and actively asking for it. And it is in the different actions of the counselor and therapist when confronted with Chantal's rejection of the intervention. And now we have to ask again: could the outcome to Chantal's therapy be equally successful if the clinician, instead of deciding to switch to process and work self psychologically in the transference, chose to focus minimally on the therapeutic relationship and more on Doing interventions? Is there scope for the clinician to bypass the self-structure building and DCT development and instead reiterate the remonstration training, delivered, this time perhaps, with more adroitness and better timing? The answer is,

---

10 Cortright, B., Kahn, M. and Hess, J. (2004). *Op. cit.*

as to every question in life and in psychology, according to San Francisco educator Mildred Dubitzky: *It depends*.[11] And now we must look into the concepts, earlier previewed, of "first-order change" and "second-order change."

Educator and consultant Simon Priest and co-author Michael Gass of the University of New Hampshire describe the difference between the two kinds of change thus:

> First order change produces change within a structured system using the same set of rules and components. This can be like pedaling a bike up a steep hill without shifting gears. As the hill becomes steeper, the bicyclist must work harder within the structure of that gear ratio, using techniques that enable her/him to keep from falling over and reach the top of the hill (e.g., stand up, pull on the handlebars, exert more pressure on the pedals). However, say that as the hill steepens and the gear ratio becomes inappropriate or dysfunctional for this task, the bicyclist shifts gears to a more appropriate ratio. Using the new set of 'rules' dictated by the more functional gear ratio, the bicyclist exerts the same amount of effort yet progresses up the hill much more effectively. This 'shift' is analogous to second order change, working in a different and new way by changing the structure of the system. First order change uses 'more of the same' rules to produce change; second order change creates transformation by changing the way change is achieved.[12]

In other words, returning to Chantal and her issues with mother-in-law, under first-order change the structure of the system would not change: the mother-in-law would still be experienced by Chantal as overbearing. She would implement some strategies taught her by the therapist and designed to give her some measure of relief from the effects of the overbearingness. Chantal remains *essentially the same person* and her transference to mother-in-law, which elicits (as from the therapist) more of the overbearing behaviors, would remain. But second-order change is systemic. Chantal has achieved horizontal development in her Sensorimotor and Formal; and, via the clinician's "*What do you make of it all?*" questioning, has made some advances into her Dialectic-Systemic. She has been able to detach from the fragile mother transference, is possessed of more self-structure and quite simply is not the same person. Chantal's Personality Style has changed. Mother-in-law's annoyingness is simply unable to trigger her as before. Because of this the two women's experience of each other changes. The issues that brought Chantal into therapy are those of a different person in the past. Her dilemma has either vanished or very greatly eroded. She is no longer so angry and upset, nor so disavowing. To

---

11 Dubitzky, M. (1993). *In lecture*
12 Priest, S. and Gass, M. A. (1997). An examination of "problem solving" vs "solution oriented" facilitation styles in a corporate setting. *In* Journal of Experiential Education, Volume 20, Issue 1, pp. 34–39 *and citing*
    Watzlawick, P., Weakland, J. H. and Fisch, R. (1974). *Change: Principles of Problem Formation and Problem Resolution*. New York, NY: Norton

the extent she has a need for the role-play intervention (she surely needs to practice the art of remonstration after so many years abstinence) she now has the developmental foundation to request and profit from it.

We asked: could the outcome to Chantal's therapy be equally successful, could second-order change occur, if the clinician, instead of choosing to work self psychologically in the transference, focused minimally on transference work and more on cognitive-behavioral interventions? The obvious answer is, yes. It could. The only rule governing the time spent in psychotherapeutic treatment on, variously, *content* and *process* is the rule of *It depends*. Some clients can achieve second-order change with relative ease and speed in treatment in which transference work plays a minimal role. And some, apparently, cannot. Our quest for the difference between adroitness and maladroitness in clinical decision making is of significance for those of us who are concerned to improve outcomes and who notice, perhaps, that our clients look to be achieving first-order change but not second-order change and—to adopt languaging from transition theory—have therefore not *completed* the clinically significant transition that has brought them to therapy.

Managing the dialectic

Our clients, then, *may or may not* be able to achieve second-order change in treatment with a minimal focus on process or the transference. We require our hypothesis to explain the difference between the two groups of clients. Transition theory (more fully explored in Chapters 5 and 7) interprets second-order change as *letting go*. Chantal is required to let go of that part of her self-image that relies on not disclosing her anger or dissatisfaction in an act of remonstrating. Is she less affected by a self disorder and with a developmental foundation that permits her to let go without her counselor and therapist focusing on process and the transference—or not? If we are to practice intentionally and adroitly we must differentiate between these two groups of clients, the ones requiring less from us in Feeling-Sensing and the ones requiring more.

Our working hypothesis is that the salient evidence comes from within the therapist's countertransference. The more active the therapist's countertransference, the more the client is projecting; the more the client is projecting, the greater the client's disavowal and incongruence; the greater the client's incongruence and disavowal, the greater is also her need for Mirroring and the reparative, intersubjective, developmental work of self-structure building and the DCT developmental sequences. And the more all these things are in evidence, the greater her problems with what we have, variously, referred to as Personality Style or self disorder.

The therapist, in sum, *already has all the information* to assess whether the dialectic will, with this patient, call for process-based techniques. The greater the necessary developmental work of self-structure building, the greater the client's problems navigating and negotiating the relationships that life has bestowed upon her. And the greater these problems, the more they manifest in the therapist's countertransference, the more, by definition, they are present in the client's transference. The more pronounced the transference, the more profound the repetition compulsion, the weightier are also the intrapsychic dynamics and developmental insufficiencies conspiring to prevent the client from benefiting, right now, from goals-based work that is not mediated by depth work.

The two kinds of client, then, are properly distinguishable—evidentially—by the *Einfühlungsvermögen* of the Good Therapist, working intentionally, whose sensorium is alert to client cues. With Chantal we saw her lean back in the first attempt at the role-play intervention. We then, via projective identification, *just knew* she would not take anything home with her from the exercise. We also had the sense there was the deeper fear. We *might perhaps* decide to reiterate the role-play intervention more adroitly; but we now have not one, not two, but *three* good reasons to believe the dialectic is calling for a switch to process. The process switch, our working hypothesis tells us, *will* deliver therapeutic gain and good outcome. A reiteration of the role-play only *might* deliver. It is not sanctioned by the evidence-based hypothesis: at this point the single leg of the evidence of the utility of the intervention is merely a probabilistic inference and the odds are shortening.

The good news for the hitherto less adroit clinician working on becoming more adroit is that the signs given by the dialectic are unambiguous and very hard to miss:

THERAPIST: What happened at the weekend when your mother-in-law came over?

CHANTAL: More of the same. I kept myself busy cooking and washing up and just left her with my husband and son. It's best that way.

THERAPIST: I'm curious: did you get a chance to practice remonstrating with her?

CHANTAL: Not really. It's easier just to use the time to get the house straightened up. Much less risky. I hope you don't mind [*with "nervous" laugh*].

THERAPIST: [*smiling*] It makes sense to me you still think remonstrating is risky. We only practiced it once. [*maladroitly and still pursuing reified case conceptualization*] Tell me more about what happened at the weekend and shall we practice again?

CHANTAL: [*silence*]

[*beginning to exhibit physical signs of discomfort*]

The signal of the dialectic [Figure 4.2], disavowed by the clinician in the previous session, is now unmistakable. Unless the clinician switches to process now, Chantal will leave treatment. The client's Default Mode Network is stirring up in her a physical discomfort that pours cold water on the Task Positive Brain of the clinician. The confabulator has been caught out and falls flat on his face.

It surely follows that the more the client is the kind of client described here, the more active the transference and countertransference system, the more likely it is that this client is among the 50% to 74% of clients in Richardson's study who achieved subpar outcomes. We already know this correlation to be the case in Waller's study, when the level of disturbance in the client's self is more than the clinician can handle. We now understand Richardson's differences in therapists' professional qualities and characteristics as *differences in therapist use of Self in client engagement*.

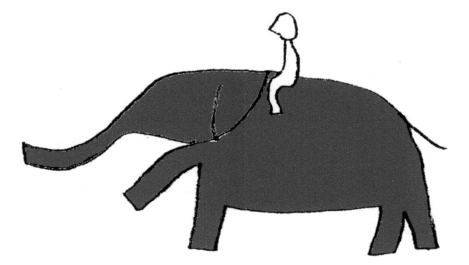

Figure 4.2 Signal of the dialectic

Summary

We now conclude, for the purposes of our working hypothesis, that use of the therapeutic relationship, use of Self in client engagement, becomes crucial and pivotal in the treatment of precisely those clients who are hard to treat, hard to keep in therapy and hard to reach. Could this idea explain the prodigious outcome variances ranging from around 25% to around 90% found by Winter between Bowenian and Satirian therapists? The Satirian therapists whose training, Aponte and Winter say, mandates self-development. We have begun to see the therapist's operationalization of Self in another way, in terms of the need to respond intentionally to the client's personality. Although goals are hierarchically prior in treatment, in case conceptualization—*what is this case about and what change is needed?*—the priority is with process.

Discussion

- "Disavowal" is here presented as a characteristic, characterological defensive structure: *have you noticed disavowal in your clients' self-narratives? Do you employ disavowal to any extent in your own self-narratives?*
- *Do you agree with the concepts of "first-order change" and "second-order change"? Do you recognize these different orders of change in your clients—or in yourself? Is second-order change "better"?*
- *Do you feel more comfortable "treating symptoms" or "developing personality" in your clients? Do you find the distinction useful to your case conceptualization?*
- *Do you find case conceptualization to be necessary?*
- *Do you agree that clients are often "unreliable" in what they tell you or in the way they tell you things?*

5
Treatment
Pathology, adaptation, transference and transition • the environmental call to let go

> Working hypothesis for Good Therapy • transition theory Continuum of pathology • assessing the transference
>
> School-based family counseling and therapy • clinician as stakeholder for family members
>
> Necessary augmentation of the Therapist-Self • developmental preparation of the client for second-order change • letting go

Harnessing the relationship

The psychotherapy client is in pain. At times this is all too obvious. At other times the affect is strangely, curiously absent and its curious absence acts as a barrier to our feeling into the client's pain. And sometimes the pain is more noticeable in the person or persons who referred the client, such as the parent or school. But, let us make no mistake, the pain is there, isolated and imprisoned in its disavowal. The client comes to therapy because of the pain and her goal, as discussed, is to be free of the pain and—with Glasser—to be happy in relationship. *She does not want to be in therapy.*

Beginning counselors and therapists have an attachment to the role of clinician, and sometimes we project our concept of professional satisfaction—a full caseload—onto our clients, especially at times when the client's transference stance is to be compliant and appreciative. But, always excepting those rare clients who come to or remain in therapy more for reasons of personal growth than of pain, it is safest to assume that even the "good client" does not want to be in therapy and would very likely prefer to be spending her time and money in another fashion.

The client's goal is to escape the pain. And the clinician's goal is to help the client to develop so as to put the pain behind her—a somewhat different formulation. The DCT counselor and therapist works toward the goal by conducting a developmental assessment of the client and generating an Empathy-based case hypothesis flowing from that assessment and a developmentally informed treatment plan flowing from that hypothesis. So much is very clear. We know we must begin by asking questions and following leads so as to feel ourselves into an understanding of the clients *story* [Greek: *logos* = "word"] of *suffering* [*pathein* = "suffer"] or *pathology*, asking ourselves what *must not have happened* or what must have happened *inadequately or insufficiently* in this client's development for this pain to arise in this way in response to environmental stimulus; and what, exactly, was and what is the environmental circumstance and challenge? How does it come about that this client is, at present, unable to respond more adaptively and happily to the environment (Love, Work, Play) even though, as we have seen, she may well already in her heart know the sorts of changes that might help her?

In conducting the kind of assessment recommended by DCT I find it helpful to look at what it is the client seems *not* to be doing. Is the client not feeling, not fully expressing Sensorimotor experience (or is she stuck in and overwhelmed by the Sensorimotor)? Is the client, like Kevin, intellectualizing—stuck in his higher Styles of Formal and Dialectic-Systemic and resistant to clinician endeavor to "descend" him into the Concrete, let alone the Sensorimotor (intellectualizing defense)? Or are there specific gaps in the client's competencies in the higher Styles, such as with Ivey's example client (p. 16), who was too Concrete in certain interactions with his wife? Once we begin thinking like this, the DCT perspective imports new insights into our case hypothesis and conceptualization: *of course* the client's abilities in the DCT Styles are as they are, given what we know about her childhood and parents. Her symptoms and behavior, with Freud, *make sense*.[1] We see, again with Ivey, how very logical is the client's best default Personality Style, and with ease feel ourselves into an under-standing of *what it is the client now wants from us in the transference*.

Story of suffering

Let us recapitulate what we know about the client from the outset, before she has even set foot in the consulting room. We know she is, with Rogers, in a state of incongruence and, with Basch and Cortright, in a state of disavowal; and we know too, with Kohut and Kahn, that these states are in some logical, under-standable fashion the product of an insufficiently or improperly Mirrored Self. We understand, with Ivey, that the client's Personality Style and way of relating may become a primary focus in treatment—again with Kahn and Kohut as well as with Rogers. This is who the client is, who she has learned to be, the set of defenses that have, entirely under-standably, in the past served best to ward off depression and pain. This is her *character* [Greek: *kharakter* = "an engraved or stamped mark"], and *this is who she is in relationship*. How she feels about herself in relation to others will, of necessity, be how she presents to her therapist: the more unhappy she is in relationship, the more this unhappiness and the relational patterns it creates will manifest in the transference. We know too, with Ivey, what has brought the client into therapy, perhaps with new symptoms: the familiar defensive structures

---

1 Freud, S. (1956–1974). The sense of symptoms [Die Sinne der Symptomen]. *In* Strachey, J. B., Freud, A., Strachey, A. and Tyson, A., (Eds.), *The Standard Edition of the Complete Psychological Works of Sigmund Freud*. London: Hogarth Press, Vol. 16, pp. 264–269

in Personality Style have begun to fail and the underlying depression and pain can no longer be warded off.

Upon entering treatment, we also know, the client's *preparedness for second-order change* will depend on where she stands along the continuum of pathology; by assembling our developmental assessment and Empathy-based case hypothesis we will with some accuracy be able to delineate both her developmental achievement and our intentional treatment plan—the likely best choice from available protocols and the likely order in which we will expect to implement our interventions. The client may require either more or less preparation in either depth work or specific development in one or more DCT Styles before being able to benefit from certain problem-specific interventions in cognitive-behavioral technique. Very possibly, and if further advanced on the continuum of self-disorders, she will need a combination of the two forms of preparation. When a client has previously done much of her developmental and depth work (perhaps with another therapist), we may find the path to second-order change has been correspondingly prepared. But when the client's functioning is hampered by much disavowal and held-in, unprocessed, un-Mirrored feelings, when she cannot operate in (it may be) her Formal Style sufficiently well to make good use, yet, of the therapist's recommendations in (for example) psychoeducation—and when the dilemma and its main feeling (a concept further elucidated in the third part of this book) have not been fully uncovered and under-stood—it is highly probable that she will not respond as the therapist would wish to such *too-early-applied* intervention. This much we know at the outset of therapy.

Transition

We know also that the client is, when viewed through another, exceedingly helpful theoretical lens, most assuredly in the "neutral zone" of at least one *transition*. A transition, according to Larkspur, California, speaker, consultant and author, William Bridges, is an *intrapsychic process occurring over time* that is not capable of direct observation and that occurs in response to a *change* or other call or prompt from the environment.[2] When a woman marries, we can see and know about this event, and the marriage is therefore a change. The woman's interior realignment or, in Bridges' terminology, *disidentification* from her unmarried self and role and *reidentification* into her new married self and role occurs *over time*, spanning periods both before and after the wedding and, being intrapsychic and therefore unseen, is a *transition*. The period between the environmental call—in the example given this may be the proposal—and the completion of the reidentification can be challenging and provoke anxiety. This *neutral zone* of the transition is where symptoms can occur; if and when the transition proves troublesome, it is these symptoms that we can observe and that bring the person to therapy. Bridges therefore follows Ivey: symptoms arise in response to a new environmental challenge. We are always, all of us, in transition and, indeed, in multiple overlapping

---

2 Bridges, W. (2001). *The Way of Transition: Embracing Life's Most Difficult Moments*. New York, NY: Perseus Publishing

transitions, some of which can last for decades and some of which can be clinically significant and the focus of therapy.

Bridges' lens instructs us to be aware that the environmental call provoking the transition (even if it is, to use one of Schlossberg's descriptors, an *elected transition*)[3] is invariably a call to *let go* of something that was cherished by or in some other—perhaps *defensive*—way important to the old, now-called-upon-to-be-disidentified Self. All of the sometimes terrible difficulties and sufferings of the neutral zone stem from our unwillingness to let go. We may "cycle" between more-or-less letting go and more-or-less holding on, prolonging our neutral zone agony and symptoms of distress. *Such cycles may go on, it appears, indefinitely.* The transition is complete only upon the final letting go. The usefulness of Bridges' theoretical matrix lies not in looking for the client's necessary reidentification and hastening the client through her neutral zone for, as Satir has cautioned us, the therapist can be of no use in pointing to reidentification, to evaluating whether the wife should leave her husband and reidentify as a newly single woman. Bridges' usefulness is rather in affording the therapist insight into the exquisite pain and difficulty involved in letting go—so that we may feel ourself into it and empathize with it, as did Joty's therapist. Letting go involves deep, profound *mourning*. And it is to the client's place of mourning that we, with our *Einfühlungsvermögen*, are to point and in which experience we are to join her intersubjectively.

The thing that must be let go is often not readily apparent at the outset of treatment—it was not so with Kevin—and when it comes into view it is often a poor, bedraggled little thing, slipping so easily into and back out of the therapeutic conversation and whose significance we are often quick to misunderstand and overlook. In the months following Kevin's death his half-brother had several conversations with the therapist treating Kevin at the time of his death and with some of Kevin's friends. The story he was able to piece together explains why Kevin killed himself and sheds light on the evidential clues everyone missed. Kevin's *content*, the focus and subject-matter of his discourse, was the terrible mistake he made in relinquishing his lease and becoming a homeowner. He was "stuck" on how he, a brilliant financial analyst and incisive thinker, could possibly have made such disastrous mistakes in planning. The poor, bedraggled little thing that nobody noticed was that Kevin had been drawn into some experimentation with methamphetamine drugs—and, as a result, had become worried that he had irreversibly damaged his brain. Of course, if he had communicated this worry to one of the two clinicians in our vignette, that clinician would have been able to address it. But he didn't, which is why it fell to Kevin's half-brother to piece the information together. Kevin had, the brother discovered, mentioned to one person that he had taken methamphetamines, to another that taking them is toxic to the brain—and to the clinician he mentioned only that he was worried about his ability to make good decisions. The case conceptualization of the clinician treating Kevin at the

---

[3] Schlossberg, N. K. (1984). *Counseling Adults in Transition: Linking Practice With Theory.* New York, NY: Springer

time of his death was that his client was a man undergoing a mid-life crisis and that Kevin's anxieties in real-estate decision making were a proxy for his existential anxieties as a still-single man of 49. This is the logical, developmentally informed case conceptualization of a Good Therapist. Yet the therapist missed something. Perhaps their conversation went something like this:

KEVIN: I'm still feeling very, very badly about my stupidity in giving up the lease of the apartment.

THERAPIST: You're still feeling that, I get that. I'm really sorry this continues to be so hard for you. The feeling you shouldn't have left is so prominent it obscures everything else. And, underneath that very prominent, dominant feeling ... is there anything else you are feeling, similarly, has gone wrong or is adrift in your life right now? [*goals-based: the therapist is thinking about his case conceptualization, which he has reified, and is trying to pave the way for an interpretation*]

KEVIN: I'm underperforming at work—I'm just unable to concentrate. I'm amazed no one seems to be noticing. At some point my boss is going to call me in, I'm sure of it.

THERAPIST: That must be very hard, Kevin, having to drag yourself into work every day and having to carry the worry that, at any point, your poor performance is going to be exposed. I am amazed at your strength in being able to shoulder these heavy burdens.

KEVIN: Yes, it's terrible [*slumps in seat and covers face with hands*]. I just so much wish I hadn't left my home. How could I have been so *stupid*!!!

THERAPIST: And ... is there anything else you are feeling, similarly, has gone wrong or is adrift in your life right now? Anything else that is, in equal fashion, stupid? [*the therapist is still clinging to his case conceptualization*]

KEVIN: How do you mean?

THERAPIST: You're single.

KEVIN: Who would have an idiot like me, someone who would be stupid enough to give up the lease on that lovely apartment?

Then perhaps the therapist, seeing the session was close to expiry, judged it best to pump up his client's spirits with a reframe:

THERAPIST: I think you left for very good reasons.
KEVIN: I did?
THERAPIST: You had the sense that this was a single man's home—you have always said "an apartment is not a house"—and you wanted to prepare yourself for finding a girlfriend by making room for her to move in with you. You had a sense that there's a correlation between outward appearance and inner psychic reality. People who live in a "bachelor

	pad" tend to be, well, bachelors; it makes sense to me that you wanted to prepare to settle down with a woman by moving to a place that is more obviously suited to two people living together. [*confabulating: wants to advance reframe*]
KEVIN:	Then why did I buy the stupid, cramped, overpriced house? It's barely big enough for two!
THERAPIST:	That's a good question. Why do you think you did buy the house that is *nearly* fit for a couple?
KEVIN:	[*shrugs shoulders*]
THERAPIST:	Perhaps out of ambivalence? Perhaps you were *nearly* ready to settle down . . . but, deep down inside, not so sure? For some of us it's often very hard to let go of the bachelor identity. . . . [*floundering amid the wreckage left by the goals-based attempts*]
KEVIN:	Hmmph.

And now the session is up. But, like the clinician Kevin saw on that first occasion, this clinician too is now troubled in his countertransference. There is something *too enigmatic* about Kevin's last utterance. The therapist feels Kevin is disappointed and discouraged. The "Hmmph" could be code for: *you can't help me so I may as well find another way out.* Feelings and thoughts of *finality* flash through the therapist's countertransference. What if the therapist then follows the dialectic to act upon these uncomfortable and alarming "internal manifestations" and, unusually, extends the session:

THERAPIST:	I sense that you are deeply unhappy, Kevin. With yourself and also with my very poor and transparent efforts to take away your unhappiness. [*the therapist abandons goals and follows process, trying hard to under-stand*]
KEVIN:	I'm just making bad decisions.
THERAPIST:	And what you seem to be saying—is it, am I hearing you right?—is that this is some sort of irreversible change for the worse in you—do I have that right? It's not because of anxiety or sadness or a midlife crisis—or loneliness—the kinds of things a therapist might think are the cause of your making, as you see it, the bad decisions. It's that *something has happened to you!* Something else. [*the therapist is feeling-into Kevin's situation and is pulling information out of his countertransference*]
KEVIN:	Yes.
THERAPIST:	Something that we have not talked about.
KEVIN:	It has been mentioned.
THERAPIST:	What?

74 • Phenomenology of clinical decision making

KEVIN: Brain toxicity.
THERAPIST: Brain toxicity? [*the therapist has no idea what's going on*]
KEVIN: Yes.
THERAPIST: Your brain has become—is it, are you saying?—poisoned? [*the therapist is again pulling information out of his countertransference*]
KEVIN: Yes.
THERAPIST: How?
[*long silence*]
THERAPIST: Ahhhh . . . You told me, it must be four or five months ago now, soon after we started working together, that you suspect one of your colleagues, another financial analyst, is using methamphetamine drugs?
KEVIN: Yes.
THERAPIST: You told me these drugs distort thinking and are toxic to the brain.
KEVIN: Yes.
[*long silence*]
KEVIN: So I've been really, really stupid, haven't I? I've ruined my life.
THERAPIST: You've been taking meth and believe it has distorted your thinking and been toxic to your brain.
KEVIN: [*slumps in seat, covers face with hands and cries*]

And now the therapist is in a position to have the conversation with Kevin that Kevin needs to have. And again we have reinforcement of our idea, with Ogden, that the projective identification countertransference is "the basic unit of study of the therapeutic interaction." It is when the therapist's countertransference finally picks up on, alights upon the truth, when the process of *Einfühlung* has run its course, that he can empathize with and Mirror his client's terrible, and, in terms of the pain and havoc wrought, terribly expensive dilemma:

THERAPIST: You've been thinking that, with your damaged brain, your life is finished! *And that thought has been so terribly frightening you have not even dared to talk about it here—you have been afraid I will simply not be able to help you because I cannot reverse the brain toxicity.*
KEVIN: Yes. I may as well be dead and so I will have to kill myself.
THERAPIST: I understand your line of thinking, Kevin, now, at last. [*reverts to goals-at-hand*] And I so completely feel the sense of devastation you are feeling and why it has been so hard for you to talk to me about this terrible, terrible fear you have that you have permanently damaged your brain. And I'm so glad you have told me because [*with congruence*] I absolutely know that you are wrong. Your fear is just a fear, it is a mirage. If your brain, if your cognitive abilities were damaged I would know. I have worked with meth users. You have absolutely no symptoms of brain damage. If you want my opinion

corroborated I can refer you to a neurologist to check that out. But first of all I'm going to ask you to promise and certify to me you will not harm yourself while we are working on dismantling these unfounded fears you have been so burdened with for so long....

Dilemma

Yes, Kevin did have a dilemma in relation to his being single at 49. And he was, very likely, in the neutral zone of more than one clinically significant transition. But Kevin's *most urgent* dilemma, the dilemma that proved fatal to him because the previous conversation did not happen, was that *he could not live with his terrible fear but he could not disclose it in case it were true*. The fear limited him to disclosing tiny incremental clues, spread among several people who were not in touch with each other. It was as if a map had been torn into pieces and each piece was given to a different person. When Kevin was talking to his therapist about meth and brain toxicity it was by way of a passing comment in an early session about another person: the ideation he projected, defensively, along with the comment was of "no need to look here." A minuscule further clue was in the tiny, transference "Hmmph" at the end of the session just reviewed. This is why Kevin was, as a therapy client, so very hard to help. Even for the two Good Therapists whose work and internal manifestations we have here reconstructed in fantasy.

I like to conceive of the client's dilemma in schematic terms. In the client's voice: *if I do X then A will happen, which cannot be tolerated, but if I do Y then B will happen, which is equally intolerable; X and Y are my sole choices, and I am therefore condemned to misery*.

The uncovering and interpreting (preferably, with Brodley[4] by the client herself) of the dilemma is the second pivotal point in treatment—the first being the point at which the client feels under-stood by the therapist. This second pivotal point in treatment is where the assessment phase more-or-less ends and the treatment plan becomes more-or-less complete in terms of content (one or more of *X* and *Y*, *A* and *B* may only just now have been fully identified). The treatment plan very likely involves the therapist's "dwelling" for a while with the client in the full experience of the dilemma. Since this is a place of pain and discomfort and since our instinctive reaction is to avoid or negate pain, dwelling for a while with the client in this place is not something that necessarily comes easily to beginning counselors and therapists. I argue however that, when a therapist is tempted to move away too quickly from the acute point of the dilemma, this impulse is most likely to be the product of an obstructive countertransference (as further discussed in the third part of this book). The client, after all, *is* her dilemma. For us to flee from it is to turn our back on who she is, trades in Empathy for pity and abandons hope.

In fact the way forward for the client is often for therapist and client together to *ruminate* upon the dilemma. "Let's be quite sure we have this all the right way round," says her therapist to our fantasized Satirian client, Chantal.

---

4 Brodley, B. T. (2006). Client-initiated homework in client-centered therapy. *In* Journal of Psychotherapy Integration, Volume 16, Issue 2, June, pp. 140–161

If you stand up to your mother-in-law, you feel you *become* her. You fear this horrible part of yourself will take you over, and you will become 'Mrs. Hyde.' Your mother-in-law will complain to her son, your husband, and you will then be unmasked as the awful monster you really are, who wants things all her own way. Your husband will divorce you, and you will die alone, unloved, unhappy and in reduced circumstances. Equally, if you lay down the law to your husband about his mother, your monstrous personality is in the same way revealed and with the same consequences. Your choices are stark. You can stay as you are, continuing to allow your mother-in-law's overbearingness to suck the life out of you—and it is, in fact, killing you to do this—or you can disrupt your marriage in an assertive, powerful way and damn the consequences! But then you are an aggressive, overbearing wolf too—and you lose the sheep's clothing of being the self-effacing victim of your mother-in-law's persecution and your husband's leaving you. So you are, really, firmly stuck in this place. I get that, and I can absolutely feel your dilemma, your stuckness. Either way you lose and are condemned to misery.

"You just can't let go, Chantal," the therapist might add, in a flash of intersubjective insight, "of the sheep's clothing. When I was the one whom, in here, you experienced as overbearing, when I kept interrupting you, you couldn't allow yourself to disclose your true response to me, trying so hard not to show me I have triggered an angry part in you. Perhaps you are feeling it now, again, my overbearingness, even as I am saying these things...."

And again empathizing with underlying process: "It . . . must hurt you very much to have to eat your responses like this—the responses of diffidence, irritation or anger—and hide your self from people." There may follow a long silence. Or sobbing. Or both. And then, as if by some magic, the rumination, the *dwelling* in what one of my students has deftly termed the "main feeling" associated with the dilemma quite suddenly and unexpectedly yields the object of the necessary, Bridgesian letting go. Thinking with one mind and in the same instant both client and therapist arrive at the interpretation together: "I/you am/are willingly shouldering all this suffering *just because* I'm/you're so scared of what will happen if I/you *get angry*." Chantal is consigning herself to unrelenting misery in her relationships because she cannot let go of her self-image as a "gentle" woman and the meaning-making she attaches to self-disclosure, in the context of a close relationship, of what does and does not suit her and when what does not suit her provokes her ire. Chantal now looks angry, tear-stained—and *alive*. "Is it so bad, after all," the therapist asks, Mirroringly, "to be so angry with me?" And, with congruence, "As for me, I have to say I think I rather like seeing this side of you—in fact, I wonder who else might be interested in seeing all of you put back together like this, with your passion and aliveness bringing color to your cheeks?"

Higher functioning clients may need very little more than the interpretation of the dilemma—with associated transference implications—and arrival at the main feeling. They have, in the long neutral zone of the transition, done significant preparatory mourning and are thus prepared for the final letting go under the therapist's Mirroring. It could be, then, that Chantal may take her new knowledge and insight back home and implement the necessary behavioral changes straight away. She has been able completely to let go in the therapy room her maladaptive beliefs governing what a gentlewoman does with her anger. "High-functioning" in her case looks to signify the ability to achieve second-order change without further depth work—and perhaps also without further intervention in cognitive-behavioral technique (she may not ask for remonstration training). Her twin developmental paths to health are dismantling the transference (Chantal's fragile mother coldly withdrew affection and "narcissistic supplies"[5] or Mirroring from her daughter when Chantal was angry with mother) in conjunction with feeling and, crucially, now as an adult surviving the feelings long defended against in the corrective, intersubjective emotional experience afforded by the therapist in the transference work.

As with every new Sensorimotor release, the re-experiencing is processed in the other three Styles to cement the corrective meaning-making: "I was four years old," says Chantal, from the perspective of resolution allowed her by her Dialectic-Systemic. "My mother was my world. She couldn't handle strong emotions; she had her own issues. It made a whole lot of sense to eat my anger. Then. But not now. If I am angry with someone now it is not a case of a vulnerable child's anger with her vulnerable mother. And it isn't even always a question of being 'angry'— it's perfectly normal to have strong preferences and express them to others!"

For this high-functioning version of Chantal everything has changed. The archaic *Gestalt* is closed and she is no longer compelled by the repetition compulsion to seek it out and replay it, and she can no longer feel as she did before at the prospect of disclosing to her husband and mother-in-law—or to her therapist— what it is exactly she needs of us and when or if any of us have upset or annoyed her or when she prefers us to do something differently.

Such an holistic re-ordering of the self-narrative is not necessarily achieved quickly and easily and all at once in its entirety. For another version of Chantal— elsewhere on the continuum of pathology and functioning—her dammed-up Sensorimotor may still overwhelm her capacity for processing in her Concrete, Formal and Dialectic-Systemic Styles. This Chantal may not be able—yet—to tolerate dwelling in the main feeling; for her the reservoir of repression is at first accessible only in brief increments. There is therefore more groundwork to do to lay the foundations for the cognitions that will make the re-experiencing safe to feel and make it "corrective." This may require some considerable, perhaps prolonged further transference work, perhaps involving a secondary clinically significant transition. And yet for these clients too their therapy enters a new phase after reaching the dilemma. Now that the therapist has fully entered and dwelt intersubjectively in the client's world, the dyad has become an intimate,

---

5 Kahn, M. (1994). *In lecture*

mutually trusting team. There can be little or no resistance, as such, where two minds are as one. The treatment plan is clear. The avenues pointed to by the dilemma must be fully explored using the techniques of depth psychotherapy. Along each avenue will be found the "main feeling" against overwhelm by which all the client's defensive structures serve to preserve her. It is, then, the holding of this main feeling—underlying both avenues of the dilemma as well as the client's Personality Style—which our client must let go, allow and feel for her healing. She must let go also of the maladaptive meaning-making associated with it and, in doing these things, find a new, corrective meaning. Now, following the pivotal interpretation of the dilemma, this version of Chantal realizes she indeed wants to be in this therapy, that she and her therapist are on the same page and, should resistance arise, she will be eager to acknowledge and discuss it in the transference.

Change

And it is *now* that Chantal is most fully prepared for our Doing Style's many interventions in cognitive-behavioral technique. Now we have interpreted and begun to dismantle the dilemma, now that, because of her—even if only partial—corrective emotional experience in the transference, the work of becoming more congruent, of entering into a full expression of the main feeling has begun, Chantal is necessarily so much more interested in the therapist's ideas in how she may disclose to her husband and mother-in-law what it is she needs of them and when or if she is angry with them. As we have seen, even the higher functioning Chantal might extend her stay in therapy to benefit from the cognitive-behavioral component, possibly, with Ivey[6] and Brodley, herself requesting it. When mother-in-law treads on her toes, when her husband doesn't support her, Chantal needs to know how to communicate her experience and preferences in a way they are able to hear. Perhaps she needs the therapist's help in how best to train them to hear her. Chantal and the therapist can practice such conversations in role-play and the therapist can set "homework." The results of these exercises are then processed in the therapeutic conversation, returning as and if necessary to the transference.

We have brought Chantal to second-order change and her dilemma is no more. She is no longer troubled by mother-in-law's Personality Style. What previously made her angry is depotentiated. With her horizontally developed ("more is better") Dialectic-Systemic, Chantal understands that mother-in-law's behaviors are about mother-in-law's developmental issues and not about Chantal. When mother-in-law attempts the overbearing behaviors Chantal therefore has, with

---

6 Ivey, A. E., Ivey, M. B., Myers, J. E. and Sweeney, T. J. (2005). *Developmental Counseling and Therapy: Promoting Wellness Over the Lifespan*. Boston, MA: Lahaska Press, Houghton Mifflin (Copyright 2005 [All quotes and figures reproduced by permission of Taylor and Francis Group, LLC, a division of Informa plc]), Appendix 4

Glasser, more choice. She can choose to shrug it off without being triggered—or, if need be, to tell her mother-in-law how she prefers things.

And now the pressure in the family system could very easily switch to the marital relationship. The husband has had an easy ride of it hitherto in that he has not been called upon to defend his wife against his mother. What if, now, his mother calls on him to defend her against his wife? And now it is he who is plunged into transition and the discomforts of the Bridgesian neutral zone. The couple may indeed split up, although we still do not know if they will. If they do, it will not be, as it would have been at the outset of Chantal's coming to therapy, because of her refusal to let go, but rather now it will be because of her husband's. The intentional counselor and therapist can anticipate the possibility and expand the scope of treatment as necessary.

School-based family counseling and therapy

Informed by the Adlerian principles of school-based family counseling and therapy, the Good Therapist will, all through Chantal's individual treatment, take care to *hold the position of each stakeholder* in the family drama. When in the initial phase of treatment Chantal demonizes her mother-in-law, the therapist will Mirror and confirm her experience *but will not condone or participate in the demonizing*. The therapist's humanistic worldview informs him that the mother-in-law and husband are fellow sufferers and his family systems theory that Chantal has become a therapy client not only on her own behalf but also on theirs. All through Chantal's therapy the therapist will be laying the foundation for an expansion of her awareness and empathy, making forays into DCT Style-shifts such as:

> You experience your mother-in-law as an absolute *witch* and you feel terribly hurt and distressed in your interactions with her. I get that. And it seems to you that this is just who this woman is, she is a horrible woman. And, Chantal, you might also have wondered this, in your distress, how did she get to be this way and why does she do these things? Even . . . how did this unattractive woman get to have this son, your husband, whom you married and whom you love?

Having in these ways avoided demonizing other family members the therapist will, at the stage where pressure is building in the marital relationship, be well-placed to help further. Chantal has changed and the husband has not (yet) and perhaps, if this painful state continues, Chantal will indeed say to herself that she needs a husband who is a husband and man and who is not a boy torn between his mother and his wife—and she will leave him. (And, if she does so, having completed her transition in treatment, she will now not be bound by the repetition compulsion to repeat her transferential mistake and marry another boy-man.) Recognizing the new goals, the therapist can psychoeducate his client further. "You have completed your transition, Chantal," he can say. "Now, let's ask ourselves, how can we help your husband complete his?" The therapist might call in the husband—and, with

Satir, the mother-in-law—for collateral sessions, perhaps including parent-child sessions; several outcomes are possible, notably the outcome that the family stays together and become more-or-less happy in relationship.

Summary

This approach, based on the developmental model and systems theory and managing the dialectic between goals and process, can have a profound impact on the happiness of several people and multiple generations of family members. Grandparents, children and often more remote relatives may also be considered, with Satir and according to San Francisco clinician Daniel Kugler, to be "part of the client base."[7] The corollary to our expanded working hypothesis is that resorting to remonstration training too early in Chantal's therapy and without preparing her by first affording her any necessary horizontal development in her higher Styles runs considerable risks. We already know a too-narrow, overly reified focus on the client-as-individual and on her problem as initially presented is not a good idea: at the very worst—and here I exaggerate in order to highlight the absolute importance of the therapist maintaining both congruence and an intentional and Dialectic-Systemic awareness of the entire context of stakeholders—we may inadvertently, via our improper Mirroring and gratifying, assist Chantal to puff up a newly "empowered" false Self, in which her higher Styles are underweight, who impulsively goes home to trash her mother-in-law and husband and grab her kids and leave.

As our quest progresses, we are seeing ever more clearly the variables distinguishing treatment that is well-conceived, adroit and intentional from that which is misconceived and may generate subpar outcome. Good Therapy reduces risk while misconceived therapy is capable of doing harm. Improper, theoretically misinformed and incongruent attempts to build client self-esteem carry significant risk, as Cambridge University's Hilary Cremin, echoing Lee, has warned.[8] Since the variables we clearly see in clinician intentionality are variables in the Therapist-Self we must now look more deeply into this construct and, with Satir, at the preparation and education of clinicians. A "bigger" Therapist-Self, we look to conclude, can better understand both the possibilities and the risks involved in counseling and therapy, which, as we have seen in Kevin's case, are matters of Life and Death. And no less, albeit in a different way, for Chantal: her fear, found, with Judith Beck, in a "picture thought"[9] in the therapist's projective identification uncovered in the full explication of her dilemma, is of dying alone and unloved and in reduced circumstances. Like all dreams and shadows—like Kevin's "Hmmph"—this cognition too contains valuable information coded within it that we do best not to ignore.

---

7 Kugler, D. J. (2001). *In supervision*
8 Cremin, H. (2008). Self Esteem: What Is Wrong With the Concept and Why We Should Not Promote It! *Presentation* to the Oxford Symposium in School-Based Family Counseling, August 11th 2008
9 Beck, J. S., *with* Carlson, J. and Kjos, D. (Eds.) (1999). *Brief Therapy Inside Out: Cognitive Therapy of Depression* (DVD). Phoenix, AZ: Zeig, Tucker and Theisen

Again, as we delve deeper, we see how therapists who ignore or cannot access certain evidential manifestations, or who are unable properly to weigh or interpret them, or, it may be, who have an insufficiently Dialectic-Systemic perspective, or who, with Rogers, are insufficiently congruent, may import into treatment omissions or commissions that may greatly impair or impede treatment or may degrade it completely. This is the concern expressed, we have seen, in their different languaging by the APA, Norcross, Richardson, Satir and Baldwin, and Turner. And we have seen that the essential task of the therapist lies in extending Self to the client and becoming vulnerable. All of these things are operationalizations of the highest order. What, then, is the Therapist-Self and how is it built, augmented and developed so as to meet the environmental challenge and enormous responsibility involved in . . . being someone's counselor and therapist?

Discussion

- *This book thinks becoming a clinician is a transition. Do you agree?*
- *Part of the "working hypothesis" here advanced is that more characterologically disturbed clients evoke more manifestations in transference and countertransference: how do you relate this to your own experience as a clinician?*
- *"Transition theory" seeks to examine the phenomenology of change, stressing that transition is a longitudinal process or series of processes occurring over time and intrapsychically—and often very painfully and troublesomely. How do you relate to this "confabulation"?*
- *"The first thing to remember about a psychotherapy client is that she is in pain." Do you agree? Do you always remember?*
- *"The essential task of the therapist lies in extending Self to the client and becoming vulnerable." Do you agree? How often do you find yourself disinclined to do these things?*
- *Do you agree that it is the job of the counselor and therapist to be the "stakeholder for absent family members" even when treating a client in individual therapy? What might this look like, and how can the clinician do this and remain concerned for the best interest of the client-as-individual?*

Part II
The Therapist-Self

6
Synthesis
Obviating the client's dilemma • therapeutic communication • the clinician's cardinal Archetypes

---

Pain, sorrow and the past • feeling the unfeelable and knowing the unknowable • intentionality and the Good Therapist

Cardinal Archetypes of the Therapist-Self

> MAGICIAN • changing the unchangeable
> RULER • authority, environment, frame • rules of engagement
> WARRIOR • doing battle for the client • upholding the weak
> LOVER • proving ourselves worthy of the client's attention

The Archetypes and their "immature" shadows (Dobson) • the environmental call to further self-development • humility

The case of Jimmy • the case of Gonzalo

> *"Using oneself as a therapist is an awesome task. To be equal to that task one needs to continue to develop one's humanness and maturity. We are dealing with people's lives."*[1]

Being someone's therapist may be a matter of Life and Death and is a daily exercise in synthesis and accountability. The client's presenting problem is accurately stated by her and also understated. What the client is telling us is the story of a person grappling with psychic pain; the story is dependent on the pain and is selective. The client is in disavowal. She has been completely frank with us—and still has a complete bombshell to drop after months of therapy, as did Ghislaine. And in the face of all of these things we are required, ethically and practically, to reconcile thesis and antithesis into a coherent treatment plan that will work. *And that we can explain.* We are required to account to the client and also other stakeholders, for example, parents, for what we are doing and how it will help further the goals.

---

1 Satir, V. and Baldwin, M. (1983). *Satir Step by Step: A Guide to Creating Change in Families*. Palo Alto, CA: Science and Behavior Books, p. 227

Constantly searching for patterns of patterns, our Dialectic-Systemic sees that, for treatment to have optimal outcome, the client must take her problem to someone possessed of formidable qualities outside the range observed in everyday life. The clinician has to be "bigger" than the client's fear, depression and disavowal and big enough also to do the many things—and not do the many things—we see are done/not done in counseling and therapy. I propose we adopt into our working hypothesis the construct of the *Therapist-Self* to explain how it comes about that the clinician, a person just like any other, nevertheless does all these things that her profession requires. Shortly after we began our inquiry into the phenomenon of the adroit clinician we discovered it is our job to help the client develop Self. Now we better understand the environmental challenge that it is to be someone's therapist, we are drawn increasingly to conclude, with Ivey and Truscott, that we have a prior task in developing *our* Self to meet that challenge.

Humility

As a beginning therapist, my greatest fear—and this was also my greatest fear as a beginning instructor—was of falling flat on my face, of looking stupid, of it becoming self-evident that I am under-qualified to do what somebody is in fact paying and *trusting* me to do. This too, I believe, is the greatest fear of my students. We know these are ordinary narcissistic fears relating to our upbringing: our successes were praised, while our earnest attempts (which happened not to result in success) and our subsequent disappointment were not Mirrored, because our parents were too preoccupied with *their* disappointment. It is not until we fully work through our archaic feelings and learn, experientially, that the Good Therapist falls flat on his face, if not "hundreds of times a day" as opined by Cortright,[2] then at least often enough to make it part of the job description, that we arrive at an adaptive meaning-making: *this falling flat is all perfectly ok*! Consider the following parent transaction:

PARENT: The school said they will expel Jimmy unless the behaviors cease. You have been seeing him for a month now, and they haven't ceased. Apparently all you do in here is play games. And *we're having to pay for this*! Do you have a plan, and when will Jimmy stop doing those things?

The clinician is required to do two things concurrently. He must give the anxious parent the reassurance that the clinician knows what he is doing and can help Jimmy. The other is to engage in what school-based family counseling calls "parent consultation." Jimmy's behaviors at school, theory tells us, arise from his experiences in the home. The clinician is also required to preserve Jimmy's confidentiality:

---

[2] Cortright, B., Kahn, M. and Hess, J. (2004). Speaking from the heart: Integral T-Groups as a tool for training transpersonal psychotherapists. *In* The Journal of Transpersonal Psychology, Volume 35, Issue 2, pp. 127–142

THERAPIST: I'm so glad to have this opportunity to sit down with you. I understand your concerns. It's important Jimmy stays in the school. The behaviors are not yet extinguished. However, the school will not expel your son. I consult from time to time with the school principal, and she is aware Jimmy is in treatment and that treatment is a process occurring over time.

PARENT: Yes. It's the *time* that's rather bothering me. In my business we have an ETA or delivery date. I don't suppose you can tell me when you are going to deliver?

THERAPIST: No I cannot, I'm sorry. What I can tell you is that I believe we are on track. If at any time I believe we are not on track and that I am not able to help Jimmy, I am ethically required to refer him to another therapist. But we are on track. We are still in the assessment phase. Therapy with children looks different from therapy with adults. Right now play therapy is the way forward. Simply talking to Jimmy about stopping the behaviors is something you and the school have already done, and I doubt I would get any further right now. The behaviors are impulses originating in anxiety, and my work is to build up Jimmy's confidence so he can shoulder his anxiety more adaptively. At the same time, I hope through the play therapy to understand the source of the anxiety. This treatment plan is on track. And I'm very glad to have this opportunity to consult with you: can you tell me anything about any sources of anxiety for Jimmy, or indeed for you and your partner, at home?

PARENT: I don't see why you can't just ask him whatever it is he's anxious about, if you're so sure....

THERAPIST: Even adults find it hard, often, to describe where our anxious feelings come from. But I do find that parents know their child better than anyone else and can point to answers and speed treatment.

PARENT: I feel like I'm in therapy too!

THERAPIST: I'm hoping you can be my consultant. You can tell me things that Jimmy can't, for example, the circumstances of the pregnancy and his birth and other things going on in the family that may shed light and speed treatment.

PARENT: [*breathes deeply*] Jimmy wasn't wanted.... [*continues*]

Hypothesis and treatment plan

Not only does Jimmy's clinician demonstrate congruence, unconditional positive regard, Empathy, curiosity and nondefensiveness but he has in addition a developmental treatment plan, the kernel of which he is able to convey to the parent in accessible languaging. The clinician has previously left several messages on the parent's cellphone and is very pleased that contact has been made. When the parent arrived, the therapist was suspect in his eyes and "wrong"—and the clinician is content, in the imagined dialogue, to be the "disappointing service provider" for as long as the parent needs him to fulfill that role. Crucially the clinician knows how to enlist the parent's interest in furthering Jimmy's treatment. And we see here further manifestations of the dialectic, carefully managed: the clinician steers between the goals elements of his authority as treating professional and the mandate of client confidentiality and the process elements of the parent's authority as parent and need to know.

The clinician must formulate an Empathy-based case hypothesis and, flowing from it, a developmentally and systems-informed treatment plan. Jimmy is eight years old and is exhibiting inappropriately sexualized behaviors in the school. The school will expel him unless he sees the school-based family counselor and therapist and treatment outcome is favorable. The stakes are high, yet the parent had not responded to the clinician's messages.

Jimmy is a client with a predominantly Concrete discourse who is also *behaviorally symptomatic*, meaning that his Sensorimotor is articulated maladaptively in the undesired behaviors and not adaptively by entering into a full expression of feelings. Almost nine, he is expected to have a basic attainment in his higher Styles, perhaps ordinarily sufficient to understanding and more-or-less adapting to environmental concepts of rules, rule-breaking and consequences. But such rudimentary Formal competencies are overwhelmed by the Sensorimotor impulses breaking through, and stakeholders have been unable to lawyer Jimmy into stopping the behaviors. He has been lectured about behaviors tolerated or not tolerated by the environment, the environment's reasons for such tolerance or non-tolerance and the series of adverse consequences likely to follow. At eight years, Jimmy shouldn't necessarily be expected to be more developed in his higher Styles—but the new environmental challenge posed by his upsetting everyone with the sexualized behaviors means there is developmental work to be done to help him find better adaptation. The clinician plans horizontal development in the higher Styles, an intentional strategy having both goals-based and process-based components: development in the higher Styles will help Jimmy better respond to psychoeducation and cognitive restructuring—while it also lays the groundwork for Jimmy's entering into a full expression of feelings more adaptively. Our aggregated theory points to insufficient parental Mirroring as well as to anxiety and asks us to rule in or rule out exposure to some kind of sexualized behavior in the environment.

While the treatment goals are very clear—to change Jimmy's behavior—a child under nine with problematic sexual behaviors (PSBs) presents unique challenges to managing the dialectic between goals and process. Parental inclusion in treatment is a prerequisite: the clinician knows that active involvement of parents or caregivers is essential to maximize the benefits of cognitive-behavioral treatment for children with PSBs. At the same time, the literature on family predictors of PSBs in children, most recently confirmed by Canadian researchers Mireille Lévesque and Marc Bigras, emphasizes the presence of developmental issues in the parents.[3] To the extent the parents may be non-responsive, absent figures, unwilling or unable to participate in or to facilitate

---

3 Lévesque, M. and Bigras, M. (2012). Persistence of problematic sexual behaviors in children. *In* Journal of Clinical Child & Adolescent Psychology, Volume 41, Issue 2, pp. 239–245

goals-based treatment, as was the case before this interview between clinician and parent, the clinician has little choice but to rely on play therapy, a process-based method. To the extent parents subsequently participate in a goals-based treatment protocol, the dialectic may call for shifts in favor of process to address their developmental issues.

Before this parent interview Jimmy's therapist was required to create an entire case hypothesis out of theory, informed, intentional conjecture based on assessment and countertransference and the literature on children with PSBs—and precious few fixed facts. Additional data yielded by the brief parent interview include the highly charged information that "Jimmy wasn't wanted." In school-based family counseling and therapy, the case hypothesis also includes a developmental assessment of the parents. This parent operates in the largely Concrete world of "deliverables" and is busy and also avoidant (not having returned the clinician's telephone calls). The avoidance—a correlate of disavowal—and the busyness allow Jimmy's therapist to hypothesize that the parent also has some difficulty entering into a full expression of feelings—which situation further correlates with insufficient parental Mirroring of the unwanted Jimmy. *Unwanted* is a bombshell. We recall Hastings: "Adequate psychological boundaries are made or lost right here." And it may be that such persons—parents of unwanted children who are also predominantly Concrete and somewhat avoidant (and therefore incongruent)—might well use sex somewhat Concretely and *carelessly* and, because underweight in the higher Styles, without fully thinking through the implications. Such carelessness could conceivably be part of the etiology of Jimmy's symptoms. While Jimmy's therapist wishes to avoid stereotyping the parents, he is aware of the clear correlation in the research between PSBs and "extensive sexuality in the family."[4] Perhaps there are marital affairs, one of which Jimmy walked in on? If the therapist can gain the parents' confidence and, using a mixture of goals-based and process-based methods, help *them* get back on track with their developmental tasks, while also helping Jimmy with his, then the family as a whole will be happier as well as the school and the desired turnaround will occur more quickly.

What kind of a professional Self operates in this world of inferences, any of which might or might not be true and all of which the therapist, practicing intentionally, must keep in mind as possible, probable, likely or too dangerous to discount? The developmental treatment plan flowing from the case hypothesis is cohesive and logical—and dependent on events. How much parental involvement will be possible? Ideally the therapist will invite the parents in for collateral sessions. From the Concrete/Formal domain of counseling the therapist will use psychoeducation to underline that parenting is not so easy in today's busy, often hard-pressed families. He will recommend parenting classes for a structured approach to developing communication strategies. The topic of family sexuality will be broached. The clinician still doesn't know when Jimmy's problem school behaviors will cease—but

---

4   *Ibid.*, p. 242

he does know the more he can assist the parents to become more congruent, using interventions intentionally from the domains of both counseling and therapy, the better will be the communication in the parental subsystem and the better will be Jimmy's parenting; and Jimmy will have less need for maladaptive Sensorimotor expression.

It goes without saying that, if the clinician comes to suspect child abuse, he will take appropriate action.

In the clinician's ideal version of the treatment plan the collateral parent sessions will entail Style-shifting the parents from their preferred Concrete Style ("deliverables") with the aim of increasing authentic expression of Sensorimotor experience; the feelings thereby accessed will be Mirrored—by the therapist and, for each spouse, by the other spouse—and processed in the other three Styles as necessary to weave an adaptive self-narrative. The parent consultation conversations will flow perfectly naturally, yet intentionally, between the domains of goals and process to afford the parents the necessary development in the Styles in which they were underweight. As the parents develop self-structure the therapist will teach the couple to Mirror not only each other's feelings, but also Jimmy's, letting them know that Mirroring is not the same as condoning. In this way the therapist lays the developmental foundation for the success of the CBT protocol for treating PSBs.

In a less ideal scenario, it may be the parents return to their place of hiding, leaving Jimmy's therapist with a simplified, yet equally cohesive treatment plan to build Jimmy's self-structure through Mirroring in intersubjective connection and via play therapy; doing so will concurrently afford Jimmy Sensorimotor release and expand his capacities in the higher Styles to process the released feelings and accrue the cognitions and processing abilities that will allow him better to cope with his situation at home and at school. It will become possible to switch to a goals-based discourse and discuss the PSBs.

Jimmy's case illustrates the profound demands of the dialectic between goals and process. The clinician preferring to do play therapy must nevertheless import goals-based methodologies and protocols as soon as parental participation or Jimmy's progress allows. The clinician preferring a structured protocol must do play therapy while waiting for the parents to come out of hiding. Such adroitness comes more easily to some than to others. We know our Task Positive Brain favors our Doing Style, in which DCT's Concrete and Formal Styles predominate, and our Default Mode Network favors our Feeling-Sensing Style, in which the Sensorimotor and Dialectic-Systemic predominate. We know that *who we are*—our personal preferences, abilities and weaknesses—informs whether we are *more comfortable* with the goals thesis and the domain of counseling and what is required of the counselor or with the process thesis and the domain of psychotherapy and what is required of the psychotherapist.

The dialectic between process and goals turns out to be a dialectic within the Therapist-Self between the Feeling-Sensing and Doing Styles, the DMN and the TPB, through which all our behaviors are mediated. The Doing and Feeling-Sensing Styles are therefore cardinal Aspects of the Therapist-Self.

Transpersonal

The demands of the dialectic and of client need are prodigious. We have wondered how the counselor and therapist does all these amazing things that her profession requires. How does Jimmy's clinician turn his vulnerability to criticism, his humility, his lack of information and his lack of progress in extinguishing Jimmy's undesired behaviors into strength and solidity—qualities he can pass on to Jimmy and, hopefully, also the hard-to-reach parents? We ask again: how do people having ordinary backgrounds full of ordinary problems—and sometimes extraordinary problems—become Good Therapists?

How does the Therapist-Self become what we have previously, in discussing development of client self-structure, described as "bigger"? Big enough to embody and emanate the essential therapist qualities (now six, if we add in *humility*), big enough to be seen as wrong by those who, like Jimmy's parent, need to project their own wrongness, big enough to love the unlovable client, big enough to feel the unfeelable feeling and to hear the untellable story? Big enough to be bigger than the problem and ... big enough to turn around the life trajectory that is irreversible? Is so much "bigness" not super-human? No. Such bigness is rather *Transpersonal* and *Archetypal*. Moore and Gillette's invaluable work on the four cardinal Archetypes of the masculine Self[5] is, I find, directly transferable to the Therapist-Self. I give them here as the cardinal Archetypes informing our work in the order in which they always present themselves into my consciousness and in the knowledge that they will present themselves in a different order—and, certainly in the case of the King, under a different styling—to other clinicians.

Magician

Magic is the process by which things change, sometimes quite suddenly and profoundly, from how they used to be experienced to how they are now experienced. Magic (with Hastings) is essential to therapy. The therapist is required to change the unchangeable: the client's worldview, personality[6] and even her

---

5 Moore, R. and Gillette, D. (1990). *King, Warrior, Magician, Lover: Rediscovering the Archetypes of the Mature Masculine*. New York, NY: HarperCollins
6 Rogers, C. R. (1957). The necessary and sufficient conditions of therapeutic personality change. *In* Journal of Consulting Psychology, Volume 21, pp. 95–103, http://dx.doi.org/10.1037/h0045357. Now in the public domain

memory.[7] The Therapist-Self is required to manifest the Magician Archetype to change the client's mood and response, whether it be the anxious, difficult, combative parent or the hard-to-reach, hard-to-retain client with a brittle, defensive personality. It is by harnessing the Magician Archetype to her Ruler that the young and inexperienced school-based family counseling intern magicks herself into the esteemed, solid collegial professional who is able to consult authoritatively with parents, teachers and the powerful and much older school principal, and sow in both family and school the seeds of systemic change. And it is by *trusting* her Magician's alchemy that the therapist who is as scared as her client can feel the unfeelable and hear the unhearable. Kevin's therapist, in the fantasized session that did not take place, summoned his Magician to convince Kevin that he *knew* Kevin's meth use had not irreversibly damaged his brain. Whenever it is necessary to create, in the therapy room, an altered or enhanced state of awareness or to invite her client to deeper interior exploration or visualization, the therapist uses her Magician. And because, in the endeavor of psychotherapy, surprise is never far away, the Good Therapist keeps ready access to her Magician.

The Magician corresponds to the Dialectic-Systemic in Ivey's schema. As said it is when things change very profoundly from how they used to be to how they are now that we experience Magic. Ivey advises us that clients who have suffered trauma are able to attain a full resolution and healing only in their Dialectic-Systemic Style:

> In treating survivors of incest and other traumas, the DCT framework suggests the need to work through the issue at multiple levels. These clients need to recover their body memories, tell their stories concretely, reflect on them, and discover how they may be systemic in nature, thus enabling them and us to take multiple perspectives.[8]

Clearly, therefore, the clinician must be sufficiently equipped in her Dialectic-Systemic to help the client enter this Style and to afford the client horizontal development in this Style. We have already seen that a clinician having a *further-developed* ("more is better") Dialectic-Systemic is in a better position to pick out the patterns of patterns in the (often conflicting) evidence presented by the client, so as to identify those systemic and contextual factors that have most relevance to the presenting symptoms of the dilemma. With the Lover in close attendance, the Magician *confronts* the client at just the right time and in just the right way so the client can see, suddenly, what she is doing and where it doesn't add up. The client has previously disavowed and separated in her awareness these disparate elements of her behavior and experience; the Magician has now conjured them up and made

---

7 Giudano, V. F. (1987). *Complexity of the Self: A Developmental Approach to Psychopathology and Therapy*. New York, NY: The Guilford Press, p. 221
8 Ivey, A. E., Ivey, M. B., Myers, J. E. and Sweeney, T. J. (2005). *Developmental Counseling and Therapy: Promoting Wellness Over the Lifespan*. Boston, MA: Lahaska Press, Houghton Mifflin (Copyright 2005 [All quotes and figures reproduced by permission of Taylor and Francis Group, LLC, a division of Informa plc]), p. 295

all of them appear together on the same stage, next to each other, so the client may not escape viewing them side by side and in the same frame. The Magician, then, guides the therapist's countertransference sensorium, *Einfühlungsvermögen* and intentionality. The Magician and the Dialectic-Systemic are implicated in the final and perhaps greatest therapist quality, more fully discussed in Chapter 8, of *emotional intelligence*, which lies behind intentionality and the importation of predictability into the work. Thus the Magician helps the client augment Self.

The Dialectic-Systemic Style is a predominant feature of solution-focused therapy and all forms of systems-imbued therapy including feminist therapy, network therapy[9] and school-based family counseling and therapy.

Sovereign or Ruler or Queen or King

The Ruler Archetype, according to Simon Fraser University's Carolyn Mamchur:

> inspires us to take responsibility for our own lives, in our fields of endeavour and in society at large . . . the developed Ruler creates environments that invite in the gifts and perspectives of all concerned.[10]

The Ruler, then, is like a parent, having the power to make the rules in the family and thereby, optimally, creating a climate that fosters developmental growth, transformation and healing. Jimmy's school-based family counselor manifested his Ruler in order to communicate to the doubting parent the parameters of Jimmy's therapy and that parental participation is implicated. It is with our Ruler that we set the therapeutic frame, interrupt the client and direct the client. Or not. The Ruler may, at times, "create environment" by choosing to defer to the client. The Queen may elect to stand in front of, behind or beside her throne. But the Sovereign is still there—and the throne still hers. It is with the Ruler's authority that therapeutic contracts are made and treatment plans are discussed with stakeholders. It is the Ruler, aided by her Warrior, who files an abuse report and who determines the content of clinical notes. The Ruler makes the rules and decides—helped by the Magician—when it is in the client's interest to break them; and it is the King, helped by both his Magician and his Warrior, who decides on the flimsy evidence of his own countertransference to hospitalize a client like Kevin if an extended session still leaves him with too much doubt.

Rules are made and decided out of experience afforded us by patterns and the Ruler corresponds to the Formal in Ivey's schema. As discussed Ivey suggests most therapists are predominantly Formal and that Rogerian or person-centered therapy and other therapies of the Self are predominantly mediated through Formal communication between therapist and client.[11]

---

9   *Ibid.* (cf. p. 154, p. 212)
10 *Accessed January 12th 2014 via* www.carolynmamchur.com/archetyperuler.html
11 Ivey, A. E., Ivey, M. B., Myers, J. E. and Sweeney, T. J. (2005). *Op. cit.* (cf. p. 154)

Warrior

According to New York University's Paul Vitz:

> The Warrior archetype stands for ... energy and aggressiveness, clear thinking in the presence of death, plus training to develop aggressiveness in a disciplined way. The Warrior shows loyalty to a transpersonal ideal.... God, or leader, or nation or another cause.[12]

In similar vein California TeacherWriter Suzanne Pitner describes eight attributes of the Warrior: "justice, loyalty, goal-orientation, strength, self-righteousness, impatience, tenacity and vengeance."[13] Therapists often find ourselves called upon to do battle for our clients, or (more precisely) to fight the fights our clients are too weak to fight. These may be battles with a legal or medical system or school system; or they may be battles involving a subsystem of which the client is part, for example, a school peer group. In such instances, using the principles of school-based family therapy and network therapy, the clinician summons her Warrior to intervene in the subsystem, supported as necessary by her Sovereign and Magician, to bring about the change that will permit her until-now too-weak client to thrive and strengthen.

> *It is with her Warrior, aided by her Lover and Magician, who help her both reach the client and avoid "therapist drift," that the clinician implements the ambitious treatment protocol with a client for whom it might well have been too difficult.*

Elsewhere the client's necessary battles may be intrapsychic. She may be too discouraged, too fearful of the darkness, dangers or emptiness within her; in such cases she will project these fears into the therapist and they will manifest in the countertransference:

THERAPIST: I'm glad to see you. You have canceled our last two sessions and I wondered if I had lost you.
CLIENT: I was frightened.
THERAPIST: After our last session.
CLIENT: Yes.
THERAPIST: When I said to you that I think in all probability we will, at some point, have to talk about the accident.

---

12 Vitz, P. C. (2010). Jungian Archetypes for Men: Jesus. *Blog Post. Accessed January 12th 2014 via* http://christianpsych.org/ wp_scp/jungian-archetypes-for-men-jesus/
13 Pitner, S. (2008). The Warrior Character Archetype. *Blog Post. Accessed January 12th 2014 via* http://suite101.com/a/the-warrior-character-archetype-a71753

CLIENT: Yes.

THERAPIST: [*drawing from her Magician*] It's almost as if—I can almost feel it—you feel that place is so dark that going there will kill you. You have avoided going there for six years; you know you cannot go there alone and you fear you cannot go there with me, here in this room. I myself can experience this reluctance as if it were my own—it's almost as if the reluctance were an entity occupying the space between us, just sitting here.

CLIENT: Yes.

THERAPIST: A somewhat friendly and helpful entity, I think. It has kept you away for three weeks but now brings you in today and watches over you carefully—and will do so as long as you need it to.

CLIENT: [*exhales*] Yes. Somehow what you just said made it seem not quite so impossible.

THERAPIST: You feel a little better now.

CLIENT: Yes. You are feeling my fear—and even giving it space—but you don't seem afraid. It doesn't make complete sense but I feel like I have more ... breathing room.

THERAPIST: [*drawing from her Warrior*] Yes. You should know that you are not alone. You and I have joined forces in this endeavor and it is my sworn duty to protect you from harm. When we go to that place I will be there making it safe for you to be there and together we will slay your demons.

[*drawing from her Magician*] Shall we ask your reluctance if she consents?

CLIENT: [*smiles*] She already left while you were talking. She said I will be ok and she is no longer needed.

It is the qualities inherent in the Warrior that the therapist draws upon to help her with the impossible tasks she must perform on the client's behalf. From the Archetype's eternal fires the therapist can rekindle in the client the flames of Pitner's tenacity, goal-orientation and strength. In manifesting her Warrior on her client's behalf the clinician reveals to the client her loyalty and impatience for justice; the fight is righteous and the vengeance lies in the client's healing. It is the Warrior who, with the Magician and Ruler, remakes theory as necessary to help her client: it is with her Warrior and Queen that Argentinian American theorist Cloe Madanes rewrote the book and remade the rules in the psychotherapeutic response of choice to cases of incest.[14]

---

14 Madanes, C. (1995). *Sex, Love, and Violence; Strategies for Transformation.* New York, NY: W. W. Norton

It will be seen that the Warrior Archetype corresponds to the Concrete Style in Ivey's schema. Concrete is about *doing*. Doing, in our case, *what is right and necessary*. The client has to be hospitalized or (with the Ruler and the Magician) the child client's classroom teacher has to be approached in a manner leading to altered teaching behaviors, to the child's benefit. It is using her Warrior that, California Jungian scholar Darrell Dobson holds, the school-based family counselor and therapist works toward the creation of a gay-straight alliance in the school.[15] Therapies mediated predominantly within Concrete communication between therapist and client include behavioral therapy and the panoply of cognitive-behavioral therapies and techniques that are so robustly informed by and make such an excellent vehicle for the goals-orientation of the Warrior and for the clinician's Doing Style.

Lover

The Lover is last in this list—and last does not mean least. "Can you love this new client?" I recall Michael Kahn asking of his students in group supervision. It is this most powerful of Archetypes that informs our congruence, unconditional positive regard, Empathy, nondefensiveness, curiosity, humility, Warrior, Ruler and Magician. Connecticut psychiatrist Scott Peck wrote:

> If the psychotherapist cannot genuinely love a patient, genuine healing will not occur. No matter how well credentialled and trained psychotherapists may be, if they cannot extend themselves through love to their patients, the results of their psychotherapeutic practice will be generally unsuccessful. Conversely, a totally uncredentialled and minimally trained lay therapist who exercises a great capacity to love will achieve psychotherapeutic results that equal those of the very best psychiatrists.[16]

And it is this last interpretation, surely, which, if there is to be one descriptor to encapsulate the essence of the Therapist-Self, is indisputable: therapists *extend Self* to their clients, as we have repeatedly seen, drawing from the Lover. Peck speaks of the "willingness to go out on a limb, to truly involve oneself at an emotional level in the relationship, to actually struggle with the patient and with oneself."[17] Clients notice it when we do this and respond accordingly.

Recalling that nobody wants to be a psychotherapy client, clinicians must prove ourselves worthy of the client's attention. This is especially to be expected with mandated and hard-to-reach clients. A student, a wonderful clinician with a formidable Lover and Warrior combination, was working in a residential facility for troubled

---

15 Dobson, D. (2009). Royal, warrior, magician, lover: Archetypal reflectivity and the construction of professional knowledge. *In* Teacher Education Quarterly, Caddo Gap Press, ISSN: 0737–5328, pp. 149–165
16 Peck, M. S. (1991). *The Road Less Travelled.* London: Arrow Books, pp. 188–189
17 *Ibid.*, p. 173

youth. Her client, an adolescent male with a long history with the agency and a poor prognosis and to whom she was, having formed a kind of twinship countertransference, enormously attached, would lead her repeatedly through the same sequence in process: on each occasion the student was put by her client in the position of choosing to break the agency's rules—using her Warrior and Ruler—to protect him from "consequences." Each time she did so, each time the sequence was repeated, he allowed her closer, until at last she found herself in the position of having earned his trust—and able to interest him in the possibility that things can be different.

"Neither shall there be any more pain: for the former things are passed away"[18]

The Lover, then, corresponds to the Sensorimotor in Ivey's schema. It is with her Sensorimotor, ultimately, that the therapist extends Self to her client and *feels*. We are again reminded that Freud's *Sichhineinversetzen* is a physiological phenomenon. As Peck suggests, to extend Self to the client and feel is to manifest an Act of Love. For Love helps us feel into rather than flee from pain. And perhaps here, more than in any of the four domains, we see the Therapist-Self as doing things that are not things generally done in the ordinary course of everyday living.

Therapies mediated predominantly within Sensorimotor communication between therapist and client include Gestalt Therapy, Drama Therapy, Focusing, Somatic Therapy and Rosen Method Bodywork, a body-based psychotherapy.

Form vs substance

Arising from this central chapter of this book is the question:

> *Do considerations of Love, Magic and the Jungian Archetypes, together with the construct of a Therapist-Self, have a place in an academic program predicated upon a goals-based methodology such as CBT?*

The cognitive dissonance is culturally imposed and must be evaluated in the context of the pendulum swing from the psychoanalytic to the cognitive-behavioral model discussed in the Preface. It is linked to David Burns' discovery that CBT clinicians may be, at times, unprepared for "a hidden emotion or problem" in the client. There has arisen (with Chaudhuri) a new movement to infuse the practice of CBT with emotion and process. Each authority in this movement in her or his own way addresses the dialectic between what *Intentional Intervention* calls the "Doing Style" and the "Feeling-Sensing Style" in the clinician's orientation to counseling and therapy. In the United Kingdom Mick Cooper and colleagues advance a new formulation—*Pluralistic Counselling and Psychotherapy*[19]—to

---

18 Revelation, 21:4
19 Cooper, M. and Dryden, W. (Eds.) (2015). *The Handbook of Pluralistic Counselling and Psychotherapy*. London, UK: Sage

encompass this way of practicing. Their reasoning is very similar to ours: in order to satisfy client need, concepts and methods from (more Feeling-Sensing) modalities such as psychoanalytic psychotherapy *must* be integrated with concepts and methods from (more Doing) modalities such as CBT.

The substance of our argument is that the CBT practitioner wishing to adhere to the best traditions of the beautiful model and to be fully true to the reality behind the concept of EBPP *must* practice within the dialectic between goals and process. While the dialectic is a given and the behaviors the Good Therapist does are givens, the form of the languaging in which you incorporate the substance of Good Therapy into your self-narrative as clinician is entirely yours to choose. You may or may not choose the expressions I use, for example, "Kohutian Mirroring." As we saw in the chapter on Theory, giving something a new name or a new focus is merely form. It does not alter what Good Therapy is.

Pain and sorrow

We have, in the foregoing pages, drawn upon the principles of depth psychology and have discussed *feeling into* client experience and *dwelling* in the client's *main feeling*. The clinician—as follows from our working hypothesis and the significance we place on the phenomena of the *Einfühlungsvermögen* and the intersubjective connection—*is paid to feel*. And we have described the clinician's bringing the client to her most exquisitely painful place and his doing this *purposefully*. There is a cognitive dissonance here too we must now pursue. We have to ask, one more time and in a different way: how necessary in fact is this dwelling in the place of pain? Can Good Therapy not be a more painless—whether for the client or the therapist—experience? Indeed clients frequently ask or instruct their therapist to avoid going certain places. "I don't want to talk about my mother/the rape" are client exhortations heard by therapists with some regularity in the first session. How is the therapist to respond? The phenomenon is, of course, one of *resistance*;[20] and the therapist, upon examining her countertransference, will realize the client is projecting his secondary dilemma on to the clinician, thereby placing her in a double-bind. The client knows the place he doesn't want to go to is also the place he probably has to reach to get to the other side of his primary dilemma. But—can't therapy be pain-free?

As we proceed, we see, with our Dialectic-Systemic, the emergence of patterns of patterns. This looks to be another case with a transference/countertransference system that is active from the get-go. Like Kevin, this client too may be forcing the therapist outside her comfort zone (itself a message in projective identification advising the therapist that the client is outside *his* comfort zone) and into an early transference interpretation. Let's call him Gonzalo:

THERAPIST: [*from her Ruler and Warrior*] You're letting me know straight away that you don't want to talk about your mother ... is it that you expect I will

---

20 Ivey, A. E., Ivey, M. B., Myers, J. E. and Sweeney, T. J. (2005). *Op. cit.*, pp. 189–192

want to talk about her? Perhaps because therapists are known to be interested in mothers?

GONZALO: Yes, I'm just very bored with that whole line. My last therapist went on and on about my mother and there's no point. Been there, done that. The woman's a bitch, end of story. Time to turn the page. I want you to help me with my boyfriend.

THERAPIST: [*from her Lover*] What's happening with your boyfriend?

GONZALO: He's this great boyfriend, on paper, but I'm becoming bored. . . . [*continues*]

In this dialogue the client ignores the tentatively tendered transference interpretation and invitation and both therapist and client collude in a retreat from a potential clash into *content*. A little later:

GONZALO: [*continuing*] . . . So he's there in the kitchen doing the dishes and thinking about our next meal—in that way he's really just like my mother!—and. . . .

THERAPIST: [*interrupting, from her Ruler*] . . . I'm not sure I know how to reply to that.

GONZALO: [*with a little irritation*] . . . What do you mean?

THERAPIST: [*endeavoring to summon her Magician to aid her Lover*] You told me you don't want to talk about your mother in here, that she's a bitch and your last therapist went on and on about her and there's no point. I get that. And I don't want to go against your specific instructions. I'm trying hard not to, right now, "lawyer" you. But right now I'm feeling I'm damned if I do and I'm damned if I don't. It seems to me that I *must* lawyer you—but at least I can apologize to you for doing this: I'm going to ask you how in the world we can between us keep your mother out of this therapy?

GONZALO: [*irritably*] All I said was that my boyfriend, in doing those things, *reminds me* of my mother. You don't have to make a big thing about it.

The therapist now knows the client is highly irritable and that she has already, no doubt like the boyfriend, attracted the irritability transference. With lightning speed it elicited, in the first therapist transaction here, the Ruler's active shadow pole of the tyrant (p. 109). Another client, perhaps having a less defended Personality Style or more fluidity in his Dialectic-Systemic, might have replied, "Ah, you got me there! Ok, let me at least finish talking about my boyfriend before you grill me on my mother. . . ." But this client is brittle, and the therapist can feel his irritation building. She has some choices, all of which involve following the resistance. One thing she must factor into her choice is the fact she is female and older than the client—in other words a perfect vehicle for the client's bad-mother transference. She reflects on the fact that, a moment earlier, her countertransference had been to feel the client was being ridiculous, to laugh at him—with not a little cruelty—at how she had caught him out in the silly game of whether or not we were going to talk about mother. She reminds herself that the client is, by definition, in pain. No doubt Gonzalo's mother too used to look past his pain and laugh, with not a little cruelty. The therapist moves past her inclination to fight the client and remembers that, before she can expect her client to become at all interested in her way of looking at and doing things, she must first climb aboard his train and let him show her around his world. Her *Einfühlungsvermögen* thus restored to functioning, her intentional choice is to say:

THERAPIST: [*from her Lover*] I apologize for my interruption, Gonzalo. You were telling me that your boyfriend is spending all this time in the kitchen, sort of acting like a househusband and—I think you feel kind of *fussing unnecessarily* about those things. You're *irritated* by his behavior and [*now, with the Magician, pulling an image out of her countertransference*]—this is my supposition here, so please forgive me if I am wrong—it occurs to me also that his time on the chores takes away, it feels to you, from *your time together*. You would rather the dishes just piled up in the sink and that your boyfriend was cuddling with you on the sofa—is that it, have I got that right? He ... he's not *romantic and loving* in the way you need him to be—is that it?

GONZALO: [*quietly*] Yes.

THERAPIST: I'm not sure but ... are your eyes a little ... ?

GONZALO: Yes. You painted quite a picture. That's what I'm missing.

THERAPIST: And does it ... hurt you to look at that picture we have painted?

And now we are, at last, and with this most defended of clients, on the verge of accessing the Sensorimotor. The question now becomes: can—or should—the therapist in this vignette try, with her client, to keep his tears and pain back? Can we help the client know what to do in his relationship with the boyfriend without dragging him, intentionally, through the pain of re-experiencing a main feeling? Perhaps it is, in any event, too soon: the therapeutic relationship is too new, and the client too brittle and defended:

GONZALO: [*irritably*] Not at all. But, yes, this is exactly why I am here. Tell me what I need to do to get Brian out of the kitchen!

The goal of Ivey's developmental counseling and therapy is, as discussed, to bring the client's development to a point at which he is able to find "balance between [entering] into a full expression of feelings, as represented by Sensorimotor experience, and the ability to become more concrete and analytical as the situation changes." While the Sensorimotor is the foundation of our experience, it is processed, and our meaning-making occurs, in the Concrete, Formal and Dialectic-Systemic Styles. "Meaning-making" is Ivey's term for how we narrate our experience: was it good or bad, profitable or unprofitable, a pointer to hope and

Eriksonian ego-integrity or a harbinger of despair? Our meaning-making is fluid, our glass half-full or half-empty depending on exactly how we process our experience. Can we help Gonzalo see the glass is half-full and thus remove from him the need to worry about being alone on the sofa?

Our client's world is rigid. Denial, disavowal and repression are the currency—along with ideation that we can somehow *make* other people fulfill our needs. Perhaps another thing modeled to Gonzalo by his mother. We will not fully *get* Gonzalo until we have done our *Sichhineinversetzen* into the world in which a more painless, "selective" therapy is indeed possible. With some clients, then, we are required *more fully* to enter the lived experience of the resistance. We have to join the client and even do the therapy the client's way before the client will show any interest in doing it our way. Since this is the only way to help, it is the way.

In another synthesis of goals and process, counseling and psychotherapy, we *must* begin by going down this path, even though our working hypothesis has suggested this avenue holds limited prospect of success. And so we come to our second "therapist's dilemma," a conundrum already previewed: how does it come about that we *must*, with the client, go down the road that will very likely not be of real help to him? In our dilemma the *thesis* is our working hypothesis, which underscores the primacy of the Sensorimotor and the goal of entering into a full expression of feelings; and the *antithesis* is the client's resistance. In such a case we are called upon, according to Chaudhuri,[21] to arrive at a *synthesis*. Here the synthesis is that we "work with the resistance" and find it in us to Love the resistance and its role in preventing the client from entering full expression of feeling. And, in so doing we in fact go with our working hypothesis, which emphasizes feeling-into, entering the client's world as our overarching, primary task.

Returning to the irritable Gonzalo and his "boring" and chores-burdened boyfriend, we can enlist our Dialectic-Systemic to the goal of helping our client feel better: we "reframe"[22] the boyfriend's actions in staying in the kitchen doing chores as "Brian's way of loving, of being fully *in* the relationship." The glass *is* half-full! The intentionality of the reframe is to precipitate a cognitive restructuring, to alter the client's experience from that of not being loved enough to that of being sufficiently loved. Even when he is alone on the couch and Brian is in the kitchen. If this doesn't work—and this is the other pole of our intentionality—we get, from Gonzalo's reactions, more information for our ongoing assessment: the client's *sense of physical separation from the loved object* is too dominant and precludes his adoption of the reframe. Being "loved" remotely from the kitchen by Brian's acts of housekeeping is not enough. And in this way we can further feel ourselves into what life is like for Gonzalo, know him better and get closer to the magic moment of intersubjective connection.

---

21 Chaudhuri, H. (1977–1989). *The Evolution of Integral Consciousness*. Wheaton, IL: Quest Books, paperback reprint: ISBN 0-8356-0494-2
22 Barker, P. (1994). Reframing: The essence of psychotherapy? *In* Zeig, J. K. (Ed.), *Ericksonian Methods: The Essence of the Story*. London, UK and New York, NY: Routledge, p. 212

Gonzalo's idea of treatment is that we discuss, in our Formal and Concrete Styles, what steps he has taken or could take to pull Brian out of the kitchen and onto the living room sofa for a shared evening. Accordingly we wonder if they should get a dishwashing machine? Do they cook twice a day, for lunch and dinner, and would they be better off, would there be fewer chores to do, if they cooked only once? Could the chores be done together, to maximize "sofa time"?

And yes, these stratagems, some of them, will have some interesting and positive results. Gonzalo leaves therapy with a new dishwashing machine, a reordered housekeeping schedule with just one fully cooked meal and one salad a day and more time on the sofa with Brian. And we didn't talk about his mother. We implicitly Mirrored his abandonment terror (as much of it as we saw in the tears pricking through his defenses) and we succeeded in reducing his experience of boyfriend boredom. He tells the clinician everything is altogether better and he won't be continuing in therapy. In compliance with the client's resistance and direction not to talk about mother we have avoided raking over the past and putting the client to pain. What now is our clinical meaning-making?

Our intentional work has brought Gonzalo to first-order change. Key at this point is the clinician's assessment of her client's potential developmental trajectory. She knows it will be better if Gonzalo continues in treatment until second-order change is achieved. Can she steer the conversation, in what the client intends to be the final session, between his goals (satisfied with first-order change, leaving) and her process (knowing the work to develop the client's personality still remains undone)?

GONZALO: It's working really well now. Thank you! I guess I won't be coming back next week.

THERAPIST: I'm happy to hear your and Brian's new arrangements are working so well! So well, in fact, you think it's right to discontinue our sessions. I'm really happy to hear you feel so good about things. You know, therapists are always cautious about terminations. Especially after a relatively sudden turnaround.

GONZALO: [*laughs*] I understand the protocol. Ok, you have fifty minutes to convince me that this relatively sudden turnaround is going to unravel!

Gonzalo has rebounded from his depression into a brittle confidence. His clinician reflects on the fact that regular weekly attendance in therapy until all valid clinical goals are met is a predominantly clinician-centered, goals-based construct. The idea works for some clients. Others like to take their therapy in bursts. This is particularly the case in some clients with attachment issues. The Ruler steps down from her throne:

THERAPIST: [*from her Magician and Lover*] Congratulations on your achievements. You are where you want to be. My door is always open to you if you want to consult further.

And it is here that we see the manifestation of intentionality. One version of Gonzalo's therapist may have a reified case conceptualization and therefore believe, when he leaves treatment with a reordered housekeeping schedule and without having explored the maternal relationship, that this is good outcome. In this event, when she says, "My door is always open," the words are pure form, the politeness of an inevitable termination, with no extension of Self. In contrast, the intentional therapist maintains an overview of Gonzalo's entire potential developmental trajectory; she recognizes that this present outcome and the client's withdrawal from treatment are both transference re-enactment and a temporary staging post. Both versions of the therapist use the same words in the final transaction. But the *nonverbal, projected* communication to the client is very different. The intentional therapist is, by manifesting the Magician and Lover cardinal Archetypes, nonverbally Mirroring the client's desire to try to move forward with first-order change. There is, therefore, encoded in what she says the subliminal message and seed idea of *when* the client will return to work on second-order change. The words are identical. The communication absolutely different.

Two months later Gonzalo is back. Brian is, again, "boring," having signed up for Spanish classes two evenings a week. And he is also thinking about joining a bridge group! Gonzalo is again alone on the sofa—unaccompanied by even the sounds of housework in the kitchen:

GONZALO: It turns out your clever ideas weren't really so very clever. Now I'm more alone than I was before!

THERAPIST: Oh dear, that is very disappointing news. We did, I think, try to work out whether something like this might happen. We talked about how it sometimes occurs in couples that one likes to spend the evenings relaxing together at home, whereas the other likes to be more occupied with the concrete activity of doing things. We wondered whether Brian is like this, someone who just likes to keep busy. If there's no housework to do he goes and takes a class.

GONZALO: You mentioned it in passing but you thought we should try those things anyway. Your gamble didn't pay off.

THERAPIST: Alas no. And, as a result, you feel quite badly about our work together; you came to me for a solution and the solution I, as you see it, gave to you, which did seem for a time to be working for you, has now resulted in your being worse off, lonelier on the sofa in the evenings, than you were to begin with. Your inclination, it would not surprise me in the least, must be to berate me and blame me for the outcome.

GONZALO: Yes. I can't believe I'm back here and paying you for this.

THERAPIST: You can't quite believe you're paying for this... this nothing!

GONZALO: You have this terrific reputation and of course David said you helped him enormously—he spoke so glowingly of you, which is why I came here. I was pinning my hopes on this therapy with you since all the other therapists were rubbish . . . and now I feel I've reached the end of the line, so much so that I'm back here with you!

THERAPIST: [*from her Lover and using her Magician*] You feel most profoundly let down by me, Gonzalo. Because of my reputation and David's recommendation you were, it makes perfect sense, *entitled* to suppose I can indeed help you, would indeed help you find just the way for you to get what you need from Brian; but it turns out I have more than failed you. And I am very grieved that you now feel *more lonely* in your relationship than before. I'm very sad indeed for you. I can absolutely feel the sadness in your aloneness. . . .

GONZALO: [*silence*]

THERAPIST: [*from her Lover*] I wasn't able to help you keep your boyfriend with you on the sofa. But I can help you, if you will let me, with this enormous, heavy, clinging sadness. . . .

GONZALO: [*sobs*]

Of course Gonzalo's profound sadness arises out of his unsatisfactory relationship with his mother. She was depressed after he was born and her behaviors toward him alternated between scorn and disinterest. Herself disadvantaged by a Mirroring deficit, she was not in a position to supply her son with adequate Mirroring, as a result of which his feelings of being abandoned, let-down, shortchanged and *angry* remain, in the main, unexpressed and unprocessed, other than by manifestations of his brittle, irritable personality. He was indeed hard to reach but our therapist has now broken through. She sat with Gonzalo to help him access his main feeling of being abandoned and failed by someone he was entitled to count on; and with nondefensiveness she afforded the client a partial corrective emotional experience in the transference. The feelings have been Mirrored, shared and tolerated (all things mother could not help him with) and a precious increment of self-structure has been built. When the client's original wounding was as an infant and therefore *pre-verbal* there can be little or no narrative attached to the main feeling.[23] It is, simply, there to be felt and grieved. After some time:

GONZALO: I don't know quite what that was all about. I do feel better, in an odd sort of way.

THERAPIST: It seems to have been about a very big sadness; just when it came on so strongly we were talking about my having failed you. You were entitled to count on me and I failed. Who else, whom you were entitled to count on, has failed you?

GONZALO: [*exhales*] Let's talk about my mother.

---

23 Baird, L. (2008). Childhood trauma in the etiology of borderline personality disorder: Theoretical considerations and therapeutic interventions. *In* Hakomi Forum, Issue 19–20–21, Summer. *Accessed October 1st 2014 via* www.hakomiinstitute.com/Forum/

The client's deep, ancient pre-verbal feelings were too big and too frightening for him to be able (until now) to bring into expression; and his defensively holding them deep within was but one result of the lack of parental Mirroring. The other result is that the client was not able to develop sufficient capacity in his higher Styles to assist with processing difficult feelings in his current life. Although gifted and intellectual in academic and business endeavors, when it comes to people and relationships he can muster very little in the way of emotional intelligence. Gonzalo cannot, when it comes to negotiating relationships, see how he is affecting others and choose to respond with a "balance between [entering] into a full expression of feelings . . . [and becoming] more concrete and analytical as the situation changes." He could not soothe himself with the idea that Brian, though always keeping himself busy, was nevertheless fully in the relationship and not going anywhere. *He could not feel into how difficult he is to be with.* His most usual response to a relational problem was, as was his mother's, to become irritated and volatile, thereby forcing the person to do it his way—or step outside the range of fire. Much as, in the transference, he obliged the therapist to do the therapy his way. And, when our spouse tends to those kinds of behaviors and we feel powerless to change him, it makes sense that we avoid rocking the boat, and choose instead to stay in the kitchen doing chores or to go out to evening classes. And, if we are the clinician, we do the therapy the client's way—intentionally, biding our time, and always laying the groundwork for the way forward that will surely present itself.

Because Gonzalo's wounding was pre-verbal, with no memory or narrative attached, no Mirroring or processing of it could take place. There is therefore much work to do. But the therapist's attachment theory and her *Sichhineinversetzen* tell her what this is about; and she can *affectively attune to* the deep yearning, the limitless lonely longing for mother. In so doing, extending Self at the point of intersubjective connection, she can transfer to Gonzalo some sense that his inexplicable, un-narrated suffering is in fact something the therapist knows about—and can therefore handle and encompass. And help him encompass and handle it.

It happened in much the same way with Ghislaine. Before she became ill the chief content of our weekly discussions, the only way of doing therapy she allowed me, were her somatic pains and consequent excursions to various physicians. The physicians were all highly educated younger men and Ghislaine took each of them over the same sequence in process. She would tell me there was a bright new doctor for whom she had high hopes that his investigations would produce a diagnosis she "liked." Telling me these things she would smile gaily and brightly and her eyes would sparkle—and at those times I became aware of how much fun had once gloried inside this woman. In my countertransference were thoughts of how Ghislaine was "dallying" with these young men earnestly attending her, like a princess in a fairytale. She held all the cards. The "suitors" had the fairytale-like impossible task of finding a medical solution to somatoform pain disorder—while Ghislaine, when they were sufficiently tortured and frustrated, could then "not like" what they told her and dismiss them. In these ways she repaid the masculinist environment for having failed to educate her and give her the means for self-support. I was thinking all of these things and able to share, Mirroringly and intersubjectively, in Ghislaine's impish delight in confounding the learned young doctors with her symptoms. One day she responded to the intersubjective moment with a transference interpretation of her own:

GHISLAINE: You agree with them, don't you. You think it's all in my mind and that there is nothing medically wrong with me.

PETER: [*urgently signaling for the Magician*] I'm not a physician. My job is to help you make sense of it all. The physicians who say it's all in your mind are talking about a phenomenon that is known to me. I know it to be *possible* that symptoms such as yours are, for some people, "all in the mind." I don't *know* that this is the case with you. I *do* know that what you are experiencing is a very real pain and that it is very painful.

It wasn't my most congruent moment, but Ghislaine gave me and my incipient Magician credit and let me get away with it:

GHISLAINE: It's fine if you do agree with them. I think I'm ok with that. You approach me in a different way. I think we can "agree to differ." [*smiling impishly*]

So we colluded in doing things Ghislaine's way—yet she knew that I knew ... and I knew that she knew I knew. But she couldn't join the dots and I didn't know then what I know now and, a beginning therapist, was not courageous or knowledgeable or "big" or adroit enough to run with the transference baton. Yet Ghislaine and I had broken through. So that later, in the hospice, when she told me about the abortion, we needed no words to co-narrate our intersubjective minds-meeting: Ghislaine's pains, which, as I had so often heard her say, "felt like wires running up my leg and through my body," were an analogue of her experience of the abortion. *So this is where they came from*. Yes, they were all in her mind. She knew, *we* knew.

Gonzalo, then, is helped by sensing that the therapist somehow knows the unknowable and is thereby making it ok. At this point the secondary dilemma of the resistance is behind us. Now the fundamental Sensorimotor has been unlocked Gonzalo, the most defended of clients, will enter into conversations with his therapist, as before described, to process each new Sensorimotor release in the other three Styles. Since he has already operated very well in his Formal and Dialectic-Systemic in the domains of Work and Play if not in the domain of Love there may be comparatively little groundwork to be laid in the higher Styles. We shall see. Our ultimate goal for our client is, from his Formal, to understand and, from his Dialectic-Systemic, to forgive his mother—she knew not what she did—and in so doing become altogether nicer for Brian (and anyone else) to be around.

It appears we need to add a further rider to our working hypothesis: sometimes, with some clients, the Good Therapist may look like she is working according to a theory that obviates pain and sorrow and raking over the past. But it only looks that way because of the defensive structures supporting the client's refusal to let go, and we should not allow ourselves to be deceived into thinking that therapy is complete and done when in fact we have only just begun. We start where we have to. We pause when we must. Our many clients with complex presentations can communicate fully only by re-enacting complete tableaux in the transference. Gonzalo's re-enactments were the initial double-binding of the therapist and the withdrawal–approach of the premature termination and subsequent return. Thus the final therapist transaction before the break was absolutely crucial: Mirroring, both explicitly and implicitly, Gonzalo's withdrawal–approach impulse sets him up for the subsequent full corrective re-experiencing while the projected message of his return to work on second-order change confers some protection upon Gonzalo for when his hopes are dashed. *Of course he will return*! (But if the therapist's case conceptualization is reified and her parting words empty, then, when Brian signs up for the evening classes, Gonzalo will be profoundly discouraged and, if he does seek therapy again, it will very likely be with a different clinician.)

Case conceptualization

Psychotherapeutic developmental repair is a process necessarily occurring over time and at its own pace. The synthesis—and our ethics—lie in our conceptualization, predicated on our assessment of the client's potential developmental trajectory. Gonzalo's therapist was practicing intentionally. When she allowed her Queen to step off her throne and to gratify Gonzalo's desire for a selective therapy, she was aware that a possible result will be a first-order change termination. Her intentionality, in colluding with Gonzalo's insistence on a problem solving approach, is manifested in her openness to the possibility of his withdrawal from and return to treatment. In this sense the staging-post termination is as much "homework" as it is ending. For Gonzalo, who is scared of process, it is a necessary precondition for *discovery*.

With a less defended client the dialectic and the discovery may be managed more fluidly. Christine Padesky, of the Center for Cognitive Therapy in Huntington Beach, California, in a keynote address delivered at the European Congress of Cognitive and Behavioural Therapies, affords us further insights into clinician conceptualization, intentionality and the dialectic between goals and process. The Socratic questioning of cognitive theory, she says, may be "to change the client's mind" (goals) or it may be "to guide discovery" (process). Padesky advocates that Socratic questioning be primarily used to guide discovery, which she describes in detail:

> As the therapist in this example . . . I had no idea when I started the questioning process where we would end up. . . . I think this is a good thing. . . .

Because sometimes if you are too confident of where you are going, you only look ahead and miss detours that can lead you to a better place... the therapist asks questions to understand the client's view of things, not to simply change the client's mind. As a result the client is more active.[24]

Padesky's intentional questioning to guide discovery and animate the client involves specific transactions that Mirror the client and "confirm self" in relation to his depression, including:

THERAPIST: Has something happened to lead you to this conclusion or have you felt this way for a long time?

and

THERAPIST: And so, because you care about your family, you then decided you were a complete failure, that you've let them down.

Elsewhere Ohio State University's Lawrence Needleman offers further clarification of the guided discovery process of cognitive theory. In his example the clinician is talking to a mother who screamed at her son "hysterically" when he jumped down a lot of steps:

THERAPIST: ... Back to the incident. What was so upsetting about his jumping down all those steps?
CLIENT: I'm afraid one day something terrible will happen.
THERAPIST: Is that a good reason to get upset at him when he jumps down a lot of stairs?
CLIENT: I guess so, but I shouldn't get hysterical with him. I was over-reacting.
THERAPIST: Is it possible that he could have gotten hurt jumping down those stairs?
CLIENT: Yes. I guess it wasn't even unlikely that he could have been hurt. The foyer door is right near the bottom of the stairs.
THERAPIST: So, do you think this was or was not a legitimate thing to be upset about?[25]

Needleman's therapist carefully balances goals and process. He avoids offering his client a simple counseling solution in the shape of an enhanced understanding of what constitutes the behavior of "over-reacting." In the last transaction he *returns the client to her dilemma and source of pain*. His doing so then brings her

---

24 Padesky, C. A. (1993). Socratic Questioning: Changing Minds or Guiding Discovery? *Keynote Address* to European Congress of Cognitive and Behavioural Therapies, London, September 24th. Accessed via www.padesky.com
25 Needleman, L. D. (2009). *Cognitive Case Conceptualization: A Guidebook for Practitioners*. New York, NY and Hove, East Sussex: Routledge, p. 58

to a more nuanced, developmentally advanced resolution than the reified, evaluative concept of "over-reacting." The client learns that her (Mirrored) reaction was understandable and evidence that she is a good and loving mother; the Mirroring augments her self-structure so as to give her choice, in this case as to her options for expressing her (valid) fears about her son's safety:

THERAPIST: You clearly don't want to respond like that on a regular basis in the future, right?
CLIENT: Right.

At this point the therapist returns to goals to ask the client to rate her disgust with herself. Having been 90 at the outset of the session, it is now 10.

> *The practice of returning the client to the dilemma after the client has apparently found a way out is further explored in Part III of this book and found to be a key component of both intentionality and "flow" in counseling and therapy.*

The rider and the elephant

Seeking to draw on the four cardinal Archetypes comes with a caveat: when the clinician does so from a position of immaturity the attempt can backfire. As Moore cautions: "An Ego that does not properly access an [A]rchetype will be possessed by that [A]rchetype's shadow and left oscillating between the shadow's two poles."[26] The Therapist-Self, then, has to *learn how to use and draw from the Archetypes*. As with Mirroring, this may be done properly or not. Addressing his audience of teachers, Dobson further writes:

> Each [A]rchetypal figure possesses a bi-polar immature shadow, one pole characterized by an active stance and the other by a passive one. For the Royal, these are the tyrant and weakling; for the Warrior, the sadist and masochist; for the Magician, the master of denial and the trickster; and for the Lover, the addicted lover and the absent lover.[27]

Dobson theorizes that a teacher manifesting the addicted lover may have "preference for one or a select group of students" or "a desire to be adored by students" or even "insecurities . . . [leading to] creating a demanding curriculum." On the other hand a teacher manifesting the absent lover "feels

---

26 Moore, R. and Gillette, D. (1992). *The King Within: Accessing the King in the Male Psyche*. New York, NY: William Morrow and Company
27 Dobson, D. (2009). *Op. cit.*

increasingly alienated from others and may be depressed" and "is merely going through the motions, not actively or authentically involved in his work or students. A persona of cold professionalism may develop" or burnout. Dobson adds, "In my own teaching . . . I have also encountered each of the shadows of the Warrior Archetype."

Moore's and Dobson's observations chime with Ivey's dictum that "more [horizontal development] is better." Clinicians, who must all the time work simultaneously in and shuttle between the domains of goals and process, are most likely to manifest one of the shadow archetypal figures in our nonpreferred Aspect. Thus a process-preferring clinician, such as myself, whose development in the Doing Style may have it gaps, is in danger of manifesting the tyrant, weakling, sadist or masochist. And the goals-preferring clinician, perhaps somewhat underweight in the Sensorimotor and Dialectic-Systemic, may invoke the master of denial, the trickster, or the addicted or absent lover. Such manifestations and their dangers will be illustrated in the third part of this book.

The ultimate synthesis we are required to make, then, is to manage the dialectic between the cardinal Aspects of the Therapist-Self, our Feeling-Sensing Style and our Doing Style. Each clinician makes and narrates the synthesis between rider and elephant, between goals and process in client work, for herself. The synthesizing cannot be reified: the wheel must be reinvented each time. The best treatment is the one we are not in a position to do, right now, either because of agency rules or client resistance or both; so the best treatment must be the best treatment we can do now. We must remain mindful of the distinction. The best treatment we can do now is intentional only if our case conceptualization extends over the client's entire developmental trajectory to full adaptation. Only then do we maintain unconditional positive regard. It will be seen how very considerable are the self-knowledge and self-monitoring skills required. When and where our horizontal development is insufficient, we limit access to one or other Aspect and may conjure up the shadows of the blocked Archetypes, risking subpar outcomes for our clients.

Summary

Good Therapy is a *synthesis*. The dialectic between goals and process is both frame and substance. The dialectic is evident in the two kinds of evidence; in the kind of client presentation demanding more from the clinician's Formal and Concrete and that demanding more from her Sensorimotor and Dialectic-Systemic; in vertical and horizontal development; in a case conceptualization and treatment plan envisaging both the client's full developmental trajectory to adaptation and a closer-in, more tangible, if more fragile, staging-post interim goal of first-order change. The dialectic connects the therapist's authority with the authority of other stakeholders. The dialectic is informed by the four cardinal Archetypes of the Therapist-Self and its disavowal evokes their immature shadow poles. Put more parsimoniously: the Good Therapist manages the dialectic between the Doing and Feeling-Sensing Aspects in the Therapist-Self.

It is evident that we cannot just step into the role of Good Therapist at will. A degree and knowledge of psychology, to echo Peck, are not enough. It takes *a particular kind of person* to manage all these manifestations of the dialectic—including the in-the-moment dialectic between now-managing and now-not-managing. It takes a particular kind of person to extend Self so as to feel and be vulnerable. To develop our *Einfühlungsvermögen* and with it our intentionality and our Dialectic-Systemic Style. We can only become such a person over time and via a developmental process; we can only do the things that Good Therapists do after we have worked on our own developmental insufficiencies and imbalances.

Good Therapist

The *Good Therapist* is itself, of course—and herself and himself—an Archetype. We have in the foregoing pages examined what Good Therapy is. Most simply defined, it is "giving the client what the client needs" and to the extent allowed by prevailing circumstances. The Good Therapist does these things and prepares her Therapist-Self to do them. But, having defined and delineated Good Therapy, how do we define the Good Therapist? Since some clients—we have seen—place lower or fewer demands upon the clinician in terms of extending Self, it is apparent that "Good Therapist" is an entirely elusive descriptor. The Socratic question arises: in terms of giving the client what the client needs, how does a clinician with a less developed Dialectic-Systemic and a less augmented Therapist-Self and a less challenging client load compare to her colleague having a more developed Dialectic-Systemic and a more augmented Therapist-Self and a more challenging client load (if we can even say these things)? Is it easier for one to be a Good Therapist—and, if so, which? Or can they both be Good Therapists? Put simply—and since more horizontal development is better—is being a Good Therapist *about the level of developmental attainment reached by the clinician*?

This inquiry is best separated into two interconnected questions. The first, goals-based, Doing Style question is about scope of competence. Any clinician is ethically required to practice within her or his scope of competence. But it is not always so simple because, as we have seen, process may be expected to intervene to frustrate the ideals of *Doing*. The client may initially present as the sort of client for whom the clinician may reasonably expect to be a Good Therapist, practicing within her scope of competence; and some time later the client may suddenly throw open the door into areas beyond the clinician's comfort zone. And now we are tackling the second, process-based, Dialectic-Systemic question: *if being a Good Therapist is not a particular level of developmental attainment—and if, in spite of this ambiguity, there is, we are nonetheless certain, an Archetype of the Good Therapist—what, then, defines it?*

The only possible answer to this question is a further addition to our working hypothesis. Let us return to the most ethically minded clinician finding herself with a client who has, suddenly, thrown open the door into areas beyond her comfort zone. *What does she do*? It is clear when there is an absence of Good Therapy.

In such a case the clinician will go to the door opened by the client and slam it shut. She does this by neglecting vital countertransferential cues. She may refuse to have the discussion with the client about, for example, the client's erotic transference. She may switch from process (the client's opening the door to the areas of discomfort) to goals (for example, dating strategies), *such switch being entirely clinician-centered*. Perhaps the clinician even heaves a sigh of relief when the client quits treatment shortly thereafter.

But, as we have already seen, each clinical choice made by the therapist may be judged ultimately not from the domain of goals but only from the domain of process, *by its intentionality*. What if the clinician indeed responds to the environmental, developmental challenge of the client's erotic transference by switching back to goals? And what if she uses the breathing space afforded by the switch to reflect on her countertransference and the evidence it brings of the insufficiencies that still remain within her Therapist-Self? What if the clinician, so reflecting, realizes she has two choices? One option is ethical according to the domain of *Doing*: recognizing that she does not want to give the client what the client needs—perhaps, right now, it really isn't the time for this clinician to be doing further self-work on her countertransference to this client—she can refer the client out to a clinician who she knows is able to handle the erotic transference.

Another option is for the clinician to *choose* (with Glasser) *intentionally* (with Ivey) to respond to the environmental challenge by acceding to the call to further self-development: "Maybe," the clinician says to herself, "now is, after all, the time for me to do this work to help this client." The clinician receives consultation, perhaps, within a group of her peers formed for just such a purpose (and as illustrated in Chapter 11). Perhaps she returns to her own therapist for a few sessions. In these ways she further expands her Therapist-Self to acquire the necessary new competencies and is able to respond to the erotic transference by giving the client what the client needs in terms of working correctively through it.

Being a Good Therapist is itself a process

So now we can under-stand the *Good Therapist* descriptor. Like the concept of cultural humility it is more an *aware orientation* to the Therapist-Self as *work-in-progress*, more *a way of experiencing oneself as a clinician* and *way of responding to client need for clinician extension of Self* than it is a particular level of developmental attainment. The Good Therapist, simply, is she who realizes when she has become stuck and who has the developmental tools to respond to and manage the stuckness challenge while always keeping sight of the main goal of the client's developmental needs.

> **The dialectic manifests between the two sets of developmental needs: the client's and the clinician's.**

We asked: how do ordinary people having ordinary backgrounds full of ordinary problems—and, sometimes, having extraordinary problems—become Good Therapists able to do all these out-of-the-ordinary things we have delineated? There can be but one answer, with Ivey: *development*. We are encountering a new environmental challenge, that of *being someone's therapist*, and to meet it we must prepare, build, strengthen and train our Therapist-Self so that we manifest all these qualities and act in all these ways of which our everyday Self has not, hitherto, had either knowledge or need—and that our continuing everyday Self is not required to follow. The Therapist-Self is by no means a false Self: it is rather an enhanced, augmented, auxiliary version of our everyday Self that we are required and are able to manifest when we are being therapists. As Rogers puts it, in further describing his third condition:

> The third condition is that the therapist should be, within the confines of this relationship, a congruent, genuine, integrated person. It means that within the relationship he is freely and deeply himself, with his actual experience accurately represented by his awareness of himself. It is the opposite of presenting a façade, whether knowingly or unknowingly.
>
> It is not necessary (nor is it possible) that the therapist be a person who exhibits this degree of integration, of wholeness, in every aspect of his life. It is sufficient that he is accurately himself in this hour of this relationship, that in this basic sense he is what he actually is, in this moment of time.[28]

We are allowed, then, to be human and to be ourselves: people undergoing all of Life's transitions, of which some may be clinically significant. What we are not allowed to do is declare a moratorium on our seeking to enhance and augment our congruence in the consulting room.

And that is the infinite benefit of being a psychotherapist. We are and will always remain our own first client.

Dialectic, development and the path of the clinician

The essential feature of a dialectic is *incongruence* between thesis and antithesis. The essential characteristic of the Good Therapist is an *ability to return to congruence* in managing the various manifestations of the dialectic. In spite of experiencing incongruence, in spite of falling flat on his face when a client rejects an interpretation. The Therapist-Self is elastic, expansionary and capable of extensive operationalization as necessary, whether in the moment or following reflection and consultation. We shall now look at ways in which an educator of beginning therapists may be of crucial help to the process by which these capacities and this orientation to the Therapist-Self as work-in-progress, are acquired.

---

28 Rogers, C. R. (1957). *Op. cit.*

Discussion

- *This chapter discusses the "Therapist-Self." Is there such a thing?*
- *The Therapist-Self is said to be required to "access" certain Archetypal strengths or attributes: do you recognize any of these attributes or strengths in your own work? Do you respond differently at different times to different clients and how do you characterize this capability?*
- *Freud once said he is his own first client. Do you agree that the counselor and therapist "cannot take the client further" than she has taken herself? How does this idea relate (or does it not relate) to your practice right now?*
- *Is it indeed the duty of the clinician to prove herself "worthy of the client's attention"? How do you understand this—and what happens if this ideal is not met?*
- *This chapter advances the idea of the "essential therapist quality" of humility; at the same time it emphasizes drawing on Archetypal qualities not associated with humility, such as those of the Ruler, Magician and Warrior; how do you understand this apparent discrepancy? Have you "fallen flat on your face" as a therapist and how did you like it?*
- *How do you feel about methods of counseling and therapy that either emphasize the pain and sorrow of the past or seek to obviate it? Do you have a preference?*
- *"The Good Therapist manages the dialectic between the Doing and Feeling-Sensing Styles in the Therapist-Self." This "management" is said to be a precondition for "intentionality" and is related to innumerable clinical choices faced by the clinician. In this chapter (and also in Part III of this book) the clinical choices portrayed as intentional seem harder, more "uphill" and even "harsh" in that they return the client to the dilemma and place of pain. This portrayal of intentionality is advanced as being in accordance with the most skilled use of the Socratic questioning and guided discovery methods of cognitive therapy and cognitive-behavioral therapy: does it seem this way to you?*

Part III

Phenomenology of clinician development

7
Transition
From good intentions to intentionality • the beginning clinician and the Feeling-Sensing Style

> Transition and life trajectory • the clinician's personal suffering • normalizing inevitable deficits of beginning clinicians • intentionality and trusting in the therapeutic process
>
> Motivations, rewards and the developmental process • disenchantment and the neutral zone
>
> Fantasies of becoming a counselor and therapist • the clinician as primary client • disavowal, "overlooking" and projection • the clinician as not knowing and imperfect
>
> The "cultural imperative" and the eclipse of the Feeling-Sensing Style

"Becoming a therapist takes ten years."[1]

When Brant Cortright made this classroom comment his students reacted with shock—as did mine when, after an interval of twenty years, I said the same thing. The shock was not of disbelief. Becoming a therapist—neither a job nor a career but, echoing Bridges, a *calling*—is a transition and necessarily occurs over time. In between these two classroom comments came Canadian journalist Malcolm Gladwell's finding, in an exploration not of transition but of the phenomena of proficiency and success, that it takes ten thousand hours of practice to become good at something: at an average twenty hours a week spent in practice, Gladwell says, the process takes ten years.[2]

People generally do not fantasize as children about becoming a therapist. Our profession lacks iconicity compared with presidents, firefighters, veterinarians and race car drivers; nor does our culture promote the therapist as role model, seeking

---
1 Cortright, B. (1992). *In lecture*
2 Gladwell, M. (2008). *Outliers: The Story of Success.* New York: Little, Brown and Company

rather to view us and our work through a more critical lens. Yet still people *want* to be therapists. Why? Since ours is, as Michael Sussman has dubbed it, "A Curious Calling,"[3] should we not be curious as to what it is that, in calling us to this transition—the environment is telling us we need to let go?

"What brings you here?"

Sussman concludes that "personal suffering is a prerequisite for the development of the empathy and compassion that characterize competent therapists" and that those entering the field are motivated by a basic wish to cure themselves. Therapists, then, according to this thesis, are first and foremost *clients*. Sussman's ideas are familiar and beg a multitude of questions not least of which is how does it come about that *only some* psychotherapy clients who wish to cure ourselves of personal suffering go on to become a clinician?

Again I can speak about myself. I was a middle-aged psychotherapy client when I decided to become a therapist. I had recently sought treatment (which I had previously believed to be for other, "weak-minded" or crazy people—not someone like me), when a crisis brought about an epiphany: other people and I are no different! My therapist, a psychologist, *listened* to me and soon I was feeling better, armed with an array of self-help books and new concepts such as "self-esteem" and "family dysfunction." A little psychoeducation goes a long way toward first-order change. I was also at the time looking for a way to earn my living and I was absolutely *enchanted* with the idea of doing what my therapist did—helping people feel so much better, as he had already helped me. This work seemed so extraordinarily worthwhile. *I could make a difference*! People are more troubled than they need to be and as a therapist I can help them become less troubled. I had fantasies of sitting in an office and putting smiles on people's faces. Only now as I write this do I realize the only face I ever wanted to put a smile on was my mother's—and that sitting in a professional office (very likely a lawyer's or doctor's) was, in fact, her fantasy for me.

So I am Sussman's typical therapist, coming to the profession through first being a psychotherapy client. I am also Cortright's and Gladwell's typical therapist. I passed my California State licensing examination in 2003, and some time in 2013, I began to experience myself as *competent*. This is not to say that I was not "good enough"[4] as a clinician and professor before then. But something strange happened in 2013 and I began doing things I have never done before. I began to admit my capability and assert my competence. When a client, student or colleague let me know she or he appreciated something I had done, instead of responding with false modesty, embarrassment or self-deprecation (worse) or (worse yet) acting out behaviors unconsciously designed to disprove my praiseworthiness, I would

---

3 Sussman, M. B. (1992). *A Curious Calling: Unconscious Motivations for Practicing Psychotherapy.* Northvale, NJ: Jason Aronson.
4 cf. "the good enough mother" *in* Winnicott, D. W. (1973). *The Child, the Family, and the Outside World*. Harmondsworth, Middlesex: Penguin Books, p. 17 and p. 44

accept the praise with gratitude and humility, thanking the praiser for letting me know my efforts were of value to her or him. And knowing they were and that I had done good.

Each writing assignment I set for my students is accompanied by a formidable rubric drawn from DCT: the writing is complete, the rubric states, only when the student has brought forth on the screen out of her keyboard and out of her Dialectic-Systemic processing *something unknown to her at the time she sat down to commence the writing*. And this is exactly what has now happened to me. I can now tell you what it is that I was called upon to let go after so many decades. It is the sense that I may never amount to anything and can muddle through only on other people's sufferance and with their express protection. I no longer self-deprecate or otherwise act out the incompetent's role.

Something happened between my parents when I was about five years old that forever changed our family life and to which I responded by adopting the identity of the "problem child" needing much ongoing management, supervision and rescuing. A role that allowed my parents to paper over the cracks that had opened in their marriage and focus on papering over the cracks in me. A role that is hard to fulfill by being, reliably, good at something and receiving recognition for that expertise. But now the final penny dropped, the veil lifted and the whole mechanism slid away. I began more fully to understand Ivey and Bridges and Ogden and Kahn and Kohut. And Good Therapy. My teaching and clinical work have attained a fluidity not previously experienced. I have completed the transition that began six decades ago when I was five years old.

I asked how we may explain that *only some* psychotherapy clients who wish to cure themselves of personal suffering go on to become a therapist. In my case, given who I was and the circumstances of my life trajectory, I cannot see how my transition could have been brought to completion in a way any other than the way it has happened. *Letting go is hard and we resist as long as we can—or longer.* I let go (with Bridges) only because I had no other way out of my (with Ivey) new environmental challenge: I *had to* let go for the sake my teaching. Else I would still be holding on. I let go for the sake of my teaching and I became an educator because I became a therapist. For now, therefore, I can propose only this much for our working hypothesis: *becoming a therapist is our best way towards completing a necessary transition—to let go of whatever it turns out we are called upon to let go.*

And now that I have, after more than half a century in the neutral zone of the transition, finally let go of the sense I must hide my competence, does what I say here mean that I can or should now take my newfound sense of competence "back into civilian life"? Should I start a business, study for an MBA or go into selling houses? *It depends*! What it depends on is what I want. Right now I want, if the environment will allow it, to continue to be competent as a clinician and educator of clinicians. I am enjoying experiencing myself as competent and not requiring to be rescued. And then again . . . I have talked about only *one* transition and one letting go. The discipline of being a therapist will surely help me in the many lettings go still to come.

> *When I first became enchanted with the idea of being a therapist I thought I was just about done with my development. Now I know I'm nowhere near done yet.*

Disengagement, disidentification, disenchantment and disorientation[5]

We, many of us, *used to think* that being a therapist is about *evaluating* what people's best options are and then persuading them to adopt our vision for them; or we used to think that being a therapist is about knowing and being expert. Those of us who came to this calling as clients perhaps thought that therapists are *unruffled*—because this was how our therapist seemed to us, this is what we needed to see in him. None of these fantasies, in my experience, turns out to be true. As we have seen, the therapist, much of the time, is in the dark and, as we have seen and will further see, the therapist's duty to feel-into client experience—at times even collude with client experience—will at some point inevitably put him into a position of discomfort. The beginning counselor and therapist is, then, in a fully Bridgesian transition involving moving from an old worldview to a new way of looking at things. The neutral zone of the transition may involve much discomfort and necessitate a leap of faith. In the neutral zone we experience dystonic feelings about ourselves and our place in the world. We have stopped being the person we were and are not yet the person we will become. We understand that our old worldview has stopped working for us but cannot see ourselves adopting any other. When another worldview is proposed to us, we are not able to "stand under" it and get it. This is often the case in the transition involved in becoming a therapist, which, we have seen, necessitates a particular developmental augmentation.

Depending on who we are, becoming a therapist may involve multiple lettings go. In the transition to becoming a therapist our disidentification from the behaviors and cognitions of ordinary good intentions is prerequisite to our re-orientation to the cognitions and behaviors of intentionality. Understanding intentionality involves disidentifying from ideas we may have had about what and how much is active and agentive in counseling and therapy. We are now called upon to operationalize and use our *Einfühlungsvermögen* to manifest Rogers' and Katsivelaris' active listening; with Winnicott, Hastings and Slavin we are further to use it to Mirror the client in the intersubjective encounter; and we learn we are to use it in addition to project communication nonverbally, as did Gonzalo's clinician when she sowed in him the seeds of his return to resume treatment.

Many facets in this schema of extending and operationalizing Self may be troubling to some students who, for reasons already previewed, like to rely on the Doing Style. Such students may experience profound disenchantment with their path when

---

5 Bridges, W. (2001). *The Way of Transition: Embracing Life's Most Difficult Moments.* New York, NY: Perseus Publishing, pp. 62–63.

invited by the instructor to grasp the concept of intentionality and experience the work of the therapist in this, for them, new way. The invitation takes the student out of her comfort zone and disorients her. A possible response is disengagement from the instructor and disenchantment with the course. The instructor is, often, in much the same position with his student as was Gonzalo's therapist with her client. Gonzalo had to let go of his reluctance to feel the feared, deep, vast, ancient and wordless feelings of abandonment. Similarly the student more comfortable with a more Concrete/Formal approach is now called upon to let go of a dualistic, paradox-rejecting worldview and have faith in the ability, as yet undeveloped, of her Sensorimotor and Dialectic-Systemic to grasp and befriend the thing she fears will destabilize her.

The transition to intentionality is a developmental process occurring over time. In its most perfect manifestation, the experienced clinician "in flow" (defined p. 178) will be able to predict with great accuracy and within a very narrow range the client's likely response to an envisaged intervention and will therefore be in a position to choose and time interventions flawlessly for maximum client adoption. Yet clinicians cannot always be in flow. Just as the dialectic between goals and process gives unmistakable clinical signals, so intentionality has unmistakable components, which may be acquired in increments.

The first is our recognition that, when not in flow, we are *always* at a crossroads. We can imagine the client will respond to our intervention in one of a number of ways. There is the set of responses we think or hope will occur and on which the intervention was predicated; there are further responses we can contemplate but do not expect; and there is always the possibility the client will respond in ways we may not contemplate or foresee. An intervention is intentional when the clinician is able to follow any path from the crossroads of client response. We must, in particular, be able to follow the path of the client's rejection of the intervention. Gonzalo's therapist, when she made the arch comment, rejected by the client, of, "I'm going to ask you how in the world we can between us keep your mother out of this therapy," had not fully analyzed her countertransference. Her (correct) case conceptualization was that her client is a man handicapped in his present relationships by archaic wounding in the primary relationship with mother. She wanted to be a Good Therapist to Gonzalo and help him achieve second-order change (with Priest and Gass, Watzlawick, Rogers and Ivey) in his defensive personality structure. With each successive intervention she was constrained by Gonzalo's defensiveness and resistance to change tack and "grade down" her approach. Each instance in grading down was a manifestation of intentionality: *the therapist had a response to it when the client's response to her was not what she had hoped.*

Each new response of the client, each discovery by the therapist contributes to the fullness and coherence of the assessment and treatment plan. This is the second component of intentionality. Having assessed the full extent of Gonzalo's defensiveness, the treatment plan is to Mirror the client in his preferred Concrete conceptualization of the problem, all the while extending Self to him until he can find *trust* in the therapeutic process and *notice* the clinician's acts in extending Self. The therapist does not know how long this phase of treatment will last—or whether it will be punctuated by the client enacting a withdrawal from therapy. It is important to realize that *not knowing* is perfectly compatible with practicing intentionally. It is, rather, "knowing" that is incompatible—the kind of knowing involved in a too rigid case conceptualization or where the therapist needs her client to respond to an intervention in only one way.

The third component of intentionality is the correlate of not knowing: *never being at a loss*. If the client hasn't profited from the intervention in, it may be, role-playing, then the clinician needs to be able to know what to do *in the moment*. While the clinician in flow is, by definition, never at a loss, when not in flow she may expect to encounter a setback that requires her to take a little time to re-group. In this case an indispensable clinical "tool" is at hand in the perfectly Rogerian, perfectly congruent therapist transaction of, "I'm at a loss and not sure I know where to go from here," followed by a Style-shift to the Dialectic-Systemic: "What do you think—what's going on and where would you like to take this?" Intentionality most certainly does not mean reiterating an unsuccessful intervention or "trying something else in case it works." Those are the behaviors of a clinician who is at a loss and feels anxious.

Intentionality is thus about having the right response when we get it wrong. As already flagged, the Good Therapist needs to be highly skilled in falling flat on her face and looking silly, all the while maintaining and modeling congruence. Perhaps an interpretation is resoundingly rejected by the client or, as in the last fantasized dialogue between Kevin and his clinician, the client catches out the clinician's too obvious and less-than-perfectly-congruent attempt at a reframe. Counselors and therapists are people and so we cannot be perfect and can be caught out.

Intentionality, then, is knowing what you want to happen or what will likely happen as a result of your intervention and also knowing what it means and what to do if the opposite happens or even if something entirely unexpected happens.

Education

When we first decide to work toward becoming a therapist *we don't have the full picture* and our Therapist-Self is as yet unmade. These things could not be otherwise. I take pains to stress that I am here making a highly generalized developmental assessment of the "cross-section" beginning therapist. She is, for reasons we can readily feel ourselves into, very likely in her transactions relating to counseling-and-therapy, to overlook something in either or both goals or process. To say this is not a finger-pointing criticism, nor wholly informed by projection. It is simply an ordinary, unsurprising, observable feature in our developmental landscape. Overlooking process elements in treatment involves disavowal (under-expression in Sensorimotor) and the disinclination to look beyond (under-deployment in Dialectic-Systemic).

The overlooking we see in the case conceptualizations of beginning therapists comes about for very good developmental reasons. Some relate to the person's own path and some are contextual and cultural. According to the DCT schema we can be expected to have developed our Dialectic-Systemic only as far as we have up until now needed to get by in a world that, as Ivey notes, operates largely from its Doing Style. Our environment likes the answers to its questions to come from the Concrete and not from the Dialectic-Systemic. If the question is *I am depressed: what shall I do?* The world prefers the answer *Take this pill* over the answer *It depends*.

The cultural imperative and the eclipse of the Feeling-Sensing Style

Our education occurs in the Doing Style and our educational system rewards us when we remain in Doing. Even at university level we are reinforced for regurgitating received knowledge and discouraged from using our Feeling-Sensing Style to bring forth new knowledge from our inner wisdom. We come to the field of counseling and therapy conditioned to copy and replicate. Thus it is no surprise that when, in the classroom, we learn a technique in, say, cognitive restructuring (more goals) or in dream work (more process) or in brainspotting (more goals) or in "draw your family" (more process) we reify. "This technique," we say to ourselves, "is what I am being taught to employ in response to this specific client presentation." We have now lost sight of *It depends* and allowed our Doing to eclipse and marginalize our Feeling-Sensing. Reification, therefore, is the immature shadow of intentionality. Conceiving and applying an intervention implies (p. xxxii) an open two-way communication between the clinician's Task Positive Brain and Default Mode Network to take account of all those things in the big picture that in some way impinge upon the usefulness of the intervention *and may require us to change therapeutic tack*.

As Ivey notes, we may demonstrate a different combination of preferred or predominant Style or Styles in different endeavors. To assess a (perhaps less adroit) beginning clinician as having an insufficient Sensorimotor or Dialectic-Systemic would be to reify the developmental phenomenon of the overlooking and reification. It is in the context of being a beginning clinician—whether goals-preferring or process-preferring—that we may, for all the good reasons here advanced, at certain moments in our client work, allow our Doing Style, the rider, to eclipse our Feeling-Sensing Style, the elephant. This does not mean we have an intrinsic weakness or unsuitability. But it does mean we likely have some un-learning to do.

Summary

The beginning therapist, then, must develop so as to un-learn certain behaviors. And it is, surely unmistakably, this sense of "I have taken my Sensorimotor and my Dialectic-Systemic as far as I need to," which we are now, in this transition to become a therapist, called upon to let go.

> *Our students, then, come to clinical programs very likely requiring horizontal development in the Feeling-Sensing Style. More is better.*

This, then, is the model proposed: building the Therapist-Self involves a Bridgesian transition in letting go of "I'm done letting go." That was how we experienced ourselves as clients in the first flush of enthusiasm for the therapy process, when we felt energized by our first-order change and a great urge to pass on our new discoveries. Once we embark upon the transition and open the door to increased self-reflectivity, reduced disavowal and enhanced perspective, our real work in second-order change begins. How can the educator facilitate it?

Discussion

- *What keeps you here? What, for you, are the personal rewards of the path of the clinician?*
- *What brings you here? Do you agree with Sussman that "personal suffering is a prerequisite for the development of the empathy and compassion that characterize competent therapists"?*
- *How easily does it happen, for you right now, whether in your personal life or professionally, that either your Doing Style or your Feeling-Sensing Style becomes eclipsed? Can you relate this concept to a client case or situation in your personal life?*
- *Did you, before embarking on this path, fantasize about being at a loss when sitting with a client? Was the fantasy ego-dystonic? The argument is here advanced that being at a loss is a perfectly normal clinician experience and that the counselor and therapist should "embrace" it: are you there yet?*
- *The argument is here advanced that the prevailing culture is predicated upon the Doing Style: to what extent would you say this corresponds with your experience in the education system?*
- *What fantasies did you have when you signed up for your graduate program? How has your experience so far matched your fantasies?*

8
Empathy
Developing clinician emotional intelligence • the *Einfühlung* group

> Empathy, boundaries and emotional intelligence • intentionality and listening • the "main feeling"
>
> Educator's developmental assessment of the student clinician: parallel process and projective identification
>
> Three typical presentations of the beginning therapist:
> - The "I don't know where to go from here" problem
> - The "education without understanding" problem
> - The "I can't stand the client's negativity" problem
>
> Experiential classroom assignment:
> the *Einfühlung* group

The duty to understand

Beginning therapists vary in every way people exhibit variation. In the professional, nuanced deployment of empathy in furtherance of theory implementation, students range from those whose Personality Style tends more to narcissistic defenses (meaning we may need to learn and practice the difference between *feeling-into* and *evaluating* another's experience) and those whose *Einfühlung* is so fluid and pronounced that they may enter into the emotions of others much too precipitously for comfort. As flagged by Ivey, the development of (lower-case "e") empathy arises along with the development of the Formal Style of cognitive-emotional processing and communication, in which we learn the *pattern recognition* and *if ... then ...* causal reasoning that helps distinguish Self and other.

Empathy involves feeling into another person's experience. The broader term *emotional intelligence* includes the faculty of self-reflectivity—the ability to feel into one's own emotions—that is so crucial to the operationalizations of the Therapist-Self. Emotional intelligence, then, according to New England psychologists Peter Salovey and John Meyer, "involves the ability to monitor one's own and others' feelings and emotions, to discriminate among them and to use this information to guide one's thinking and actions."[1] This complex interplay corresponds closely not only to Lipps' concept of the *Einfühlungsvermögen* but also to Ivey's descriptions of the Dialectic-Systemic Style in which we are able both to recognize *patterns of patterns* and to put our Self aside.

A natural readiness to empathize is a great asset to the beginning therapist—and by no means the whole story. The Good Therapist's operationalized *Einfühlungsvermögen*, or Rogerian Empathy, includes empathic ability, self-reflectivity and the ability to predict—with Ivey's intentionality and Salovey's emotional intelligence—within a range how the client will respond and how the encounter will go. How, then, do we turn ordinary people—who may or may not also be psychotherapy clients but who very likely, we have surmised, are exhibiting disavowal—into psychotherapists manifesting (upper-case) Empathy in a manner characterized by replicability, dependability and intentionality?

Experiential training

It has, since Freud, been thought desirable that those practicing psychotherapy should themselves have experience as client. However the *requirement* that a trainee clinician shall receive or shall have received therapy is not universal. Yale University's Jesse Geller and his colleagues find that:[2]

> In most European countries a requisite number of hours of personal therapy is obligatory in order to become accredited or licensed as a psychotherapist. In the United States, by contrast, only analytic training institutes and a few graduate programs require a course of personal therapy.

The contrast between the United States and Europe in the emphasis placed on the personal work of the therapist is not limited to pre-accreditation training. In California a licensed clinician may practice entirely without supervision or consultation, needing only to keep up with "Continuing Education Units," which are often taken online and which tend not to focus on the kinds of skills identified in this book as necessary for Good Therapy. In stark contrast, in the United Kingdom, every accredited clinician, however senior or professorial, *must* retain a supervisor.

Whether or not requiring personal therapy, graduate programs in localities across the globe take pains to afford students experiential training in psychotherapy microskills, an approach to the education of counselors and therapists developed by Allen Ivey and colleagues following his 1971 book *Microcounseling: Innovations in Interviewing*. The instructor asks for a volunteer for a live demonstration and the class subsequently splits into small groups. The frame and context varies: the encounters may be entirely role-played—or the student in the client role may talk

---

1 Salovey, P. and Mayer, J. D. (1990). Emotional intelligence. *In* Imagination, Cognition and Personality, Volume 9, Issue 3, pp. 185–211
2 Geller J. D., Norcross J. C. and Orlinsky D. E. (2005). *The Psychotherapist's Own Psychotherapy: Patient and Clinician Perspectives*. Oxford: Oxford University Press

about a live issue of concern. The course may provide for continuity to the encounters, in which case students bringing real issues to the table have a real chance to work on them and their classmates in the clinician role have a real chance to practice not only psychotherapy microskills but also clinical decision making. In these ways each student gains a degree of firsthand experience of what it feels like to sit with a therapist as client: how it feels to be listened to and to be empathized with; how it feels to have a therapist perform a particular intervention or therapeutic technique; and, since training is by definition given to those who are not yet expert, how these things all feel at those times when they are inexpertly delivered.

Inherent in this educational model is the expectation that the student will, during the course and in supervision, become entrained into the skillset and behaviors modeled by instructor and supervisor, perfecting them in increments. And yet there remains what has brought us here: the problem of the less adroit clinician.

Our working hypothesis tells us that becoming a therapist is a transition, which requires the development of a Therapist-Self, which is possessed of an *Einfühlungsvermögen*, which requires the person to have certain levels of competence and fluidity in the Feeling-Sensing Style of, in Ivey's terminology, the Sensorimotor and Dialectic-Systemic Styles of cognitive-emotional functioning. Further specific competencies in the Dialectic-Systemic are implicated in our flexible use of theory, our curiosity and our Magician's ability to correlate disparate elements in the client's story.

The Therapist-Self is, additionally, required to manage, in a way optimal to client work and with self-reflectivity, the interface between the clinician's Feeling-Sensing and Doing Aspects so as adroitly to recognize when the dialectic requires a shift between goals and process. But what if (as surmised in the foregoing chapter) the student's developmental trajectory has been mediated by the cultural imperative to over-reliance on her Task Positive Brain? What if she is not yet fully there, not yet best placed adroitly to optimize treatment of her client cases? What if she has not yet fully or sufficiently emerged from disavowal? What if she herself (alongside her clients) requires horizontal development in her Feeling-Sensing Style?

In this case her position as student in the classroom will be analogous to that of the client in therapy. Will the instructor subject her to "education without understanding" (a phenomenon described later in this chapter)? Or will the instructor first assess whether his student's level of development permits her to make good use of and under-stand his exhortations—will he tailor his instruction *intentionally* to the student's level of development? For unless he is able to engage the student, she will (like the client in parallel circumstances who is unable to profit from the help offered) disengage from the instructor and disidentify with the course.

If our working hypothesis is sound, we should be seeing some student therapists floundering and disengaging. And indeed we do. I myself was in this position at one point and there is, as Freud said in the different context cited (p. 10), no shame in that. A therapist in training is, after all, in training and with an inchoate Therapist-Self: if he cannot flounder now, then when? The educator is required to respond in a way that shifts the discourse for the floundering student from the at-times over-dominant Doing Style (*correct* vs *incorrect*, *right* vs *wrong*) into the at-times marginalized Feeling-Sensing Style (*you responded to your client in the way you did and then this thing happened: now how do we feel about and what are we to make of the sequence?*). The Style-shift to the Dialectic-Systemic opens possibilities for the student to notice it when he is overlooking something that can help advance the client case.

Three typical presentations of a beginning therapist

The—eminently understandable—symptoms of a floundering student clinician have at least three clear "Voices."

Voice #1—The I-don't-know-where-to-go-from-here problem

[Student-therapist discussing female client aged 17] "*I started out building rapport and mapping the problem; she doesn't know whether she should dump her boyfriend; she likes some things about the relationship and some things she is not so sure about; I don't know where to take it from here; shall I make an inventory of the boyfriend's pros and cons?*"

Process

The student is anxious. The supervisor must determine, with Satir and Baldwin, to what extent this is beginner's anxiety (whether appropriate or excessive) and to what extent it is the anxiety of the client, communicated via projective identification. Wanting to escape her anxiety, the client exhibits disavowal and reifies her goal into coming to a decision about her relationship. To make a decision one must know what one feels, which implies Sensorimotor development: in the conversation about the boyfriend the clinician will help the client untangle her feelings and own her disavowed experience, prompting her to develop beyond the dilemma underlying her indecision.

Goals

Within DCT's overarching, Dialectic-Systemic goal of the client's developmental adaptation, lie our Concrete goals of reducing/eliminating her depression and helping her build self-esteem. Underpinning our endeavor is *Einfühlung*. We must under-stand the client's frame of reference, hopes and disavowed anxieties—including the boyfriend's pros and cons as the client experiences them. The predominantly goals-based technique of making an inventory is an excellent way forward, since it follows the path indicated by the client and furthers assessment and information gathering.

The beginning clinician has unconsciously absorbed the client's indecisiveness and colluded with her conceptualization, reifying her presenting issue into a binary decision over whether or not to stay with her boyfriend. In consequence he is more inclined to give precedence to his (favored) Doing Style. His Feeling-Sensing Style subordinated, he is more inclined to overlook self-disclosure of clinician process as a facilitative and intentional intervention. And this is why he feels stuck.

The I-don't-know-where-to-go-from-here problem is a very slight problem, expectable in a beginning counselor and therapist. And it is right here that the prospective Good Therapist's intentionality is made or unmade by the educator's response. An inventory of boyfriend's pros and cons is the clear next step. But, before we affirm and reinforce the student's proposal, we must deploy our Dialectic-Systemic ability to look beyond content and examine communication. Do we share each other's constructions and inferences around the inventory? What does the student *intend/expect* in making the intervention? Does the fact he is asking the question mean part of him doesn't really think it's as simple as that? And does that idea bring on feelings of anxiety? Informed by a DCT assessment of both student clinician and client, the best educator response distinguishes between considerations in goals and process and opens the discourse, modeling looking beyond and encouraging the student to cognitions in intentionality, *constituting a DCT Style-shift to prompt the student to development in the Dialectic-Systemic.*

The student has asked a Concrete question. If the educator gives a Concrete answer, simply advising the student to proceed with the inventory, the student hears the advice in his dominant Doing Style and maintains the eclipse of his Feeling-Sensing Style. If the educator subjects the student to too long and too academic a lecture in intentionality, this may provoke disengagement. The educator therefore plans a developmental response incorporating encouragers to Dialectic-Systemic thinking. Again it should be emphasized that we do not assess the student as "Concrete and insufficiently Dialectic-Systemic" or "Doing and insufficiently Feeling-Sensing" *globally as an individual.* We are assessing the Styles of cognitive-emotional processing he is presently using, or of which he is allowing himself the use, *right now in supervision as he attempts to understand this client.* "Doing and insufficiently Feeling-Sensing" is merely where we must meet him now, in this consultation, to take him forward in the transition of becoming a therapist. A possible avenue for responding to the student's question is:

EDUCATOR: When you say 'I don't know where to go from here,' what are your instincts are telling you?

STUDENT: It's the logical next step. She said 'I have to make a decision about DeWayne' and *really made it sound like* it's about weighing up advantages and disadvantages. Making this decision is why she came to me.

EDUCATOR: It *sounds like* a logical next step—but it also seems like *you're not sure.* What would make you sure?

STUDENT: I guess it's right if it works?

EDUCATOR: Is it that you don't really think it will work and that, after you have done the inventorying exploration, she will be no nearer a clear decision?

STUDENT: I'm sure this will be the case. I will feel like we hadn't gotten anywhere—and so will she. I will have failed her.

EDUCATOR: Seems the client has convinced you the case is about, simply, good decision making. Which makes the inventorying intervention right if it works and wrong if it doesn't. I can understand, then, why you are undecided. And what you are thinking is true: if the case *is* about good decision making, then you *cannot possibly know* whether to do the inventory!

STUDENT: Ah…

EDUCATOR: So one way of looking at your indecision is that it is projective identification stemming from your client's indecision.

STUDENT: I am in the same boat as my client! There are some things I like about the intervention and some things I do not. Just how she feels about the boyfriend.

EDUCATOR: What you like about the inventorying intervention is that it matches client discourse in logical pursuit of her goals. What you don't like is that you don't know how she will respond. You *might not be prepared* for one or more possible responses. Let's review them…

STUDENT: #1–she makes her decision, is happy about it and treatment is successful; #2–she cannot decide even after the inventory; #3–something else happens.

EDUCATOR: What might the something else be? #3a–she gets angry with you? #3b–she becomes more depressed or anxious? #3c–she realizes there is more to her problem than she first thought? Can you see any of these responses as more or most or very likely?

STUDENT: I get it now. I soaked up her conceptualization that her case is a simple decision-making problem to be solved by weighing up the evidence. But the case is at some level surely also about her indecisiveness and its developmental roots in how she feels and how to ask for what she wants. *I* think there's more to her problem than she at first thought. Probably, after the inventorying, she will too.

EDUCATOR: Exactly. The realization will be intersubjective. You can—and will—say to her: 'Seems we are right back where we started: you don't know where to go from here. I wonder—are you wondering—if your decision is more complicated than we thought?'

STUDENT: I get it. The inventorying intervention is not intentional if I need it to succeed! Nevertheless it's the clear next step: she needs the process of inquiry for her development and I need it for my ongoing developmental assessment. If, as a result, she arrives at a decision and no longer needs treatment, we are happy; and if not, the result of the intervention will be that I am better able to pinpoint, with her, what she does need in terms of how she feels and asks for what she wants.

EDUCATOR: Exactly! And…*before* making the inventorying intervention: it is always good technique to *return the projection to the client* once you are aware of it. You will deepen the discussion of boyfriend's pros and cons by first saying to her: 'I don't know where to take it from here—you tell me you don't know whether you should dump DeWayne; there are things you like about the relationship and things you don't…you are in a place of uncertainty and *just don't know where to go from here* and I can feel that….' Hold up a mirror to the client to give her back her feeling, which you have introjected. Develop her horizontally in the Sensorimotor by helping her own and feel her anxiety.

The instructor makes his thesis accessible and interesting to the student by first joining with the student in his temporarily dominant Doing Style and then immediately Style-shifting to Feeling-Sensing. The instructor Mirrors the student's indecision and uncovers the underlying cognitions and dilemma. At the same time the educator models for the student the Socratic process of arriving at synthesis. The value in the inventorying intervention results from the intentional conceptual frame within which it is done—and, now the educator has helped the student broaden his conceptual frame, the student therapist can, in parallel process, help his client broaden hers, *beginning with the inventorying intervention.*

Voice #2—The education-without-under-standing problem

[Student-therapist discussing female client aged 45] *"My client is very anxious. She is overweight, single and frightened of public situations in which she is on display, as in the cafeteria line. I have been psychoeducating her about anxiety: studies show that typical fears—she will drop her tray or will pass out—are vastly exaggerated in terms of likelihood these things ever could or will happen; I told her this is a thought she can consciously import into her mind in the cafeteria line when feeling she may be triggered. Next session she was right back where we started; it was as if she hadn't taken in a word. It's like there's something different she wants from me that I'm not giving her."*

DCT assessment

At age forty five the client may be expected to have developmental attainments in the higher Styles and to have a foundation in, respectively, empathy and emotional intelligence; in other words, she knows something about how people respond to each other. She knows she is shy and awkward and (with Glasser) not happy in relationship. In terms of finding place in the world of Love, Work and Play she is surrounded by other people who look through her. No one in the cafeteria line pays much attention to the client; yet she is wracked by thoughts that they judge her punishingly—or would do if they noticed her. DCT assessment reveals her Sensorimotor is constrained by disavowal. The constraints impinge equally upon the higher Styles: saying things that *sound* Formal and Dialectic-Systemic, she has the *appearance* of adequacy. The combination produces a depressive, uncomplaining and conflict-avoidant personality, which closes the system and serves to reinforce the defense of disavowal. Until the recent exacerbation of symptoms she was only just getting by.

Goals

The client wants to feel better about her place in the world—and, right now, about her place in the therapy room.

Process

Are the two linked?

The therapist's tone is of objectivity: the practitioner-specialist delivers necessary strategies and *information*. The student's countertransferential anxiety to help his single, overweight, anxious client leads him to a too quick over-reliance on the (perfectly reasonable) Doing Style idea he can teach her to discover she is, in fact, bigger than her anxiety. It would be good if she can use the thought replacement tool. She also lacks the tools to confront her clinician when, for whatever reason, she feels dissatisfied with him. There has thus arisen an impasse in the transference, and an air of incongruity, *of things not being said*. The student feels uncomfortable. He has lost touch with his curiosity (an attribute of the Dialectic-Systemic) about the client and what she is feeling. Again we encounter a student who responds to the environmental challenge of being someone's therapist with an eclipse of his Feeling-Sensing Style. Again we must meet him in the temporarily ascendant Doing Style. The best educator response Mirrors without condoning and encourages the student to develop in Feeling-Sensing and in intentionality. A possible avenue for the educator is:

EDUCATOR: You were quick to note the change in your client's demeanor—how she was seemingly engaged in the psychoeducation and then, between sessions, seemingly erased all trace. It's the more frustrating because you feel this intervention is a crucial component.
STUDENT: Yes. The literature is very clear on that. But she can't hear me.
EDUCATOR: What does the literature say about when the client can't hear you?
STUDENT: It doesn't comment. I was hoping you can tell me what to do.
EDUCATOR: Before we look at that, may we just bring your intentions into focus? You hypothesize a goal to depotentiate her anxiety to traverse the cafeteria: your idea, I take it, is she will then gain more freedom to experiment with new interpersonal behaviors and will embark on a virtuous cycle (which the psychoeducation is intended to jump start) of adopting learnings, restructuring cognitions and changing behaviors? Seems like a sensible treatment plan.
STUDENT: So how do I get it back on track when the client can't adopt the jump start?

EDUCATOR:	The APA talks about 'adjustment of treatment as needed.' Does this suggest anything? Look at the client's DCT development; look too into your own countertransference ideation…
STUDENT:	For her to hear me I have to do something different. She's predominantly Concrete. So is much psychoeducation. But thought replacement is complex: it asks for Dialectic-Systemic self-reflectivity and Formal recognition of patterns; and Sensorimotor awareness of triggers. I keep thinking—well hoping—she will just get it.
EDUCATOR:	You keep hoping she will not need you to adjust treatment from goals to process.
STUDENT:	She needs development across her four Styles. I find it difficult to know where to start.
EDUCATOR:	It's tough to have these feelings. You have a reasonable case conceptualization and goals-based treatment plan in response to her present pain—to which her response is a process of disengagement, which leaves you discouraged. All your feelings are entirely understandable. And I believe what you are experiencing with this client is transference and the projective identification countertransference.
STUDENT:	She can't hear me. And that's how she feels in the cafeteria line!
EDUCATOR:	Very good. For various reasons the client is overlooked and unheard by those around her. As well as feeling unheard you also feel aggrieved. One way of looking at your aggrieved feeling is that it's part of the projective identification—the client also feels aggrieved. Another interpretation is that you *over-relied* on the psychoeducation intervention. Did this sound critical?
STUDENT:	Only a little! You emphasize intentionality and being prepared to respond if the chosen intervention falls flat and she disengages. You talked about Burns' 'hidden emotion or problem' that prevents the client from adopting the clinician's interventions and tools.
EDUCATOR:	For your client in this case, what could this be? She cannot adopt the intervention you administered; and the only way she can tell you this is by communicating to you projectively. Can you say more about the kind of person she is in relationship?
STUDENT:	She is a person who just skims along under the radar without expressing her thoughts, doubts and resentments. She is actually showing me in her relationship with me the things she does in the relationships with coworkers. I feel trying to reach her is a waste of time—as do they!
EDUCATOR:	Good! Don't feel bad about having succumbed to the projection: this client needed you to over-rely on some aspect of your treatment plan so she could communicate her frustrations to you accurately. Now you get it, your intentionality can return. You can revise and

	clarify your assessment and treatment plan. If she needs to project, it follows she needs development in the Sensorimotor together with development in the higher Styles to help process the feelings. As you just said. And you may be able to accelerate the developmental process by talking about what's going on between you.
STUDENT:	You mean talk about her response to the thought replacement?
EDUCATOR:	Now I can answer your earlier questions of what to do and where to start. The dilemma having surfaced now in the transference, I encourage you to pursue what I call a transference discussion. Your other instructors and supervisors call it immediacy. Can you in some way let her know you completely get her experience of being on a different wavelength from you? Perhaps say: 'I notice a lack of energy in you just now; it seems like you don't remember what we talked about last week; somehow your heart isn't in what we are doing in here; very possibly you think I am off-base in wanting to focus on combatting your anxiety in the cafeteria?'

Is the educator's thesis sufficiently accessible to the student? The educator will be alert to parallel process: just as the student therapist is trying to teach the tools-resistant client, so the instructor is trying to teach clinical tools to a student who may exhibit similar resistance. Beginning clinicians are often shy to work in the transference. Such conversations with clients are confrontive, requiring the student clinician be skilled in nondefensive self-disclosure and exposing him to potential hurt from any one of his many narcissistic vulnerabilities. We should not be surprised if:

EDUCATOR:	Oh dear…
STUDENT:	What?
EDUCATOR:	You were, just then, slumped in your seat with a glazed expression. I think I have provoked in you the same reaction you provoked in the client. [*Mirroringly*] Can you tell me: how does it feel to have someone—a person in authority who is supposed to know something—try sell you a strategy and a solution that, for you right now, doesn't hit the spot of where you're coming from?"

Employing such complex Style-shifts from Doing to Feeling-Sensing, the educator hopes to awaken the student's interest in his message by demonstrating it experientially. Feeling safe in the Mirroring and with Self thereby confirmed, the student might just become interested and not disengage:

STUDENT:	[*after a silence*] Yes. Thank you. This part is difficult for me.
EDUCATOR:	That's ok. That hidden emotion or problem preventing your client from profiting from your psychoeducation intervention…I can imagine you already have a sense of what it is.

Beginning clinicians often find ourselves called upon to help clients with issues touching on ones we have ourselves not fully resolved. The education-without-under-standing problem, which preserves clinician disavowal, is a behavior of the neutral zone of the beginning clinician's transition. Where the student is close to second-order change the supervisor can help; should the student appear to need it, the educator will recommend personal therapy.

Voice #3—The I-can't-stand-the-client's-negativity problem

[Student-therapist discussing female client aged 17] *"This is the client who doesn't know whether to dump her boyfriend; I found out a whole more stuff about her through making the inventory of boyfriend's pros and cons; it seems like she's quite sad and feels like she's never going to find what she's really looking for in a relationship; she keeps saying she's not sure she knows what love is and perhaps there's something wrong with her; every time I tell her how much she has to offer, every time I bolster her self-esteem, she relapses into the negative narrative..."*

Goals

The client wants to feel better; the therapist's reified case conceptualization is to build her self-esteem as swiftly as possible to reduce/eliminate her depression; along the way he will help the client acquire the relationship skills she presently lacks.

Process

The client wants to feel better about herself, with Glasser, in relationship. What process element prevents her from feeling better, now in this therapeutic relationship, in response to the therapist's earnest affirmations?

Some student therapists too easily enter the emotions of others and fear being overwhelmed by the sadness and hopelessness, the painful uncertainty and other difficult client feelings which in some ways touch on the student's own pain. What then ensues is an unconscious, countertransferential war in which the campaigns are, alternately, the clinician yanking the client forcefully into a positive narrative and the client, equally forcefully, yanking the clinician back to the negative story. Again the student therapist manifests a reified conceptualization with apparent reliance on the single intervention of iterating the positive narrative—and the single purpose that this intervention will prove curative. The student *needs* the client's cognitions and self-esteem to be capable of being changed by persuasion, argument and reiteration.

In the education-without-under-standing problem the client is having a hard time remaining engaged in the therapeutic process; in the I-can't-stand-the-client's-negativity problem it is the clinician who is loath to remain engaged with the client's negative affect and process. The projective identification is overwhelming the student. As with Kevin and his clinician, in this case there is some crucial, fundamental aspect of the client's negative experience that the client has not been able to communicate to the student therapist; there is *something about the sadness* that the clinician needs to know. But first he must escape the crippling effect of the projective identification. The pressure can be relieved and the session put back on track via the technique of appropriately feeding the countertransferential information back into the therapeutic conversation. A possible avenue for responding to the student's question is:

EDUCATOR: You have noticed a *distinct pattern* in the process of your recent sessions. *If* you drag her up, bolster her self-esteem, *then* she just drags you down again, goes back into negativity.

STUDENT: Yes exactly. It's like a tug-o-war!

EDUCATOR: Yes! Why do you think this tug-o-war is happening? What does it tell us?

STUDENT: She doesn't believe it when I tell her how much she has to offer? She doesn't like hearing me say it?

EDUCATOR: Why might she not like hearing you say it? Let's go deeper into your countertransference: what feelings arise in you as a result of what you're experiencing in this war?

STUDENT: I feel really discouraged and *depressed*. It's like her depression is infecting me. *I can't stand her negativity.*

EDUCATOR: You're struggling with these painful negative feelings of the client, which are almost too much for you to bear. And I would like to ask you a similar question to the question I asked you last week—what is your *intent and expectation* when you, as you put it, bolster her self-esteem…?

STUDENT: She will realize she is a valuable, good and acceptable person and begin to feel optimistic about her impact on others.

EDUCATOR: When we discussed the inventorying intervention we talked about being prepared for client nonadoption: what if it doesn't work? If you aren't prepared for it when she drags you down again, then your reiterated attempts to boost her self-esteem are not intentional. How come?

STUDENT: The alternative is I stay with her in the negative narrative!

EDUCATOR: We have talked about self-disclosure as a technique to shield yourself from the projective identification. Have you tried this with her? To recover, you can say something like: 'I feel there's an important part of what you are telling me about you and about knowing what love is that I'm somehow missing. And…as you show me how easy it is for you to lose hope and feel so badly about what you have to offer a boyfriend, I feel flooded with terrible sadness and searing pain—is this something like what you are experiencing inside?'

STUDENT: My fear is that I *will* feel too flooded with the sadness.

EDUCATOR: I get that. Have you noticed we are in parallel process? You are trying to sell your client your theory about self-esteem building and I am trying to sell you my theory on avoiding being flooded by the sadness. If you and I are stuck, now, in the same way as you and she are stuck, then it means I haven't listened closely enough to how hard it is for you to sit with this kind of negative affect. Can you, now, tell me more about this?

The educator now extends Self to the student, operationalizing Empathy to soak up some of the student's fear and sadness and help him shoulder them. If the student can then do the same with his client, she will very likely then acknowledge her projected feelings and begin to sob. Feeling her feelings in the presence of an empathic other who also feels them in the intersubjective encounter allows the client, as we have previously seen, to build self-structure and, with Cremin (p. 80) and Kohut, *true* self-esteem: the client learns she can tolerate or cope with the feelings and does not have to resort to projection or other defense. And she learns further from the intimacy conferred by the shared experience with the therapist and may be encouraged to transfer some of the learnings to relationships outside the therapy room.

If the student allows himself to sit, with curiosity, with the client's depressive story and feelings it will allow her underlying cognitions to emerge. Their emergence will highlight the workings of the family system in a way the presenting discourse cannot. This particular teenager is the same age as her mother was when she was born. The mother, who is single, is extremely strict and also demeaning. The client's solution to her difficult life at home is to find, *soon*, a man with whom she can live independently of mother. Mother's developmental and consequent relationship and parenting problems are an important component of the client's depression and can be accessed by the clinician only by looking beyond the presenting discourse of whether or not to dump the boyfriend. To see this as a case about self-esteem is to reify an aspect of it. This is a case about a family whose daughters become pregnant at around seventeen years of age and a mother who projects her guilt onto her daughter. The clinician is now in a position to decide to intervene as appropriate.

More Feeling-Sensing

Some students with an ascendant Doing Aspect pursuing reified goals of dispelling the client's pain may feel it is "not what a therapist does" to sit with a sobbing client and may take considerable time to develop the necessary skills. While such skills may be legitimized according to theory they must be acquired experientially. The task of the educator is to prepare the student for the particular client presentation and support the student very closely when it manifests.

The three student voices share certain characteristics. In *case conceptualization*, an inclination to take the referral narrative at face value and a reluctance to look beyond the presenting discourse lead to a reified view of the problem and to applying goal-specific interventions perceived to be remediating and curative. In the *therapeutic relationship*, a reluctance to use transference work or immediacy as a tool or technique leads to apparent curtailment in Empathy, *experienced as such by the client*. A countertransferential avoidance of the client's negativity may also be present. The Feeling-Sensing Style has become subordinated and the dominant Doing Style has propelled the therapist into a laudable but doomed impulse to fix the client's problem. The Feeling-Sensing Style is eclipsed for reasons that are entirely under-standable in terms of the DCT hypothesis: in each of the three presentations the student therapist is defending against his fear of his vulnerability. The behavior precludes intentionality.

As I noticed such presentations in my students and began to pick out the patterns I wondered how could I help them—and, through them, their clients? Could I design a developmentally coherent educational plan to afford the students the horizontal development in the Sensorimotor and Dialectic-Systemic Styles necessary to obviate their situational, defensive and obstructive need to reify?

Feeling-into the dilemma

Like their clients and like us all the students are beings engaged in development. DCT proposes that *development across the four Styles occurs in response to need or environmental stimulus.* For the client who is predominantly Concrete in her Style of cognitive/emotional functioning and communication, Ivey recommends vertical development with Style-shifts into the Sensorimotor, Formal and Dialectic-Systemic and associated horizontal development in those Styles. What if we structure into the course similar developmental opportunities for the beginning clinician whose therapeutic Style has become, temporarily and reflexively, dominated by Doing? It is not accurate to see the students' problems as capable of being corrected simply by emphasizing *Einfühlung*, process or Dialectic-Systemic thinking. Such (goals-based) attempts would be bound to fail if the educator does not first lay the developmental groundwork. The DCT schema allows us to conceptualize less adroit students as people who haven't hitherto in their lives particularly needed more development in their Dialectic-Systemic—or who best access it under conditions that do not expose them to emotional risk. In this conceptualization the students are responding in an entirely under-standable, predictable way to the challenges they face (and in a context—education—that usually rewards manifestations of Doing). As with our clients, the development of our students occurs via a dialectic between goals and process. We must educate *with* under-standing.

The *Einfühlung* groups

Experiential small-group practice is the hallmark of counselor education. Counseling-and-psychotherapy is best taught with alternate components of the experiential (process) and the didactic (goals) and students generally appreciate the experiential component. I devised a series of exercises in *Einfühlung* designed to give the students the experience of practicing Empathic feeling-into as a process-based psychotherapeutic intervention in its own right. I introduced the exercises to the students within a discourse distinguishing goals-based from process-based working and opening rather than closing off possibilities for looking beyond. This frame allows the students to see the exercises and my instruction as complementary rather than antithetical to input from their placement setting supervisors and concurrent instructors teaching more goals-based methodology. I advance the rationale that it is necessary—and certainly interesting—to see how far one can take things with a fundamentally exploratory, guided discovery or Rogerian approach. Only after a clinician has this understanding can she be *truly* intentional in choosing and applying a specific remedial intervention from the goals-based armamentarium.

Splitting the class into, first, triads (clinician-client-observer) and then dyads (clinician-client), I asked the clinicians to "be like Carl Rogers." They can track the client, reflect the client's feeling, summarize, empathize and, as they feel into the client's experience, use information from the projective identification countertransference to do these things in an ever deeper way. What they cannot do is *help* the client Concretely: there are to be no goals-based interventions and no advice-giving. Questions of the client are, with Brodley, permitted *only* in the service of the therapist's greater understanding of the client's lived experience. If there is a silence, it is to be waited out as Rogers would—or discussed with the client. Those in the client role were asked to talk about an actual problem and not to role-play a problem. This is because the clinician's task of feeling into the client's situation—and into what is "real" in the client's account of it—is sufficiently complex without the artificial layer of role-play, and I felt it to be necessary to give students a fully authentic experience. No student took the client seat unless she wanted to. Very soon everyone wanted to.

I went around the groups and helped those clinicians with the most need to get back on track. Afterwards the class reconvened and the students shared their experiences. All the clinicians agreed that the exercise was *incredibly difficult* and *counterintuitive*. They all wanted to help the client and fix the problem. Questions such as: "Have you thought of . . . ?" or "Have you ever tried . . . ?" come so naturally to the naturally helpful person and, once flagged down by the observer in the triads as *suggestions masquerading as questions*, had to be unlearned by the clinicians, not without difficulty. All the clients on the other hand loved the experience.

The student clients didn't in the least bit mind the absence of Doing Style interventions.

While individual client experience varied, the directionality was clear: the client got to *explain and explore more* in and around her presenting problem and got to understand herself better—and this self-understanding and exploration, under the therapist's active, operationalized listening and Mirroring, was experienced as therapeutic gain, whether or not any specific advances had been made in tackling the presenting problem or issue.

From the pedagogic perspective, even those students who were still floundering in the therapist role, whose suggestions masquerading as questions were flagged down by the observers and whose attempts at reflection of feeling were wooden, became nevertheless *interested* in the directionality of the group experience, thinking: "*could it be there is something in this for me*? If I can master this strange, uncomfortable way of doing therapy (which still feels like doing nothing very much!)—perhaps my clients too will report feeling like they are getting somewhere, just like these classmates."

The following week we did more of the same. Student clients chose, in the main, to continue their work of the previous week—another vote of confidence in the method—and I began to see a second pattern emerge out of the sessions in which the student therapist was more proficient in feeling into the problem. Although each client had a different issue in terms of content, I began to see the clients, each of them, as experiencing a *dilemma*. A dilemma that, moreover, is in each instance reducible to the schema: *if I do X then A will happen, which cannot be tolerated; but if I do Y then B will happen, which is equally intolerable; X and Y are my sole choices and I am therefore condemned to misery.*

The subsequent week therefore, in the experiential portion of the class, I shared my observation with the students, importing a rider into the assignment. They were to continue as before, attending to the client, following her process and feeling into the experience of her inner world but now *with the aim of reaching and identifying the client's dilemma*. Identifying and describing the client's dilemma is, of course, an *interpretation*. Finally the students were to be allowed an intervention other than reflecting the client's feeling, summarizing and empathizing. As I made my rounds of the dyads I noticed that in most cases the client—who in our practice sessions has the benefit of being a beginning clinician and knowing the goal of the exercise is to feel into the dilemma—would get to the interpretation, again with Brodley, first.

Interpreting the dilemma

The students were now clamoring for multiple demonstration sessions in which I am the therapist and one of them is the client. In these demonstration *Einfühlung* sessions we found that I was doing something in a somewhat different way from the way the students were pursuing the assignment: I was asking a very great many questions in order not only to understand the entire context of the client's problem but also—more significantly—to bring my feelings and experience into alignment with hers. Each time the context broadened I, with Brodley, resummarized the problem with the new information. Having a well-developed Dialectic-Systemic I would bring together in my summary those specific elements of the client's narrative in which I saw relevant correspondences or parallels—or incongruities. And it was at these stages in the therapeutic conversation that we would both together, as if arm-in-arm, stumble upon the interpretation of the dilemma. Whichever of us first voiced the formulation, the other would immediately say, "Yes."

The main feeling

While the interpretation of the dilemma was an *Aha*! moment, this was in many or most cases quickly overtaken by a deepening of the client's Sensorimotor experience. The feeling was a deeper, older feeling, which had been underlying and informing the more accessible, surface feeling response to the presenting issue. One of my students called the phenomenon the *main feeling* and I see no reason not to adopt this convenient term.

When fully in the experiencing of the main feeling the student became who she really was. The muscle-holding in the body and face that is in all of us part of our characteristic defensive structure and Personality Style was seen to be relaxed. There would be, often, floods of tears, frequently followed by laughter. The client felt much better. And now we had arrived. It was often unnecessary for me to ask the client (who of course was also a student therapist) whether the re-experiencing of the main feeling "reminds" her of anything. The client usually went directly and without a pause from the experience to discussing her mother or father.

I am here talking about these things in detached, Formal languaging, describing patterns of behavior seen across several years' teaching. The student client's main feeling was, invariably, heart-wrenching and often full of dread, evoking in me—and also in others witnessing the interaction—a painful somatic countertransference. At times, it was reported to me, some of the students in the group, whose own issues became triggered, thought it best they slip out of the room for a while.

The instructions for the experiential small-group portion of the class were once more modified. As before, the therapists were asked to use only techniques in *Einfühlung* to feel themselves into a full understanding of the client and her problem in context. They were to look to the goal of reaching the dilemma and its main feeling. Once there they were to allow the main feeling to develop and spend time there with the client, for as long as she needed. They were specifically asked not to recoil away from the main feeling. And I gave a further set of instructions. Inevitably some of the clients were exhibiting some resistance. For whatever reason—the therapist's proficiency, the dual relationship, the time, the place—the nature of the underlying issues—it didn't feel right to these students to follow the process through. In such cases the therapist was instructed to enter the transference and discuss the resistance. And/or, after some clearing of the air, switch roles. It goes without saying that any student who wanted to stop knew she could do so at any time and every student was secure in the knowledge that I was at all times available to be called upon.

Specific instruction to use projective identification in the "dwelling"

Arriving at an understanding of the dilemma can bring an uncomfortable feeling of stuckness to the client-therapist dyad. The therapist's reflexive, Doing-Style response may now be to help the client choose the least of the two identified consequent evils, *A* or *B*. The problem with this approach is that it reifies the case conceptualization as a binary choice between *A* and *B*. In actual fact the developmental, Bridgesian solution lies in embracing the main feeling and its message. The clinician must indeed pursue each side of the dilemma, the content element, while assisting the client to dwell in the main feeling, the process element. The intentional strategy allows for one of a number of resolutions: the client may indeed become sure in choosing either A or B as lesser evil; or she may express, tolerate and integrate the main feeling to such an extent that both A and B disappear and she is free to choose whichever she prefers of either X or Y. Therefore the students are asked to repeat the exercise but with a further rider: the instruction for the final modification in the *Einfühlung* sequence is that when/if the point of the impasse or dilemma is reached and the main feeling emerges, the student in the therapist role should "dwell" there with the client and feel into the experience of the stuckness, the pain of the main feeling and the logic of *if I choose X then A will happen—and if I do Y then I will feel B*.

The strategy has considerable educational value. It is desirable in classroom practice to accrue impulse control skills in *holding off* applying a remedial intervention; far from being the expert and taking the lead, the student therapist should practice hanging back in an observer role assistive to the client's experience of the dilemma and stuckness. In this way, if there is a message or if there is growth/development to be found in the stuckness, it can more readily emerge. It is equally valuable that the beginning clinician, who, we have seen, may easily absorb and become derailed by client affect, build capacity to tolerate negative affect and the terrible stuckness feeling.

All students, not only those inclined to the I-can't-stand-the-client's-negativity problem, are encouraged to hone their awareness of projective identification and guided in analyzing and using the information to assist the unfolding of client process via the technique of appropriately feeding the countertransference data back into the therapeutic conversation; use of metaphor, another vehicle for the Dialectic-Systemic, is encouraged:

THERAPIST: Hearing you talk I feel so *boxed in*!
CLIENT: Yes! That's just how I feel. . . .
THERAPIST: See if you can *tolerate* the boxed-in-ness just a little . . . does it remind you of anything or suggest a message to you?

Beyond the dilemma

Dwelling in the dilemma and its main feeling and affording the client a chance to ruminate in the two equally unacceptable options, and the clinician joining her there intersubjectively in the ruminations, can bring a magic moment of swift and sudden change. It may become suddenly apparent to the dyad of client and therapist that one of the poles of the dilemma is simply no longer true. It has vanished. Either the client no longer minds the thought of A happening if she chooses X or it is no longer true that she will feel B if she does Y. This is the cognitive restructuring of second-order change, born of dwelling in the main feeling with the therapist. A and B are simply not the things they used to be.

In second-order change the client develops beyond her dilemma.

The progression to the full experiential sequence here described spanned the entire period of my teaching. However from the very beginning the students responded positively, seeing value in the approach. They would at times allow the class to be extended late into the evening. When tired and busy students are keen to extend class running time from 10:00 pm to 10:30 pm it is indeed a vote of confidence for the experiential component! As discussed, for a few students the dilemma became annihilated upon its interpretation and upon the re-experiencing of its main feeling. For others the way forward was equally clear and some decided to enter therapy to continue the work begun in our course.

Choice

Overall the *Einfühlung* groups brought about the following observable phenomena:

- The clients all advanced without a specific remedial intervention being applied
- The clinicians were pulled out of positions similar to the three typical presentations of a beginning therapist here discussed
- The clinicians gained insight into their own personal process as well as into the client's process
- The clinicians were pulled into a position of having to look beyond
- All students advanced in the Sensorimotor and Dialectic-Systemic Styles

As predicted by our working hypothesis, Empathy or *Einfühlungsvermögen*, an operationalization of the Therapist-Self predicated upon emotional intelligence and precursor of intentionality, indeed turns out to require of the therapist a certain developmental attainment in the Feeling-Sensing Aspect. We are able further to refine our working hypothesis. "Less adroit" means less able to manage the dialectic between the clinician's TPB and DMN and prone to over-reliance on either Doing or Feeling-Sensing. Among students enrolled in an academic program emphasizing Doing, the clinician who is *less developed* in her Sensorimotor and Dialectic-Systemic or, it may be, who is *more inclined* to allow her Concrete and Formal to over-dominate will have more problems of the kind here illustrated.

The way forward for such students is therefore development in the Sensorimotor and Dialectic-Systemic.

Again I take pains to stress that when I describe a student as "inclined to allow her Concrete and Formal to over-dominate" this is not an indictment of him as a person or clinician. It is simply a DCT assessment of the parts of himself the student is now manifesting to me in our journey together in this course or in discussing this client case. There is no shame in it that a student should present this way. The role of the educator is to put the student in the position of, with Glasser, *choice*. To build her Therapist-Self and become a Good Therapist the student will surely, as I did, choose to let go.

Discussion

- *The idea is here advanced that the educator of prospective counselors and therapists in a graduate program will make a DCT developmental assessment of the student. How do you feel about this idea? When you signed up to your graduate course did you realize you were also signing up for a process of development?*
- *Do you recognize in your own client work to date an element of the "I don't know where to go from here" problem?*
- *Do you recognize in your own client work to date an element of the "education without understanding" problem?*
- *Have you ever experienced the "I can't stand the client's negativity" problem?*
- *You have read here about the Einfühlung group and have possibly also participated in such a group or a sequence of groups: what was this like, or what might this be like for you? Do you believe in using an exercise such as this to advance your capabilities in the Feeling-Sensing Style?*
- *The idea is here advanced that "feeling-into the client's dilemma" and dwelling in the place of stuckness and in the "main feeling" of the dilemma affords the client therapeutic gain; do you agree (or not)? Can you reconcile these practices with the guided discovery of cognitive theory?*

9

Congruence

Client negative affect and the low experiencing clinician • neurobiology of upholding the dilemma

---

Educator countertransference, congruence and parallel process • neuroscience and negative affect

Student development in the Feeling-Sensing Style

Sensorimotor: authentic disclosure of negative feelings
Dialectic-systemic: writing to bring forth new knowledge

The student's predominant Style as clinician • the "Ivey Instrument"
Educator Mirroring and confrontation: "Elena" and the case of Alexei

Experiential writing assignment: the response emails

---

*Education **with** understanding*

Our course was called *Individual and Family Life Transitions Therapy*, and our texts were Ivey and Bridges. The syllabus placed clinicians and clients equally on the same developmental continuum and self-assessment was a key course objective. To begin the first class I asked students to self-administer the "Ivey Instrument" (see Appendix), which Ivey describes as: "designed to help you examine your conceptual style, the way you think about relationships and the way you make meaning in the world."[1] If you have not already done so, you may wish go to the Appendix and take the Instrument before reading on.

In the Ivey Instrument the scores are plotted on the wheel diagram (p. 193) in which the four cognitive-emotional Styles, Sensorimotor, Concrete, Formal and Dialectic-Systemic, are shown as quadrants of a circle. A line is drawn from point to point between the scores, drawing a pattern onto the circle. Patterns produced

---

1 Ivey, A. E., Ivey, M. B., Myers, J. E. and Sweeney, T. J. (2005). *Developmental Counseling and Therapy: Promoting Wellness Over the Lifespan*. Boston, MA: Lahaska Press, Houghton Mifflin (Copyright 2005 [All quotes and figures reproduced by permission of Taylor and Francis Group, LLC, a division of Informa plc]), p. 423

are varied, some closer to an even square and some having pronounced peaks and troughs. My own result, which I disclose to the students, shows a significant predisposition to the Dialectic-Systemic, consistent over time, with a subsidiary preference, also consistent, for the Sensorimotor. My dominance in the Feeling-Sensing Aspect correlates, as expected, with my personal preferences and therapeutic style as a predominantly process-preferring clinician.

The Ivey Instrument gives some indication of vertical development in relation to the task of being someone's counselor and therapist, but it cannot measure horizontal development. It cannot measure competencies in one or more Styles *relatively between clinicians* nor is it a developmental assessment of the clinician as individual or prognosis. If the Ivey Instrument discloses a peak in one or more Styles, what this says is that the student, as clinician, tends to exhibit preference for one or more Styles of cognitive-emotional processing, conceptualization and communication. While the significance of Dialectic-Systemic capability in the clinician has been flagged repeatedly in the foregoing pages, having a peak in the Dialectic-Systemic in the Ivey Instrument does not demonstrate the clinician is a Good Therapist or can make good use of her Magician—it discloses merely the inclination to prefer a Dialectic-Systemic perspective in clinical work. Thus a clinician with a prodigious Therapist-Self and who has accrued substantial horizontal development in all four Styles may take the Ivey Instrument and show a slight trough in the Dialectic-Systemic—while another may show a peak. Both can be Good Therapists—the one with the greater and more balanced horizontal development being perhaps less likely to eclipse either Doing or Feeling-Sensing.

Many students' final shape drawn on the Ivey Instrument is close to a square—they are more-or-less perfectly balanced in terms of the dialectic between goals and process, Doing and Feeling-Sensing, rider and elephant, Task Positive Brain and Default Mode Network. If the Instrument has an ideal outturn it would be this shape, any peaks and troughs being relatively shallow. These are the more adroit students. For it is not so much the peaks that are assets as it is the troughs that are weaknesses. My peaks in the two quadrants of the Feeling-Sensing Style do not mean that I am uniquely blessed with an ability to bring forth my Magician and my Lover optimally on each occasion and with every client and every student. It means rather that, as a clinician, my elephant can dominate my rider and I must therefore guard against allowing my Feeling-Sensing Style to eclipse my Doing Style.

Again, the Ivey Instrument cannot measure horizontal development or predict whether the student's Magician, Ruler, Warrior and Lover will be strong enough for a particular client case. Ivey has already told us that, in terms of horizontal development, more is always better. Whatever our result from taking the Instrument it is merely a snapshot taken at a fixed point upon the ongoing journey towards augmentation of the Therapist-Self. All and any result is equally "good." The point is not to reify a particular score or pattern but rather, as I ask the students, to use their taking the Ivey Instrument as a basis for developmental self-reflection and choice, inviting them to observe themselves during our course and to see if the

Instrument does or does not have any value for them in helping them along their path. I say that the hurdles experienced by most beginning therapists in developing their own therapeutic style as they learn to work with clients are what Ivey would term "environmental challenges." To the extent the student has not been challenged in these ways and in this specific context before, she may be called upon to accelerate her development in one or more of the four Styles in order to rise to the challenge. It may be the client case is difficult or triggers some personal issues. In a course focused on how to work with the developmental hurdles of clients, we will be able also to apply the teachings of Ivey and Bridges to our Self. Thus primed, the students are motivated to extend themselves outside their comfort zone by the idea that doing so will be *useful* both to them and to their clients.

Our students are working adults. Each class meeting is scheduled for six hours. Outside the classroom itself the course's written assignments are my primary tool in fostering the development of the students' Therapist-Self. The requirement is to send me an email after each class meeting to respond to what occurred in the class and, before each subsequent class meeting, to send me an email responding to the required reading. As discussed (p. 119), each writing assignment is accompanied by a rubric, drawn from Ivey's exercise for "discovering your developmental blind spots"[2] and requiring students to imbue their writing with each one of the four DCT Styles. The assignment helps students both with self-reflection and with understanding DCT and its method of developmental assessment. I set no minimum or maximum page or word length for the writing; the student will know the writing is complete only when she has brought forth out of her Dialectic-Systemic processing *something unknown to her at the time she sat down to commence the writing.*

Students are, to begin with, baffled. Their education has, up until now, been conducted mainly via the Doing Style and reliance on the Formal and Concrete domains of the Ruler and Warrior. It is in these Styles, Ivey believes,[3] that most of the everyday business of the world is conducted. Some students, accordingly, deliver the early email assignments in largely Concrete and Formal communication, describing what occurred during our class meeting and seeking to summarize or paraphrase the content of the readings. I explain the best emails cover the least ground but in the greatest depth; was there just *one thing* that Carl Rogers said or did in the video we watched in class, or *one thing* Ivey wrote in the book, which caused a *particular* feeling response in the student? Might the student explore that? The rubric for the emails has specific instructions for the Sensorimotor component: expressions such as "I enjoyed . . ." or "I was pleased to see . . ." are not considered expressions of the Sensorimotor but rather expressions of the Formal Style, since these are, in fact, *evaluations*—the student is passing judgment on, it may be, the book or the video or something that took place in the classroom. I suggest that one way of being sure the Sensorimotor is engaged is to write about a *negative* experience. Particularly if it is directed at me. I tell them the students

---

2 *Ibid.*, Box 7.3
3 *Ibid.* (cf. p. 114)

achieving the highest scores and most success in our course are those who have had most trouble with the course material and with my approach to it. It goes without saying that the email assignments are entirely confidential.

So the student tries it my way and tells me, it may be, she was slightly bored during the Rogers video and, perhaps, she didn't like something I did or said in class; perhaps I allowed one of the other students too much time talking. I respond to each disclosure by Mirroring. It's absolutely lawful and laudable[4] that she should experience those feelings when watching the video or while listening to her classmate rattle on or upon observing my weakling's (p. 109) failure to rein in the classmate. And after the Mirroring I generally go on to ask a question, draw a parallel or discuss a hypothetical client having a presentation or issue that is in some way relevant. At this early stage in the course and with a student who is somewhat more reliant on the Doing Style and who finds the email assignments challenging, my replies are often of much greater length than the student's writing.

At this point in the sequence the student is, typically, stunned. With each course I am told that no one, no other professor, has ever *replied* to a writing assignment—or never in such a generous, Self-extending way. The student has, then, been afforded the first corrective emotional experience and displays the kind of gratification—and gratitude—Basch would expect. Before too long the writing assignments cease being a chore and become something the busy student *wants* to make time to do. And as the emails become longer—and, from the perspective of the educator's goal, better—the student's experiential learning gathers momentum along with her development. The writing assignments, then, become my way of working individually with each student for the duration of our course on just what it is she or he needs to be working on.

Because students have different learning styles and needs I expand the parameters of the writing assignments to be both more inclusive and more relevant. So long as there is some point of contact with the class process and the reading assignments a student may write, as she feels the need, about current or past clients or about an issue in her family, or experienced by a friend. I tell the class that students preferring to be more private and circumspect in their self-disclosure to me can import the Sensorimotor into their writing in these or other "once-removed" ways.

Confrontation

Ivey is at pains to stress the importance of the therapeutic use of "creativity, perturbation and confrontation"[5] as an essential impetus to the developmental process. Angela Molnos agrees, saying:

> The therapist's fear of confronting the patient's resistance is one of the lengthening factors in analytic psychotherapies. We can talk about confrontation

---

4   Kahn, M. (1994). *In lecture*, describing Mirroring
5   Ivey, A. E., Ivey, M. B., Myers, J. E. and Sweeney, T. J. (2005). *Op. cit.*, pp. 171 *et seq.*

whenever the therapist points out a contradiction or discrepancy without trying to explain or interpret it. The discrepancy might be between what the patient is saying and his actual behaviour, between his own statements or between the patient's and the therapist's perceptions.[6]

Failure to confront, then, in the therapeutic relationship delays the client's healing and developmental gain. Echoing Ivey and drawing from Austrian American philosopher and psychotherapist Eugene Gendlin, a student of Rogers', and his concept of "low experiencing,"[7] Arkansas psychologist Kathleen Boukydis notes:

> I feel that 'caring confrontation' is another way of increasing experiencing level. I see 'low experiencing' as actually being a variety of behavior patterns learned by the person as child as ways of avoiding feeling feelings, or experiencing. 'Caring confrontation' enables the person to step around these learnings and right down into experiencing, or the feelings that are there.[8]

The same must be true in relation to therapist education and the necessary developmental augmentation of the Therapist-Self. Our working hypothesis is thereby further advanced: by using caring confrontation in my replies to student email assignments, I am likely to be of help to precisely those students who need it most, those students we identify as, in their case conceptualization, manifesting a temporarily eclipsed Feeling-Sensing Style and, now with Gendlin and Boukydis, somewhat inclined to the low experiencing Personality Style defense. These presentations, eminently understandable in terms of the developmental trajectory of the beginning clinician, limit ability to respond optimally to clients.

What follows is an illustration of one of these email exchanges and an indication of what they can accomplish. The student, Elena, and her client, Alexei, are composites. Like many first-year clinicians Elena is drawn to using interventions from the Wellness model. An excellent, committed student and an enthusiastic and literary correspondent in the emails, Elena is in the first email concerned to discuss her response to the first class session and, in the second, a client case. The correspondence shows how the educator can assist the beginning therapist working to achieve mastery in the interplay of the cardinal Aspects of the Therapist-Self.

---

6 Molnos, A. (1998). *A Psychotherapist's Harvest: A to Z of Clinical Practice and Theoretical Issues With Special Reference to Brief Forms of Psychoanalytically Based Treatment.* Accessed via http://fox.klte.hu/~keresofi/psyth/psyhthr.html *and quoting*
   Hill, C. E. (1989). *Therapist Techniques and Client Outcomes: Eight Cases of Brief Psychotherapy.* London: Sage Publications
7 Gendlin, E. T., Beebe, J., Cassens, J., Klein, M. and Oberlander, M. (1968). Focusing ability in psychotherapy, personality and creativity. *In* Schlien, J. M. (Ed.), *Research in Psychotherapy, Volume III.* Washington, DC: American Psychological Association
8 Boukydis, K. (1979). Caring and confronting. *In* Voices: The Art and Science of Psychotherapy, Volume 15, Issue 1, Spring, pp. 31–34

In the first email Elena describes her own experiences of transition, discussing events leading to her happy marriage. Here I reproduce my comments as the student receives them, interwoven into the text of her email to me:

ELENA: After ... the big setback, a huge and painful ordeal, I was feeling quite bad about myself, with much second guessing, anxiety and *even* [PG's italics] depression. I recognized a pattern—I'd been here before. I knew I was responsible and I had to pull myself out of it. This pattern ... holds good for me even with an elected transition. There is one in particular which comes to mind, a decision I considered a very well thought out and conscious choice. Being very aware of the pattern, I attributed my difficulties with transition to be indicative of a weakness or deficit on my part.

PETER: The narrative therapists would see this *weakness* as a "story" into the narrative of which we are "recruited" by those in the environment who have certain beliefs about how one can best be "strong."

ELENA: Especially because after every such emotionally tumultuous process I have returned to my typical optimistic and upbeat self, and in all but one instance I did so without significant assistance from anyone else.

PETER: Yes. Our two theorists, Bridges and Ivey, tell us that (as you conclude below) we humans have within us the tools for self-development to meet environmental challenge. *On occasion* (as you describe) we may go get a developmental boost from a therapist.

ELENA: The one exception was when ... I decided to move to a different state. My anxiety on that occasion started when I signed the listing agreement with the broker to sell the house. With each step in the process—finding a buyer, accepting the offer, looking for a rental—my anxiety grew and grew. This extreme anxiety quickly developed into severe depression, at which point I sought assistance from a therapist. I was stuck. But I was determined not to give in to *what I considered to be a character flaw*. [PG's italics]

PETER: Dear me. And . . . what you say here begs the question: do you still, now, consider that you, at that time, manifested "weakness" and a "character flaw"?

ELENA: I also did not want to lose the respect of the people I was leaving behind by appearing indecisive.

PETER: I take it that indecision means "bad" and makes you "less-than"?

ELENA: After all, this transition is what I wanted and spoke to them all so enthusiastically about. Ultimately, as in the other major transitions in my life, I did return to a state of positive emotional equilibrium. Which is the point I'm making here. In fact this most difficult of transitions transformed my life in wonderful ways, leading directly to meeting the man who is now my amazing husband. Based on these experiences I believe that, just as the body has a natural tendency to return to a state of physical health, so too does the psyche to emotional health. The way I see it, the therapist's role is best described as assisting people to navigate their way through the transition process back from temporary weakness to normal emotional equilibrium.

PETER: Many thanks, Elena, and I greatly value your describing to me the pattern of these different experiences you have had with "weakness" and depression. Bridges' view is that the therapist's role is to help the client "embrace life's most difficult moments" while Ivey's view is that the therapist's role is to accelerate or repair development so that the client can *process* experience so as to move beyond the (as I conceptualize it) dilemma. Each of these (to pick up on your word) *navigational* paths is arduous and uncertain; and each, most likely, involves the basic dilemma you describe above: *how can I be "weak" and also not "lose respect"... be discouraged and depressed and yet be lovable and loved*? After talking about your "difficulties with transition indicative of a weakness or deficit" you quickly change tone and go on to talk at length about our "natural tendency" to return to a "positive mental equilibrium." I certainly congratulate you on your return there and on the happiness you have found. What you do not say here is what became of your dilemma—*can I be weak and also loved*? To the extent that you perhaps may not yet have answered this for yourself, I hope our course will help.

In this email Elena iterates her belief in a "positive" state of mind and discloses that her meaning-making is to associate negative experience with the possession of a character flaw. While our humanistic and developmental theory tells us we all do indeed possess a "natural tendency to return to a positive mental equilibrium" Elena, it seemed to me, in some way *really needed this to be so* and *really needed to escape the depression and consequent meaning-making*. Things she had said in class came into my mind and I saw something defended in the way she told her story in the email. My sense of Elena was that her default defensive Personality Style is to find any and all necessary means to avoid or negate negative experience—matching Boukydis' theorizing—a stance that necessarily lowers her experiencing. Ivey holds "we often find that so-called blocks in the counseling relationship are really blocks and impasses in the counselor or therapist."[9] Elena's tendency to want to escape the negative narrative could be expected to manifest both in the *Einfühlung* groups and in case conceptualization. Shortly thereafter it did. From the emails:

ELENA: My client Alexei has been married for eight years. About eighteen months ago his wife had an affair and they separated. This was devastating for Alexei for two reasons: he still loves her, and he is a traditionalist and cannot imagine getting divorced—or his family's reaction if he does. Also, what if the same thing happens the next time he gets married? In an effort to save their marriage Alexei and his wife entered couples therapy. However this ended when he discovered that the wife had restarted the affair. . . .

---

9 Ivey, A. E., Ivey, M. B., Myers, J. E. and Sweeney, T. J. (2005). *Op. cit.* (cf. pp. 215–216)

So he is again separated. His presenting problem is he is unclear how to proceed, whether he should seek a divorce or continue his attempts at reconciliation.

I asked Alexei to describe his vision of a perfect world. He answered that it would include a happy and emotionally connected marriage, a family and a nice home. I explored the importance of family in his culture. He indicated they typically have very closely connected families. Although his family of origin is very spread out geographically, they speak frequently on the phone and hold reunions whenever possible. In contrast his wife comes from a very emotionally disconnected family, who rarely see or communicate with one another despite the fact that most of them live in close proximity. This difference has always been a concern for Alexei.

. . . I have observed that Alexei displays primarily abstract thought and emotion. He is very reflective and aware of his patterns in relationship. This contrasts sharply with his wife, who, based on his description, is a very Concrete thinker and communicator. He states she is quite matter of fact and emotionally distant. He is extremely frustrated by the fact that his wife's manner of communication is very "superficial," typically devoid of any true expression of emotion or personal insight.

Consistent with the Wellness Theory aspect of DCT, I then began exploring Alexei's strengths *in an effort to take the focus off his problems and help him build for the future in a positive way* [PG's italics].

When I asked Alexei how he has coped following his wife's affair, he said he leaned heavily on his family, who have been a tremendous source of emotional support, although not knowing the whole story. When I told him he has a great way with people and a very good sense of humor, he told me his current job requires him to have strong people skills. Alexei is very social and has always made friends easily; whereas his wife was always reluctant to get to know people. When we discussed his future, should he decide to divorce his wife, I highlighted all of these strengths, and that they would certainly help him find a wonderful partner. We also talked about the fact that he is so emotionally available, unlike many if not most men, which would serve to make him very attractive to most women. Finally we discussed the fact that, during the recent period of separation from his wife, Alexei once again began to pursue hobbies he had enjoyed before the marriage, taking violin lessons and playing tennis. He stated he had found himself starting to adjust to his new reality and reported he was generally becoming happier and had even begun dating again. This conversation really seemed to build his sense of hope for a new and positive beginning, and served to take the focus off of what he was potentially "losing."

PETER: I am greatly impressed by your account and your very keen observation of Alexei and astute ability to relate your work to the course material. I also see how completely committed you are to helping him reach the rainbow at the other side of his dilemma. The discourse here is that Alexei's wife is "broken" and unable to be the wife he needs. He is minded to "decide to divorce" her—in spite of the fact that this might look bad to family members and that he "still loves her." And you, if I understand correctly, see your task as helping him build himself up for the big push to change this old, broken, un-fixable wife for a new, better one. On the face of it you and the client are on the same page and it's looking very good.

Yet I can't help thinking there is more. It's true Alexei's wife is acting the part of someone who is broken and psychologically damaged; it's *also* true Alexei mentions in passing a Bridgesian concern that he may turn out to be a serial divorcer. Oftentimes the things clients say to us in passing turn out to be significant. You don't say whether you picked up on this comment or not. The phenomenon in countertransference is of being *rushed past* something trivial. Yet I believe he is asking you *in a very quiet, all-but-inaudible voice* a question of great concern to him. Is there something wrong with him? How come he chooses women who perhaps seemed suitable at the beginning and then it goes wrong? Might that in some way be his fault? Bridges observes that people "make changes *so they won't have to make transitions.*"[10] Is not Alexei's exactly the kind of situation Bridges has in mind and to which the client himself is—all but unnoticeably—pointing?

You have explored one side of Alexei's dilemma, an avenue pointed out to you by the client himself, and your interventions in the Wellness model have taken you a great distance in that direction; my recommendation is you do not allow the other side of the dilemma to slip completely away from your focus. A new wife (a Bridgesian "change") seems a most attractive way out and we can certainly Mirror Alexei for entertaining this enticing fantasy. Yet are we to condone it? Is it, really, "for the best"—the best long-term answer? The awful reality on the other side of the dilemma, the prospective reconciliation, is that it involves very hard work on the couple's intimacy issues. It is, ultimately, the client's choice, not ours, and it may be too late to save the marriage. But it is not for us to say. If Alexei has intimacy issues then, unless he is super-lucky with the next wife, the problems will recur. Therefore in order to help him make a fully informed choice and to practice intentionally, you should at this point, in my opinion, Mirror the part of Alexei that he has rushed by you too quickly and from which he has diverted you: the part that wants to know what happened to destroy the marriage, the part that wants, *even now*, things to be different with his wife.

I press this with you for a specific reason: I am concerned at a kind of "cold-hearted" countertransference that arose in me upon reading it above where you say Alexei experiences his wife as "emotionally distant" and "superficial." I found myself wondering, *Hmmm . . . did he notice this before*

---

10 Bridges, W. (2001). *The Way of Transition: Embracing Life's Most Difficult Moments*. New York, NY: Perseus Publishing

he married her? What if he is the superficial, cold one and is projecting his intimacy issues on to her? The discourse in your three sessions has gone *all one way* and the way looks to be turning the wife into the scapegoat. Ivey shows us in his book how problems can arise when one spouse is predominantly Formal and another is predominantly Concrete. You have assessed Alexei as Formal and the wife as Concrete. Yet my countertransference tells me the wife is also Sensorimotor and angry; Alexei *appears* to have sufficient Formal capability and certainly evidences this outside his marriage; yet he shows us no understanding of his wife's feelings and responses to him, only late Concrete/early Formal *evaluations* of her behavior. As to the Sensorimotor, from what I can see, this couple express it only obliquely in passive aggressive actings-out (her affair, his trashing his wife to you). Through your excellent writing I can feel the anger poisoning the waters between them.

What I think has happened in your three sessions is that your client's anger has been channeled into the negative evaluations and scapegoating of the wife, which you have Mirrored. I wonder what would happen if you Mirror the client's underlying anger? When he can "enter into a full expression of [this] feeling" you may discover a further, more vulnerable layer underneath—and that may help you with the other pole of Alexei's dilemma, the one presently eclipsed.

Elena, then, is enchanted by the idea that she, putting the weight of her professional opinion behind Alexei's tentative evaluation of his situation and options, can cause him to blossom and put a smile on his face. Her bringing in the cultural component was skillful. I should have Mirrored her for all these things (without condoning the former) but didn't. Why?

I was indeed conscious of my countertransference to Elena, which was informed by my longstanding and defensive suspicion of the Wellness model. As someone hitherto prone to be depressive, I am inclined to feel criticized by the model and am correspondingly resistant to it. I believe it neither so easy, nor so wise to eclipse the negative narrative *as a default position*. I was accordingly struggling with an obstructive inclination to feel critical of Elena, who had in class discussion manifested zeal for using Wellness. It is now evident to me I could have better managed my countertransference (after all I have—with Truscott—something yet to learn from the concept of Wellness, something I have hitherto feared fully to understand) and spent some time Mirroring my student's evident delight in the Wellness model and in applying it to this client and in seeing the Wellness well up from within Alexei. But my Feeling-Sensing became temporarily eclipsed by my goal of pointing out to Elena her over-reliance on Wellness and I lost sight of the fact that Mirroring her delight is not condoning the over-reliance.

As I write, I notice what I believe to be a parallel process in the dynamic of withholding. . . . I *withheld* Mirroring from my student. Elena Mirrored her client selectively, withholding Mirroring from one side of the dilemma. And the couple's problems with intimacy, very likely, stemmed from the fact that they withheld

Mirroring from each other. And, since withheld Mirroring frustrates love and since frustrated love turns to hate, they had come to hate each other.

It appears we have competing developmental assessments for this couple: the first is *she is predominantly Sensorimotor and he predominantly Concrete* and the second is *neither Mirrors the other*. In process terms these are, in fact, the same assessment. As Michael Chabon, author of *The Pleasure, Regrets of 'Manhood'* observes: "Everyone wants to be loved and to be understood by someone who loves the things that he loves."[11] We want our spouse to under-stand and Mirror the passions animating our life—our golf, our yoga, our unpaid work for the charity we believe in fervently and the way we like to vacuum the cat hair off the sofa. If spouses love too-different things, from whom will each get the Mirroring for which we all, according to Kohut and Kahn, retain a lifelong need? The answer is clear: each spouse will seek Mirroring outside the marital dyad, from friends, a therapist—or, as Alexei's wife, from someone with whom she is acting out sexually. The ability to Mirror arises developmentally, with empathy, in the Formal Style. If Elena were treating the couple, her intentional treatment plan would involve Style-shifting both spouses into and then horizontal development in the Formal Style, along with the Sensorimotor.

Chabon's perspective helps us feel into the concept behind arranged marriages. Cultures valuing "unarranged," romantic pairings are peopled by couples who fall in love and marry in the fantasy we have found such a person, who does love the things we love. It is only after the honeymoon we find we have to learn to under-stand and Mirror our spouse for loving other things. Chabon gives us a nuanced perspective on Alexei's dilemma: he may divorce and then find a new wife who loves the same things, or enough of them; or he may repeat the sequence of finding a wife who turns out to have loves of her own that he does not share. And this is Alexei's fear, in his throwaway question, "What if the same thing happens the next time I get married?"

Elena's stance in case conceptualization manifests a version of the education-without-understanding problem. She was educating her client to be Well without understanding she was thereby suppressing the other pole of the dilemma. The client, like the others we met in the first part of this book, wants the therapist to rubber-stamp an easy way forward that does not involve completing a painful transition. Having allowed her Therapist-Self to collude with the client's anxiety for an efficient resolution, Elena has, momentarily, forgotten the other side of Alexei's presenting discourse, which is that he says he still loves his wife and feels it would be better, in a whole lot of ways, if only he could achieve his goal of a happy, emotionally connected marriage with the woman he is now married to. There are several doors to caring confrontation of the client but Elena's eclipsed Magician is too weak to open them. But Elena can get back on track. She does not

---

11 Chabon, M. (2009). *Interview* with Terry Gross on *Fresh Air*. WHYY-FM, Philadelphia, aired October 7th

need an awareness of Chabonian nuances—she needs only to employ the technique of returning to revive the suppressed pole of the dilemma.

It can never be right or intentional to pursue only one side of the dilemma.

The student has accepted the client's conceptualization of the problem and does not keep an open mind in relation to the client's assessment of his wife, a stakeholder and (albeit absent) part of the client base. Elena colludes with the client's inclination to see the failure of the attempt at couples therapy in very Concrete terms: the couple is beyond any help, divorce is a foregone conclusion and the therapist's case conceptualization and role is to support the husband, her client, and extol the virtues of this, the *only* choice, to go ahead with the divorce.

Elena's stance also has elements of the I-can't-stand-the-client's-negativity problem: in seeking to help Alexei avoid the agony of his dilemma, the therapist risks projecting her own meaning-making into the treatment, the meaning-making of her own vulnerable self that feels the need to escape quickly from depression. We can easily imagine how superbly this decisive, Wellness-boosting Warrior-like attitude of his therapist suits Alexei at this stage of the therapeutic endeavor. Only the Warrior is, in this instance, sent off on a detoured quest by the improperly accessed shadow archetypes of the subordinated Feeling-Sensing Aspect, the master of denial and the addicted lover. We now see in this case how accurate are Dobson's descriptors of the immature shadows of the four cardinal Archetypes. It is after all our job as therapists to hold up to the client a mirror—small m—so that he or she can, thus caringly confronted, see in its entirety what is really going on. In conjuring up for the mirror only *selective* facts assistive to the persistence of the client's disavowal, the manifestation has been not of the Magician but of the master of denial. And the Lover has indeed become "addicted"—with Elena becoming completely countertransferentially *enchanted* by the conjured-up vision of the client, divorced, as a happy, well-rounded being who can very likely attract all manner of good women to him.

My challenge as educator came in the form of a student somewhat prone to low experiencing, somewhat averse to negative affect and very keen to return her client to mental equilibrium by employing interventions from Wellness. I could better have assisted Elena and, through her, Alexei if I had then been familiar with the literature in neurobiology. The existence of a dialectic governing the clinician's decision to steer between the positive and the negative narratives is confirmed by neuroscience. As Lane reports:

> There are two broad themes in psychosomatic medicine research that relate emotions to physical disease outcomes. Theme 1 holds that self-reported negative affect has deleterious effects and self-reported positive affect has salubrious effects on health. Theme 2 holds that interference with

the experience or expression of negative affect has adverse health consequences. From the perspective of self-report these two traditions appear contradictory.[12]

The Theme 1 and Theme 2 traditions constitute a culture war in psychosomatic medicine that Lane now seeks to resolve into a synthesis, using a model distinguishing between "implicit" and "explicit"—unconscious and conscious—emotional processes and between "ruminating and catastrophizing" and "primary" negative emotional states and concluding:

> the possibility exists that sustained implicit emotional states may be more pathogenic than sustained explicit emotional states, particularly if the duration of the former exceeds that of the latter.[13]

Lane and his colleagues therefore greatly assist our discourse in relation to the I-can't-stand-the-client's-negativity problem and the use of interventions in Wellness in preference over the return to the negative narrative. "Sustained *implicit* emotional states" are bad for the client: negative affect that is repressed or disavowed or otherwise ignored over time is pathogenic and can lead to psychosomatic symptoms. It follows that the clinician's duty in relieving pathogenesis is to reflect underlying feeling and make the unconscious conscious. To that extent counselors and therapists *must*, with Needleman, revive the negative story. However when encountering clients' "sustained *explicit* emotional states," which are "ruminating and catastrophizing" and not "primary" (reasonable response to a stressor) clinicians *must* revive the positive story in Wellness.

The evidence from research in psychosomatic medicine corresponds with the phenomenological mandate to uncover the dilemma—even if doing so means provoking negative affect in the client.

Parallel process

Alexei's explicit emotional state had become highly positive. Any danger in pathogenicity could be found only in implicit, unconscious repressive processing. From this perspective it is clear Elena should indeed confront Alexei to bring back the repressed pole of the dilemma. This Formal argument, not available to me at the time these things took place, would have greatly helped my endeavor to engage Elena's Doing Style in support of necessary horizontal development in her Feeling-Sensing Style.

---

12 Lane, R. D. (2008). Neural substrates of implicit and explicit emotional processes: A unifying framework for psychosomatic medicine. *In* Psychosomatic Medicine, Volume 70, pp. 214–231, p. 214
13 *Ibid.*, p. 226

It is desirable, then, for the educator to confront the student in order to help the beginning therapist attain a greater level of congruence, being, in Rogers' definition, the state in which "there is a close matching . . . between what is being experienced at the gut level, what is present in awareness, and what is expressed. . . ." If I can help the student to a greater awareness and *tolerance* of her own negative thoughts then she will be less inclined, surely, in her client work to collude with her client's—equally under-standable—desire to subsist in a "lower" and more painless experiencing. And if I confront my student in just the right way, she will confront her client, also in just the right way. What if, in the case under discussion, Elena goes back to Alexei and says:

ELENA: We have talked in here about your heartfelt wish to have this happy and emotionally connected marriage and family life. You were depressed and discouraged finding your wife to be emotionally distant and superficial, then completely shocked to find she was having an affair and then further wounded by the failure of the couples therapy and her quite outrageous behavior in continuing with the affair! You separated—which for you was very hard to do, to *be seen to do*—and in the past months you have become a new person. You have re-entered life! [*Style-shift to Dialectic-Systemic*] Why wouldn't this future we have imagined for you, where you divorce and find yourself another wife who can give you what you want . . . why wouldn't this be the best way forward for you!?

ALEXEI: Yes. I am in good shape now and I love feeling this way. And . . . I have been wondering the same! It feels so right . . . and yet . . . it comes back to what I told you when we started: what if it doesn't work out like that—what if I make a mess of it a second time?

ELENA: You mean . . . what if you divorce, find yourself another wife—and then, somehow, it all goes wrong again? You mean in the same or in a similar way, is that it?

ALEXEI: Yes.

ELENA: If that could happen . . . then are you saying, "Oh, maybe there's something inside me I need to look at?" Is that what you are saying?

ALEXEI: Yes.

ELENA: I see. Well, if that's true, or could be true, we should look at that. It would also mean, wouldn't it, that our idea about your wife, that she is, in some way, not very well-developed emotionally, that this idea might, somehow, not be the whole story? Because in our discussions up until now we have been inclined to heap all the blame on her, haven't we?

ALEXEI: Yes. I have more than once wondered whether how she is . . . is somehow because of the way I am.

ELENA: Oh. You mean, I take it, *if* you act in certain ways *then* she will respond in certain ways—disconnecting from you emotionally? Is that it? And then it goes from bad to worse in a kind of downwards spiral . . . she feels more disconnected, you feel more critical . . . and. . . . [*pulling from countertransference*] perhaps also *cold*?

ALEXEI: Yes.

ELENA: You must tell me . . . what are these things you think it possible you may perhaps be doing that may trigger those responses in your wife?

ALEXEI: She says. . . . [*continues*]

Elena meets Alexei in his late Concrete/early Formal, then, in a Style-shift, accesses the client's Dialectic-Systemic thinking: why wouldn't the imagined future work? Having successfully opened the discourse the therapist then uses "if . . . then . . ." markers for her client's horizontal development in the Formal. It turns out that Alexei's emphasis on his wife's problems is indeed defensive, serving to mask his own low experiencing and his own issues, with Glasser, in relationship. And it also turns out that the client and his therapist, my student, have been engaged, on parallel tracks, in the same quest for congruence, for a closer matching between what is being experienced at the gut level, what is present in awareness, and what is expressed. The same quest, in fact, upon which we have all, in our various ways, embarked.

The educator's intervention with the student in the composite case just discussed is shown to have had good outcome. Yet some questions remain, not least among them being: what if the outcome had not been good? What if Elena had gone back to the client and iterated the other pole of the dilemma, as recommended to her—but without the skill and success here demonstrated and after which Alexei abandoned treatment?

Evidence in countertransference

Clients abandon their therapist when they feel the therapy isn't helping and the therapist is insufficient. Beginning trainees and interns—and also more experienced clinicians—lose clients when under stress. The Therapist-Self has become diminished, with all that implies: the intrusion of the shadow archetypes or, it may be, an Aspect eclipse, combine variously to cause too many clinical mistakes and missteps and too much overlooking. The client experiences the therapist as *incongruent* and simply not "big" enough to be of help.

These things are of concern in supervision. Her Therapist-Self incompletely prepared and developed, the student may not be fully ready or fully able to implement with congruence an intervention recommended by her supervisor. Congruence, we recall, is Rogers' *first* essential therapist quality. An intervention delivered too much from the Doing Style ("my supervisor told me to do this") with the Feeling-Sensing Style and its adroit grasp of timing, Mirroring and client cues temporarily eclipsed, is incongruently delivered. The effect on the client can be devastating. In this case Alexei has a sensitivity to withheld Mirroring, no doubt arising from archaic wounding. Were Elena to reassert the suppressed pole of the dilemma incongruently, we can imagine that he could experience the shift in therapist discourse as a betrayal and the therapist as perpetrator. The client feels slapped in the face—and responds with a similar slap in the face to the clinician, not showing up to the subsequent session and not returning messages.

The educator wishing to attempt a DCT Style-shift to the Dialectic-Systemic to further development of both student and client in parallel process must forestall these risks. The educator intentionally feels into the student's likely range of responses, including resistance, to the supervisory encounter and clinical recommendation. He may choose to delay the recommendation or qualify it. I like to tell my students and consultees: "When I make a recommendation it is based on my countertransference response to you presenting the case. You have to decide when and in what manner to implement the intervention I propose—or whether to implement it at all. You are 'the decider.' Only do it when you experience it as fully yours, fully natural for you, fully congruent."

Summary

We can say, then, that Good Therapy and Good Education follow a similar process. If the educator is fully congruent and fully operationalizing his *Einfühlungsvermögen* he will be in the same position as the experienced clinician, knowing and under-standing at a profound level the student's likely response to the clinical recommendation. His intentionality will be so finely honed that, when he believes his student has overlooked something and that he should bring this, with Boukydis and Molnos and with caring, to the student's attention, when he asks his student, "Have you thought of . . .," then his act in asking will be fully well-intended, done with humility, and a timely intervention assistive to the student and the client. Conversely, where the educator is not fully congruent, not in control of the full spectrum of his countertransference and not fully intentional in his ability to assess and predict what the student will do, this may not be the case: in the fantasized example in which Alexei abandons his therapy with Elena we see again, this time from the perspective of a failure, the differences between when Good Therapy and, in parallel process, Good Education are present and when not.

There is more at stake than the supervisor's correct case conceptualization, sanctioned by both theory and neuroscience. Congruence is an ideal and in practice every clinician from time to time falls short. This need not prove fatal. Many clients give their therapist the benefit of the doubt when they encounter incongruence or an break, and return for the next scheduled session, by which time the therapist may well have figured things out and be primed to interpret the transference and work on what has happened, for the client's great gain as discussed in Part I of this book. And this is exactly the point: while good luck always helps, *intentional* intervention, whether by clinician or educator, minimizes dependence on it.

The next chapter is an account of another educational tool and another case consultation in countertransference. The educational intervention was swiftly and flawlessly adopted by the student therapist; and the ensuing intervention was swiftly attended by validation in the shape of client adoption and a good outcome to the case.

Discussion

- *Do you see parallels between "Good Therapy" and "Good Education"?*
- *What is your result on taking the "Ivey Instrument"? Do you feel the exercise has any value or accuracy?*
- *How do you feel about being asked to disclose your negative feelings to your instructor in the manner here suggested?*
- *Do you think the email correspondence between "Elena" and her instructor was helpful to her? What are the risks in this approach to a student and the student's client if the educator is not in complete control of his "obstructive" countertransference?*
- *If you had been "Elena" would you have allowed your client "Alexei" to blossom in the fantasy of reinventing himself through his divorce?*
- *Neuroscience is enlisted to justify the clinician behavior of returning the focus to the negative; earlier this behavior was linked with the Socratic inquiry of cognitive theory. Do you agree—and "can you stand" the client's negativity?*
- *Do you agree with Chabon that "Everyone wants to be loved and to be understood by someone who loves the things that he loves"? What value does this principle have for us as clinicians in the endeavor of helping our clients? How does Chabon's principle tie in with the concept of Mirroring here advanced?*

10

Unconditional positive regard
Clinician susceptibility to client disavowal • projective identification and the countertransference group

---

Client discrepancies and incongruities • using process to perfect goals

Student development in the Feeling-Sensing Style
Teaching and learning projective identification

Mirroring but not condoning: "Cai" and the case of Norah

Experiential classroom assignment:
The countertransference case conceptualization group

"Many times it has happened to me, while listening to a patient during the first appointment, that I will be able to measure the intensity of his or her aimance. Beyond the words used, I hear the patient tacitly inquire of me, 'Are you available for me to love, hate, or fear? May I idealize you? Will you accept being honored one day and mistreated the next? Are you ready to enter my fantasies and play a role?'"[1]

The therapist's unconditional positive regard lies essentially in a position of deep respect for the client: there is an under-standable, *human* reason for the client's being in this predicament. The therapist's unconditional regard presupposes not only that the client is doing her best in the unique circumstances but also that she has already done a lot of thinking—and that, in the course of thinking, she has very likely alighted on some things that she knows would help her and her situation *if she could only bring herself out of disavowal to do them*. The clinician is therefore interested in what is so obvious: the client cannot bring himself to do the things he knows he should do. The husband in the case just reviewed *knew all along* that there's something he's not doing quite right in relationship. But it hurts us to look into the things we know we are not doing optimally; we know we

---

[1] Nasio, J.-D. (2012). *A Psychoanalyst on the Couch*. Albany, NY: State University of New York Press

simply cannot let go of whatever it is that's keeping us doing the flawed behaviors. So we go to our therapist and try to get him to *agree* with us. Our wife *is* impossible. Our mother-in-law . . . *shouldn't have done* those things. The way out *is* clear, isn't it? Or, alternatively, *it's never going to get any better so I might as well save myself the trouble of trying*!

Along these lines some very defended clients, we have seen, will do almost anything to deflect attention from the real, underlying issue. We know we can help our clients only by keeping it in mind that their reporting is unreliable. We cannot take at face value everything the client tells us, and must fact-check with the "internal manifestations" of our countertransference sensorium (with Satir, Ogden, Norcross and the American Psychological Association). Our Feeling-Sensing Aspect sifts the evidence and alerts us to the discrepancies and incongruities in the client's story. In Alexei's case just reviewed my countertransference upon reading Elena's email was to become cold-hearted and critical towards the client, thinking, "Ha! How come it was 'only later' he noticed the wife's 'superficiality?' The narrative presented to Elena doesn't make complete sense."

As a low experiencer, Alexei's method of dealing with inconvenient feelings is to disavow and project. He projected into the therapeutic conversation feelings of being—somehow, in spite of all the wife's evident transgressions—himself in some way at fault as regards the state of his marriage. The projective identification remained unconscious in the student therapist who, nevertheless, encoded the countertransferential information into her writing on the case. I then found the client's projection in my own countertransference response to reading Elena's writing: I felt a coldness toward Alexei for being so cold-hearted toward his wife whom, at any rate in the first session, he said he "still loved." My coldness replicated his. He was prepared, if his therapist endorsed the (easy, obvious) course of action, unhesitatingly to cut off his wife. It inevitably follows that Elena's positive regard for her client was, in fact, *conditional*: it was conditioned upon the collusion that they would conspire to write off the wife.

Elena describes Alexei as saying, in the first session, he is "unclear how to proceed, whether he should seek a divorce or continue attempts at reconciliation." Having disclosed two equally plausible avenues, the client then began to wage a propaganda campaign designed completely to discredit the avenue of reconciliation. At the very least, surely, the therapist manifesting *unconditional* positive regard should caringly—and Socratically—confront her client with his incongruence, saying, "Look at this one-sided thing you are doing—how do you account for it?"

My task, then, as an educator of beginning therapists was to devise ways of restoring the students' full sensorium, so they can *notice* when something does not quite add up. To notice instead of overlook. To develop and strengthen their Feeling-Sensing Style, in which noticing occurs, and their Dialectic-Systemic ability to *pick out relevant information*—including the information coming from their countertransference that *something is missing*. To achieve my educational goal I added another process component to our course.

The countertransference group

The instructions to the students for the countertransference case conceptualization group were to "say all sorts of things that come up for you in relation to the client; say the kinds of things you wouldn't necessarily say in your other classes or supervision groups." The students were initially quite unsure of what to make of this strange enjoinder. Students having a high allegiance to the Doing Style seemed taken aback: was it not much more professional to talk about diagnoses, goals, interventions and techniques than to muse on the fact that, say, they felt a strange sense of unease about the client and her story or that they felt very critical of the client or cold towards her? But many of the students had clients they had already presented in supervision group and with whom they were still struggling. They were curious about this new forum and different manner of presenting. And, from the beginning, the countertransference group *worked*! Each presenter took away something from the group that helped unlock the case. Here is an early example.

Cai, a student in her late thirties in a school-based family counseling traineeship placement, presented her client, Norah, sixteen. The italicized expressions in the following sections are Cai's and reflect her preferred, Sensorimotor Style.

> The presenting problem was a self-referral: Norah *needed to talk to someone right away*. Bursting into *a pool of tears* she wept through the entire first session. She said she was having problems with her mom and her stepfather. She wanted to go live with her dad in another part of the State but mom won't allow it. She said her stepfather is very *mean and nasty* to her and she feels *left out* and *trapped in her room*. History-taking in the subsequent sessions revealed that:
>
> - Norah's parents divorced when she was 11 years old; to begin with she lived with her dad, while her mom moved to another part of the State
> - At 13 years old Norah was drinking alcohol secretly for a year; it was during that time that a close guy-friend was killed by an opposing gang member
> - When Norah was 14 years old, her dad was arrested and put in jail for six months for assault. It was then that her mom took custody and moved her upstate to live with mom, the new stepfather, his two sons and Norah's half-brother Ben; Norah stopped drinking and her grades improved
> - Ben, 18, was killed last February on a visit to the city where dad lives; this was nothing to do with gangs; he *was in the wrong place at the wrong time*
> - A cousin is in hospital in a coma

In her presentation to the countertransference group, Cai characterized Norah as a young person bewildered by grief and multiple tragedies; although knowing people who knew people in gangs she emphatically—and it was very important to Cai that we understand both the emphasis and Cai's belief in and trust for her client—was not herself in a gang or an adherent of the gang culture and lifestyle. Cai's writing continues:

> I presented my client, Norah, for class instruction and feedback. I felt I had established a good empathic rapport. She had already divulged deep emotional feelings and stories of her personal tragedies. After presenting the basic facts, members of the class began commenting and the discussion got very lively. I felt Norah was being labeled a gang member, a liar, someone who believed in family curses. Some class members inferred I was naïve in my approach to Norah, saying I am a *genteel lady who doesn't know what life's like in grittier parts of the State*. I agreed that might be true in some respects but insisted I was not being a *Pollyanna* in my therapy with Norah. It seemed almost everyone had countertransference feelings to my case. I felt very protective of Norah: even though I hid her identity, I somehow felt like I was betraying her trust to talk about her tragedies, especially when certain class members were so judgmental of her.
>
> I reacted in an immediate Sensorimotor way, since this is my predominant Style of relating, and I felt as if classmates were *attacking* me. I strongly identify with Norah's grief and multiple losses since I have had much grief and multiple losses in my life as well. People were *throwing out* their opinions and I felt they were *way off base* and not perceiving my client correctly. I believe I am an intuitive person and I usually know when someone is not being honest with me. I feel I am a good judge of character.
>
> My hypothesis is that Norah is seriously searching for some deeper *existential* meaning in all these tragedies. It appears she wants to understand *why* these things have happened to her and her family. She also is seeking her *true identity* and *purpose in life*. Norah has been in *identity diffusion* for some time and she is moving towards *identity moratorium*, exploring different identities, trying them on, seeing what fits.

Cai has a developed Feeling-Sensing Aspect. And in her conceptualization of Norah she has eclipsed Doing. Her Dialectic-Systemic Magician should deploy her Queen and Warrior to investigate Norah's odd need to explain each family tragedy as "nothing to do with gangs." But the Magician is unavailable. Cai's Sensorimotor elephant has assumed control. Her rider, urgently confabulating justification, has summoned the shadow archetypes of the master of denial and the addicted lover. Cai was *enchanted* with her conceptualization of Norah. As Elena projected into her treatment of Alexei her own need to believe in Wellness, so Cai projected into the case of Norah her own need to seek meaning in adversity and loss. Cai's Sensorimotor holds her tightly to the reified case conceptualization: this case *is* about a very fine young woman needing support struggling with existential loss. Cai reaches the reified conceptualization not, as in the cases previously examined, through over-reliance on Doing but through over-reliance on Feeling. She is flooded by the client's urgency in disavowal.

Cai's account also perfectly illustrates the mayhem in the group. Her and Norah's disavowals and projections had emerged in the group to ricochet around the room. The upside was that we were all alive and excited and Norah herself had become alive in our midst. We *under-stood* Norah and her ambivalent presentation to her nice genteel lady school-based family counselor, Cai. We insisted that Norah's *actual* problem was whether to go back to father and gangs—or to remain with mother, indifferent stepdad, their toddler and an altogether less exciting life. The reason stepdad, we said, didn't allow Norah to help with the toddler was because he felt Norah was too drawn to the gangs.

Cai was taken aback. In this, one of the very first countertransference groups, I had not properly accessed my Ruler and Warrior and, invoking only their passive shadow poles of weakling and masochist, had failed optimally to control group process. Attempting restitution I now commented to the group that what we were experiencing was *uproar* in the sense described by Murray Bowen;[2] this manifestation is diagnostic insofar as the client is concerned, the polarization in the group reflecting the polarization of the lifestyle and identity choices facing Norah and represented by, on the one hand, staying in her present situation and, on the other, moving back downstate and, it seemed to us, likely gang involvement. I said that Norah's focus on her family's "many tragedies" was not so much grief as it was a question: is the involvement in or closeness to the gang culture going to lead to yet more tragedies, yet more deaths of males close to her? *Is this how it's going to be?*

The downside of the group process was that Cai felt attacked and left feeling upset. I have since grown more adroit in managing the group and become more conscious of its powerful dynamics. To overcome countertransferential blind spots in the clinician, the unspoken, unconscious projections between client and student therapist and, in turn, between student therapist and group must necessarily struggle to come to the surface. Where the client's issue involves extreme polarization, each pole, each antagonistic thesis, will locate inside one or more group members, who will become conduit for its expression. But in this case there was more. Cai's addicted lover refused to let go of her collusion in the client's disavowal; at the same time her Warrior became replaced, in the countertransference group, by its negative shadow, the masochist. And this brought out the sadist in some group members.

Cai was unshakably identified with her view of Norah. Having experienced much grief and tragedy herself, she was inclined to focus on this vulnerable side of her client's story; she unconsciously elided over key cues and clues. The client *wanted not to see* the gang-relatedness all about her and Cai was hooked into collusion. Cai's conscious volition was to fight against what the group was telling her, which is why she felt attacked. What she was in fact fighting for and projecting into the group was her client's desperate attempts at denial, which had prompted the client's desperate self-referral. Norah's dilemma was that gangs were part of her life, but she was also terrified of what that might mean.

---

2 Abraham, L. (2010). *The Husbands and Wives Club: A Year in the Life of a Couples Therapy Group.* New York, NY: Touchstone, p. 228

As before discussed, a Good Therapist experiencing herself under attack responds not with defensiveness but rather with nondefensiveness and curiosity. Cai's narrative continues:

> I saw Norah again and told her I was confused about some things she told me last time. I did a *Columbo* [*referring to a 1970s TV detective, who cracks his cases by gentle, puzzled, insistent confrontation of incongruity*], in other words, I acted dumb, about the details and time periods involved. I started drawing a timeline of her life events and tragedies between the ages of 11 and 16. At first Norah wondered why I was doing this but then started correcting me and became more interested as I encouraged her to write the details on the timeline drawing. This was a good medium for eliciting the precise circumstances that led to her parents' divorce, *getting in trouble* when she was 14 years old, her dad's incarceration and moving in with mom. After the countertransference group I was determined to find out the truth about her possible gang affiliation and the reasons she moved back and forth between her parents.
>
> Norah divulged that she had friends who were gang members; she claimed she was never *officially initiated* into the gang because the leader liked her, was protective of her and allowed her to *hang out* with them without being an official gang member. It seems that the leader also wanted to protect/save her. . . . She claims she was not involved in violence but did drink alcohol when hanging out with the gang (and she managed to hide that from her father). She also told me that her mom had spent time with gang members when she was younger but had reformed completely as she got older and is now "*a hard worker and a good influence on me; she doesn't even keep alcohol in the house.*"
>
> She does not think that her brother was in a gang. She . . . thinks he was killed by an opposing gang member because he was in the wrong territory—perhaps he went to see a girl there.
>
> Norah started to tell me all the areas around where her dad lived that were not safe to go *if you threw up a sign of an opposing gang from a different territory*. She seemed to know a lot about gangs and was greatly influenced by the gang lifestyle. So I came to realize that, in our earlier conversations, **she had kinda rushed me by some key details—as if she had not wanted me to examine them too closely.** So the feedback I received from classmates was helpful in moving me to find the truth in her stories. I think it was important for her be honest about her life choices and know that I still accepted and cared about her. [*PG's bold type*]

Cai responded with unconditional positive regard and Mirroring—not condoning—to each of Norah's disclosures, thereby helping Norah build self-structure for the final assault on her dilemma. Again in Cai's voice:

> The uproar in the countertransference group does point to the strong conflicts within the client and the possibility there is more going on than meets the eye . . . it also perfectly reflected the client's exploration of the different identities.

When we were finished detailing the timeline, I asked what she thought about her life from 11–16 years old? Her eyes grew wide and she said, *It's terrible, really terrible!* I agreed and reflected back to her that *these situations were really terrible and that she had seen more tragedies in a few years than most people see in a lifetime!* Then, I drew a line between where she now lives with mom and where dad lives and asked what she thought about the difference? She thought for a moment and said: *why would I want to go back to that life?* (This realization comes at a crucial time when her parents are deciding whether she should stay with mom or return to dad).

A *chill ran down my spine* as I realized **those were nearly the same words someone had said in class: Why would she want to go back to her old life down there where the gang life was?** [PG's bold type] I may not have dug so deeply if my classmates hadn't brought up the possibility of Norah's gang lifestyle.

This young client was—as are all clients—in a dilemma and in transition. She liked all the things there are to be liked about belonging to a gang. Her friends in the gang, particularly the males, seemed more accepting of her, more understanding of her and more generous to her than did either of her parents. They allowed her a unique status in which she enjoyed all the privileges of being one of them while being able to disavow the gang, saying that she was not herself a gang member. So Norah had nothing to fear from being around those young men who were nice to her and also just happened to be gang members. But the other side of the dilemma was the evidence piling up in the shape of all the family tragedies. Norah tried to experience herself as untainted by gang membership and the seamier side of life; but the seaminess was impinging uncomfortably into her awareness. Cai was right: Norah did indeed seek Cai out to discover whether she might have "higher hopes" for herself.

Participation in the countertransference group restored Cai's curiosity and with it her intentionality. She realized the client had rushed her by key details. The group was the place of the environmental call to Cai to let go her incomplete case conceptualization and understand and acknowledge the projective identification. After removing from her positive regard for the client the conditionality of their collusion in disavowal, Cai was able to bring Norah to insight and to her letting go. The story has a happy ending: Norah's dilemma disappeared. Her strengths, with the environmental support available, allowed Norah to achieve second-order change and she stayed where she was and withdrew from involvement with gang members. And her stepfather noticed and relaxed and started to appreciate her help with the toddler.

Our clinical choices are, according to our working hypothesis and with Boyatzis, mediated by interaction between our TPB and DMN antagonists. Cai's difficulty lay in her twinship countertransference: her history of multiple losses made her more susceptible to Norah's projection of her faulty hypothesis. Thus within Cai's Feeling-Sensing Aspect the Sensorimotor temporarily eclipsed the

Unconditional positive regard · 169

Dialectic-Systemic. And the rider did the elephant's bidding, rationalizing and justifying the elephant's impulse, with Haidt.

In the correct case conceptualization, while loss, grief and shock are present, *in relationship* Norah is a young woman wanting to be loved, cherished and Mirrored by people who demonstrably love the things she loves. Norah, in common with us all, wants to feel *specially accepted* and this was, for her, the benefit of the association with the gang members. Yet in flirting with the gang lifestyle she also replayed her parents' conflicts; and these had previewed it to her that the special acceptance of the gang comes at a price she might regret. This was her dilemma.

The case confirms a key feature of our working hypothesis. It is by no means only goals-preferring clinicians who may evidence maladroitness in case conceptualization. The reifying behaviors are equally accessible to process-preferring, more Feeling-Sensing clinicians. Also confirmed is the salience of the Dialectic-Systemic Style in perfecting the goals. Had Cai maintained access to her Dialectic-Systemic she would not have reified the case conceptualization. As soon as her Dialectic-Systemic became again accessible she called forth her Magician to engineer the intervention of the timeline.

The dialectic, then, between goals and process is again reinterpreted: it is to use the process to perfect and precisely delineate the goals.

Cai might have got there another way, using a combination of process and the Socratic method:

CAI: Last time we met you mentioned that your brother had not been involved in gangs.

NORAH: That's right.

CAI: When someone emphasizes a negative, saying that something or someone is "not like that," the speaker usually is worried that the listener might think those things. Were you worried I might think your brother belonged to a gang?

NORAH: No.

CAI: It would certainly make sense to me that you might think that I have views about gangs. I am the school counselor and school counselors warn people like your brother to steer clear of gangs. It's what we do.

NORAH: Yes. My brother was just in the wrong place at the wrong time [*cries*]. I wanted to be sure you understood that. It's very important to *know about* gangs and how to stay safe.

CAI: Yes. It's very important. And everyone knows that. What happened to your brother was an outlier. But for young men who are members of gangs, being killed happens all the time. Have you ever wondered about that?

NORAH: Why it happens that gang members get killed?

CAI: No. Why young people become gang members when there is so much evidence that bad things can happen, including getting killed. Why would people seek out danger? Why would they not run a mile?

NORAH: Well some young guys are just thrill-seekers....

CAI: That's true. But what about the girls? They become part of the gang too.

NORAH: [*silence*]

CAI: It's because belonging to a gang feels *wonderful*!

NORAH: I can't believe you just said that!?

CAI: Many kids have a very hard time of it growing up. Their parents are under pressure in various ways and have insufficient time for them. The school doesn't seem to care. The young people get parked around among caregivers and feel like they're a burden to everyone; how the kids feel is that they caused the parents' divorce, the bad grades are their fault and they are a big disappointment to everyone.

NORAH: [*silence*]

CAI: That is why belonging to a gang feels *wonderful*!

NORAH: [*exhales*]

CAI: It's almost impossible to understand how something can feel so *wonderful* and yet be so laden with likely adverse consequences.

NORAH: It's ... it's not like that....

CAI: I have never asked you about gangs, Norah. Each time you have told me about a family tragedy you have added the information. This event, you said, is unconnected with gangs; this person is not a gang member; and so on....

NORAH: [*exhales*]

CAI: I heard a story once. It was about a girl who was lonely and felt no one understood her. She felt she had nowhere to go. There was this young man and he liked her. He was a member of a gang. He said to the girl, "Come hang out with me; you will be safe with me; you won't have to join the gang."

NORAH: What happened then?

CAI: She discovered it wasn't so simple. That's what this is all about, Norah, isn't it?

NORAH: Yes. You "heard" that story very well. It really isn't that simple [*cries*].

Reflecting teams

The countertransference case conceptualization group is an analogue of the *reflecting team* approach in family therapy. In both cases the idea is the treating therapist may be—under-standably—overlooking something or may have become temporarily coopted by the clients into a particular conceptualization. The team, or group, *reflects* back to the treating therapist what has been overlooked.

Summary

It is worth repeating that both our last two clients did the same thing in successfully projecting their flawed thinking and disavowal onto their student therapist who was thereby encumbered by a false premise on which to base conceptualization and treatment. And, as previewed, it would be quite incorrect to hold that this does not happen with a more experienced clinician. Such processes in collusion are, we have hypothesized, both inevitable and useful. Inevitable surely. Useful only if the clinician can find her way out of the collusion and apply the information, in time and intentionally, to discern and refocus upon the client's ulterior, clinically more significant goal.

Austrian British theorist Melanie Klein developed our concept of projective identification as an enrichment of Freud's idea of projection.[3] Projective identification is omnipresent. It has become a widely quoted (if disputed) cliché that 85% of our communication is nonverbal. Columbia University experimental social psychologist Robert Krauss and his colleagues use the following formulation:

> Quite apart from its semantic content, speech may convey information about the speaker's internal state, attitude toward the addressee, etc., and in the appropriate circumstances such information can make an important contribution to the interaction.[4]

Since clients by definition are unable to tell their full story accurately in words it follows that extensive missing information, vital to treatment, is available for access within the pre-conscious and unconscious of the clinician.

Projective identification is the precursor of intersubjectivity. The difference it makes in treatment when this information is accessed—accurately— cannot be overstated.

Of our two indivisible components in effective treatment, counseling and psychotherapy, projective identification informs all key aspects defining the latter. The ability, located in the clinician's Feeling-Sensing Aspect, accurately to decode and use, with Ogden, the vast flows of the client's projected communication is an essential clinical skill *and it can be both taught and learned.*

---

3 Klein, M. (1946). Notes on some Schizoid mechanisms. *In* International Journal of Psycho-Analysis, Volume 27, pp. 99–110
4 Krauss, R. M., Chen, Y. and Chawla, P. (1996). Nonverbal communication: What do conversational hand gestures tell us? *In* Advances in Experimental Social Psychology, Volume 28, pp. 389–450, p. 397

And teaching and learning projective identification, and affording the beginning clinician the necessary horizontal development in the Sensorimotor and Dialectic-Systemic, is not the preserve of the analysts. Clinician adroitness, that hallmark of what we, variously, call Good Therapy or, it may be, evidence-based practice, that ability to steer the therapeutic discourse between goals and process so as to give the client just the mixtures she needs as those needs change, exists and applies in one and the same way to every clinician, including clinicians preferring a theory offering increased scope for *Doing*, such as CBT.

Discussion

- *How susceptible are you to client disavowal? Is such susceptibility "bad"—or does it, ultimately, further the client's development?*
- *Projective identification, "intuition" or contrivance? How do you respond to reading that "Cai's" client's words were "nearly the same words someone had said in class"?*
- *Do you agree that using projective identification for client clinical gain is "essential" and that it "can be both taught and learned"?*

11
Intentionality
Flow and the Good Therapist •
the final letting go of neediness

Science and proof • end of the debate

Flow • intentional intervention
The "autotelic" personality of the clinician
Completion of transition

Student susceptibility to collusion with client • clinician development in the Feeling-Sensing Style

The neediness countertransference • clinician "working harder than the client"

Intentionality and the client's dilemma • clinician as stakeholder for the disavowed pole

---

"Proofs only exist in mathematics and logic, not in science."[1]

In the Preface I described theories of counseling and therapy as being more goals-based or more Doing—or more process-based or more Feeling-Sensing. Each theory, I then suggested, is a construct attempting to represent a single, infinitely faceted reality—the human psyche. Since the psyche *is* both goals and process, rider and elephant, our theories *must necessarily* address both. Goals *and* Process. Process *and* Goals. It is therefore inaccurate to describe CBT as a "more Doing" model of counseling and therapy *in the sense of less Feeling-Sensing*. CBT is, rather, a model of counseling and therapy—an endeavor encompassing both Doing and Feeling-Sensing—*offering an expanded scope for Doing*.

The great debate is over. The key to adroitness in practicing CBT is to embrace its expanded scope for Doing while (with Burns) maintaining our capacity for Feeling-Sensing. The key to adroitness in practicing therapies offering expanded scope

---

1 Kanazawa, S. (2008). Common Misconceptions about Science I: "Scientific Proof". *Blog Post* of November 16th 2008. Accessed *July 11th 2016* via www.psychologytoday.com/blog/the-scientific-fundamentalist/200811/common-misconceptions-about-science-i-scientific-proof

for Feeling-Sensing is to maintain and (with Owen) wherever possible expand our capacity in Doing. Both domains underpin all Good Therapy and Good Theory.

The countertransference case conceptualization group gave Cai a better appreciation of the possibilities latent in Norah's communication and her adroitness returned. She chose the diagrammatic chart, an intervention neatly straddling the goals–process continuum and constituting an adept DCT Style-shift from Concrete to Dialectic-Systemic. Cai's Magician confronted Norah with the full picture. Because development in the higher Styles allows further and more adaptive Sensorimotor processing, Norah's disavowal eroded and, her wisdom potentiated, she was able to see her situation clearly and experience, with Glasser, *choice. Why would I want to go back to that life!*? The words Norah spoke were those imprinted in Cai by the countertransference group participants. This is no coincidence. It is, rather, a demonstration of the science discussed in these pages: intersubjectivity, projective identification and the reality of the highly complex construct of evidence-based practice in psychology.

We have built a cohesive working hypothesis that explains—and solves—the phenomenon of clinician adroitness. We have used the DCT developmental model to explain phenomena in client and clinician self-development and in client response to clinical intervention—and to guide assessment and planning in both client treatment and in the education of counselors and therapists. We have refined the concept of intentionality. We have framed all these things within the dialectic between goals and process in counseling and therapy. And we have located the entire working hypothesis within the discourse of evidence-based practice.

We have seen how the Good Therapist *looks beyond* the presenting discourse, *feels-into* an understanding of the client, her experience and frame of reference, and works *intentionally* to uncover the *dilemma* underlying the presenting narrative, at all times *managing the essential dialectic between goals and process*. Clients like Kevin, Chantal, Gonzalo, Joty, Alexei and Norah are depicted as having superior outcomes where the therapist's actions conform to our working hypothesis and inferior outcomes where they do not. The evidence presented all fits together beautifully and makes good, logical sense. Clearly there is such a thing as clinician "looking beyond" and its absence. Clearly there is such a thing as working "intentionally" and for maximum client adoption of interventions. Clearly the DCT assessment schema is a key component in predicting client ability to adopt an intervention. Clearly the idealized version of Kevin's therapist whose *Einfühlungsvermögen* helped him decode Kevin's "Hmmph!" was possessed of more skill, more clinical adroitness, than the prior version. *And we must now return, intentionally, as Elena with her client Alexei, to the negative narrative. We are enchanted by our working hypothesis: have we proved it?*

London School of Economics evolutionary psychologist Satoshi Kanazawa suggests this is not a profitable question. Indeed our Socratic perspective informs us that, if a working hypothesis is true, it is true whether or not it has yet been or even can or should be tested in a randomized controlled study. It would be neither easy nor ethical to design a study assessing the impact of clinicians' failures to heed the signal of the dialectic. Yet we can test our working hypothesis nevertheless, every day, within our Therapist-Self. We can, with Satir and Baldwin and in memory of Kevin, test and re-test our working hypothesis against the evidence to be found within our own Feeling-Sensing Style, our Default Mode Network, taking care to draw from elephant and (nonconfabulating) rider in just the right combination.

As Kanazawa writes:

> There is no such thing as final proven knowledge in science. The currently accepted theory of a phenomenon is simply the best explanation for it among all available alternatives. Its status as the accepted theory is contingent on what other theories are available and might suddenly change tomorrow if there appears a better theory or new evidence that might challenge the accepted theory.[2]

Evidence-based practice is therefore, ultimately, what we the clinician determine is "simply the best explanation" right now for this client. What Norcross and our other authorities demand of us is not only that we keep up to date with the literature but moreover that we be adroit in assessing, discerning and determining phenomena—and in changing our mind in the face of fresh evidence. This adroitness, according to our working hypothesis, we may need to augment or acquire by developing specific competencies in the Feeling-Sensing Style. The true question before us is this: *if the working hypothesis presented in this book appears to us the best explanation, why would we wait to use it to benefit our clients?*

Intentionality and the educator's dilemma

In particular, if we have a natural inclination, even a passion, for modalities of counseling and therapy that offer expanded scope for Doing, how do we respond to it when we wish to raise outcomes? Waller writes:

> Therapist drift is a common phenomenon and usually involves a shift from 'doing therapies' to 'talking therapies.' It is argued that the reason for this drift away from key tasks centres on our cognitive distortions, emotional reactions and use of safety behaviours. A series of cases is outlined in order to identify common errors in clinical practice that impede CBT (and that can make the patient worse, rather than better). The principles behind each case are considered, along with potential solutions that can get us re-focused on the key tasks of CBT.[3]

---

2 *Ibid.*
3 Waller, G. (2009). Evidence-based treatment and therapist drift. *In* Behaviour Research and Therapy, Volume 47, Issue 2, February, pp. 119–127

The clinicians studied by Waller drift away from doing and into talking. Their training has not equipped them to respond adroitly to certain client transference presentations and they evade implementation of the CBT model because of obstructive countertransference. These therapists' talking at these times with these clients does not help and may harm. Our working hypothesis, on the other hand, suggests that an augmentation of the process component will assist treatment if it is an intentional response to the signal of the dialectic. We have observed that intentionality involves preparedness for a range of client response to a given treatment strategy, joined with an ability to use the goals–process decision tree appropriately in furtherance of safety and clinical goals and in a manner informed by a developmental assessment of the client.

Intentional clinicians do not make the "common errors…imped[ing] CBT" identified by Waller. Whether by natural, instinctual adroitness, by good modeling and supervision or by adjunctive training in the process methods that are an inescapable part of the goals-based theory, the intentional clinician knows that more Doing does not mean less Feeling-Sensing—and more Feeling-Sensing does not mean less Doing. That subpar, even damaging outcomes are with regularity generated by clinicians desiring to practice according to history's most effective therapy and most perfect model is not about CBT. The model is beautiful. And, as a vehicle potentiating Good Therapy, it is more complex and multifaceted than many of us realized. The distinction between the closed descriptor "more Doing" and the open "offering expanded scope for Doing" is key to our meaning-making. If we are a less adroit clinician more inclined to disavowal and reification and to eclipse the Feeling-Sensing Aspect and Dialectic-Systemic Style, we may misunderstand and misapply CBT by trapping ourself in the closed discourse of more Doing. And when CBT is misapplied the antagonists misinterpret the misapplication. As Waller laments:

> Cognitive-behavioural therapy (CBT) has a wide-ranging empirical base, supporting its place as the evidence-based treatment of choice for the majority of psychological disorders. However, many clinicians feel that it is not appropriate for their patients, and that it is not effective in real life-settings (despite evidence to the contrary). This paper addresses the contribution that we as clinicians make to CBT going wrong. It considers the evidence that we are poor at implementing the full range of tasks that are necessary for CBT to be effective—particularly behavioural change.[4]

We now know that what the CBT antagonists and the CBT clinicians "going wrong" have in common is the need for developmental augmentation. The antagonists tend to prefer and over-rely on Feeling-Sensing; and the drifting CBT clinicians studied by Turner and Waller, we believe, are insufficiently equipped by their training with competencies in Feeling-Sensing to manage the demands of the dialectic in the more complex client presentations. Thus the solution to the problem of the "likelihood of evidence-based interventions being delivered in routine

---

4 Ibid.

clinical settings" now suggests itself: it is the kind of horizontal development in the Therapist-Self discussed in the previous chapters.

Intentionality and the client's dilemma

Our journey to intentional intervention is paved with elusive concepts. Gonzalo's therapist's developmental case conceptualization and treatment plan envisaged an ideal outcome affording the client second-order change; but the circumstances were not ideal and she had to content herself with the lesser goal of first-order change and symptom relief—the only outcome available immediately to hand. The benefits turned out to be of short duration ... but might not have. Some clients, as we have discussed, will go on to achieve second-order change on the foundation of first-order change. And, yes, environmental luck (or its absence) plays a part.

Our overarching consideration is the need to manage the dialectic between goals and process and, in so doing, practice Good Therapy. We have seen and *known* the Archetype of Good Therapy. When manifested it uncovers the divorcing husband's problems with intimacy (thus possibly but, with Satir, not necessarily saving the first marriage), saves Kevin's life, improves family life for Chantal, her husband, their children and their grandmother—and, at just the right time for client adoption, confronts Norah with her disavowal and puts her adolescence back on developmental track.

The case in which Elena colluded with her separated client's fantasy of giving up on his marriage and divorcing his wife pointed us to refine our working hypothesis: *intentionality is present only when the therapist's case conceptualization and treatment plan involve upholding both sides of the client's dilemma*. As Stanford psychiatrist Irvin Yalom reminds us, the Latin root of the word *decision* involves killing.[5] The dilemma exists because we cannot bear to kill off one of the possibilities. Elena, countertransferentially, couldn't bear to kill the fantasy that Alexei's second wife would indeed, with Chabon, better understand her husband's love for the things he loves, and he hers, so their need for mutual Mirroring would not become frustrated and turn to hate. And indeed, it seems so true to us, from our goals perspective, that this would be an ideal outcome. In seeking a new wife Alexei can make a better choice, perhaps arranging to pre-screen her for potential incompatibility in terms of DCT communication and the things each loves. When the alternative may be years of couples therapy and continued unease in the relationship with the present wife, we hate to deny Alexei the chance of an easier path. Is it not healing to help him choose the path that will likely minimize pain?

We must resist this obstructive countertransference. We can never know the path that must be sacrificed and we can never collude as executioner. Should Joty's daughter kill off her intended marriage? Some daughters in these circumstances do make the sacrifice, knowingly, willingly, lovingly and indeed intentionally. As

---

5 Yalom, I. D. (1989). *Love's Executioner*. New York, NY: Basic Books

Satir cautions, these are not our decisions to make. Better, if we have such obstructive countertransference, to self-disclose it, since it is but a projection of one of the poles of the client's dilemma:

ELENA: I keep thinking how much easier it would be for you to go down the path of choosing a new wife. Carefully choosing someone who has the personality and interests to dovetail with who you are. I keep thinking how hard it would be for you to go back to your wife and try to make a success of your marriage. I keep wondering what to do with these thoughts. . . .
ALEXEI: You and me both! I want to kill off my marriage. But I can't.
ELENA: There's *something you need* before you can make the decision. Let's see if we can find out what it is. . . .

Intentionality and the clinician's dilemma

The clinician's dilemma is solved by the technique of feeding the information from the projective identification countertransference back into the therapeutic conversation. The dilemma is the client's and must, with Satir, be returned to him. To do otherwise is to become *personally invested* and to reify case conceptualization. These clinician behaviors lead to *working harder than the client*, an obstructive countertransference for which no citation is needed and which leads inevitably to clinician burnout and poor client outcome. Only if the therapist can disinvest, can let go of the maladaptive, obstructively countertransferential need for the work to go a certain way and can *become curious* as to how the work is in fact going can intentionality return and with it Good Therapy. Full operationalization and extension of Self—and thus true caring—lies in an unflinching approach to what is there in the psyche of the client.

Flow

When the clinician manifests curiosity and not neediness it has profound implications for the clinician, the client, their relationship and its outcome. The burden of needing the work to go in a particular way, of having an attachment to a particular outcome, is so crushing that, when finally freed from it, the therapist can suddenly begin to experience doing therapy as "easy!" Counseling-and-therapy is of course as we have seen in these pages highly complex. Yet *detachment* from therapist neediness brings with it the great peace of being able to focus exclusively on the client and the client's developmental needs. It brings the therapist to the state of *flow*[6] as proposed by Hungarian American psychologist Mihály Csíkszentmihályi. Flow is correlated with an *autotelic personality* elsewhere described by Csíkszentmihályi as:

"Autotelic" is a word composed of two Greek roots: *auto* (self), and *telos* (goal). An autotelic activity is one we do for its own sake because to experience it is

---

6 Csíkszentmihályi, M. (1975/2000). *Beyond Boredom and Anxiety. Experiencing Flow in Work and Play.* San Francisco: Jossey-Bass

the main goal.... Applied to personality, autotelic denotes an individual who generally does things for their own sake, rather than in order to achieve some later external goal.[7]

It will not surprise us that the traits of the autotelic personality experiencing flow are described by Csíkszentmihályi and co-authors as: "pure curiosity and the need to achieve; enjoyment and persistence; openness to novelty and narrow concentration; integration and differentiation; independence and cooperation."[8] These are the powers of the Magician and the Dialectic-Systemic abilities of the Good Therapist. Good Therapy, then, is done, with Csíkszentmihályi, ultimately *for its own sake*. That is the test. The synthesis of goals and process is, finally, to be found in pure *curiosity*.

The curiosity that persists until the dilemma is uncovered, the import of both sides is fully explored and the client's inherent developmental nisus is brought back to life.

Intentionality and client-centeredness are thus two sides of the same coin. The pivotal phenomenon of flow in the practice of psychotherapy is above described as occurring when the therapist is able to "let go of the maladaptive, obstructively countertransferential need for the work to go a certain way." And surely this is it—*this* is the letting go that finally completes the Bridgesian transition of becoming a therapist.

We can infer that, while we cannot always know, with Satir, whether the husband should divorce his wife, we can and should uphold what we know to be true about the practice of Good Therapy. The task of the autotelic practitioner is to equip our client with the developmental assets (Ivey) that will allow the choice (Glasser) to kill (Yalom) that which must be let go (Bridges). If the client's dilemma is to be properly resolved, we must maintain impartiality and uphold both poles to her scrutiny. This is how we know the scrutinizing is done:

ELENA: I keep thinking of your two paths. Choosing a new wife appeals in so many ways and seems so much easier. Going back to your actual wife seems like choosing the long, hard road....

ALEXEI: Yes. It will be. You have shown me here just how hard and how long that road will be. And, yes, a cute new wife would be terrific! But, you know, I just can't bring myself to go down that path. The attractions it holds pale before the importance of my duty to myself and to my wife and my family.

ELENA: What do you mean?

---

7 Csíkszentmihályi, M. (1997). *Finding Flow. The Psychology of Engagement With Everyday Life*. New York, NY: Basic Books, p. 117
8 Csíkszentmihályi, M., Rathunde, K. and Whalen, S. (1993). *Talented Teenagers: A Longitudinal Study of Their Development*. New York, NY: Cambridge University Press

ALEXEI: I'm not the same person I was when we started working together. The old Alexei wanted the easy way out. Now I want the right way out, the way I can live with.

Thus the bedrock motive from which springs the well of Good-Therapy-in-flow is the allegiance to exhuming that which the client has buried but which can, if brought to light in the therapy room, save him. And we almost missed the final twist to the Bridgesian letting go that completes the transition of becoming a clinician. Whatever obstructive countertransference we may harbor toward our client, perhaps the hardest to manage is the false premise under which we embarked upon the path of becoming a counselor and therapist: the idea that the clinician fixes the client. Once detached from this fallacy we now are able truly and fully to see, with Ogden, that our projective identification countertransference is indeed the basic unit in the therapeutic interaction. Once flow is attained we experience a heightened ability to attune to the client's nonverbal cues and disavowed experience. We do not miss Kevin's "Hmmph!" We can unerringly find Chantal's dilemma and uphold either pole and employ, variously, process-based and goals-based methods to allow her to access her own solution. And in flow we can do all these things with a therapeutic dexterity that seems almost shocking.

In flow the clinician uncovers the dilemma and main feeling with the unflinching, tender precision of a surgeon. Client resistance either yields to flow or responds to it peaceably. Whatever the client response, the clinician in flow is never at a loss. The flow is in the sure direction of helping the client develop to second-order change, if need be via a staging-post in first-order change, *as directly as possible using goals-based methods and as indirectly, using process-based methods, as is necessary*. All is equal: the flow is in the synthesis of goals and process into the most effective treatment continuum. Flow in counseling and therapy is the manifestation of the Archetype of evidence-based practice in psychology: all three legs of the stool are, finally, fully supporting theory and practice.

The client is given just what she needs because the clinician does not need to give her anything else.

It is, in the final analysis, the neediness of the counselor and therapist that informs maladroit clinical decision making and ineffective treatment. The need to be a good student and a good clinician; the need to maintain disavowal; the need for the client to respond a certain way; the need not to do some essential personal developmental work. The need not to be annoyed or surprised by the client; the need to be loved by the client. The need, perhaps, to come to a decision about whether we should leave our spouse. It is these ordinary, humble, very human needs that are the real face and authentic lived processes behind the reification of "maladroit clinical decision making." At the times we are not prey to these needs we *are* Magician, Sovereign, Warrior, Lover.

Maintaining intentionality

And at the times we are prey to these needs and temporarily lose access to the Archetypes we can work to regain flow. The scene is a licensed clinicians' "Good Therapy" case conceptualization group of six experienced counselors and therapists. The newcomer, Mona, a marriage and family therapist in private practice, is a pleasant woman of middle years and of down-to-earth appearance. Introducing herself to the group, she tells the other five members why she has joined. She fears she is suffering from burnout. Her clients are mainly females with characterological and relationship issues. She has for twenty-five years diligently extended Self to her clients in predominantly process-based work and she has been very successful in helping her clients achieve second-order change, "so much so they keep sending me their friends, daughters, sisters and mothers!" A new client, Jennifer, has just presented herself. Mona discusses her ambivalence to her new client with alarm:

MONA: I simply don't know what to make of it. On the one hand, Jennifer (not her real name) is the sort of client I have been seeing for years and know how to handle. Taking her on should be a routine experience for me. On the other hand I just simply do not want her. I'm kinda horrified at myself for feeling this way. In our first session she spent all the time glancing around the room—at me, my clothes, my things. *She was totally checking me out!* Appearances seem very important to her. She's just *too much*! I keep thinking *how shallow* she is. While I have other clients about whom I could say the same thing, Jennifer strikes me as somehow over the top.

ZARA: I get the feeling, Mona, you have thoughts around people—women—for whom appearances are very important.

MONA: I keep thinking maybe all she really needs from me is some self-esteem work and some dating strategies. Perhaps this treatment won't be as long as some of my other clients.

ZARA: Self-esteem work?

MONA: She keeps blaming her dating mishaps on trivial superficial stuff like her complexion, or the shape of her breasts. Honestly! That woman really is infuriating.

ZARA: Your practice, Mona, is very like mine. Every once in a while I get a new female client who pushes all my buttons. I keep thinking I did all the work the last time around—yet still these clients come.

MONA: Aaaaaarghhhh! Ok, you got me. I confess. This is why I came to this group. Jennifer reminds me of my mother. Obsessed about her looks, supremely narcissistic and forever criticizing me. She loved me, of course, in the best way she could but it certainly didn't feel like it at the time and it took me years of therapy ... and [*laughing*] look, I *still* bear the scars.

Jennifer needs so much more than self-esteem work and dating strategies. She needs Mirroring, so much and so badly that I fear it will suck me dry and leave nothing left—for me, for my family or for me to give to my other clients.

THEO: You don't have to see her, Mona. You can refer her out.

MONA: Or I can work on myself to build the capacity I lack. I know that. At other times in the past when I have been challenged like this I was happy to take up the challenge. I'm just not sure why now, with this client, I don't want to and it feels like *too much*.

THEO: *Too much*! That's the second time you have said that. *This* new client, who is obsessed with appearances, like your mother, her eyes darting around the room and *evaluating* you. ... What is different now, so as to make Jennifer too much?

MONA: [*sighs*] Lately I've been confronted with the fact that I'm letting myself go. I always wanted to be the opposite of mother and don't care about my shape or signs of aging. None of that has ever bothered me. But a few months ago I had a blood test and was told I have pre-diabetes. Suddenly diet and exercise and aging *are* important.

ZARA: So you are *doubly vulnerable* to Jennifer's evaluating your signs of aging. You have a new health concern that now upsets the pact you made with mother and women like her. You feel that, in allowing your blood glucose to climb you have let yourself down; you can almost hear your mother berate you for doing so, through Jennifer's darting eyes.

MONA: [*sighs*] Yes. And the nurse practitioner who counseled me after the blood test ... I could have strangled her! Telling me I can't squeeze oranges for breakfast and asking me if I know what a four-ounce serving of meat looks like. I'm fifty-five, for God's sake—I have been eating for fifty-five years!

THEO: So if you can't have your morning orange juice, then Jennifer can't have her Mirroring and must make do with a bit of self-esteem work and some dating strategies.

MONA: [*smiles wryly*] It's true. Yes. I'm wanting to punish her. And the nurse practitioner. Ok. Let me see if I can get over this. Poor Jennifer ... I guess.

TERRY: All the process in the room seems to be around her evaluation of you and yours of yourself. How might it be to talk to her about how she sees you?

MONA: Yes, that's the question. If I can get up to speed there I can take her on. If I feel I can't—or I need too much help—then I will refer her out. I will not punish her with a treatment plan of half-measures that will prove ineffective. She isn't my mother and she isn't my blood sugar—and she isn't the nurse practitioner!

In this way the Good Therapy group helps clinicians recognize it when they are incongruently motivated to project a need of their own into the clinical encounter. Sometimes they choose to step back from the case. Mostly they choose to continue—with the client and with the personal work triggered by the client. Reality, we remember, with Kanazawa and Satir, is found *in experience*. I do not know how well your next client similar to Gonzalo will do with first-order change; I do not know whether your student's next client like Alexei contemplating divorce will, if he goes down that route, find happiness; and I do not know if Kevin's suicide could have been averted in the way we have here imagined. And I still do not know how best to measure outcomes. If Mona "punishes" Jennifer with an ineffective treatment plan affording "only" first-order change, she may yet go on to marry the millionaire—our lighthearted fantasy at the beginning of our quest. But we know now that if Mona were to treat Jennifer in a way in which, as clinician, she refuses to extend Self to the client, then it would not be Good Therapy.

The working hypothesis is now entrusted to your client work. You who are to follow will prove this thesis.

Discussion

- *"Flow in counseling and therapy is the manifestation of the Archetype of evidence-based practice in psychology."* How do you understand this assertion?
- *Is your personality, as clinician, "autotelic"? How do you feel about the descriptions of such a personality here given: do you want to be like this?*
- *"The client is given just what she needs because the clinician does not need to give her anything else."* Is it as simple as that?
- *Mona in the vignette is portrayed as harried and inclined to withhold from her client Jennifer for reasons in obstructive countertransference: has this sort of situation, or an analogue, occurred in your own practice?*
- *Has this book "proved" its thesis and working hypothesis sufficiently for you to attempt to practice in the ways outlined?*
- *The "more process-based" techniques here advanced are presented as being within the discourse of cognitive theory. Do you, as a student identifying more easily with more goals-based theory and methodology, agree? Do you agree as a student identifying more easily with more process-based theory and methodology?*
- *Is it, as this book suggests, a "given" that all manifestations of counseling and therapy occur on the same continuum between goals and process?*

Epilogue
Working hypothesis for intentional intervention • implications for the education of clinicians

> Primary themes in counseling and therapy • definition of the Good Therapist

"Shoulda coulda woulda. We didn't."[1]

We have come to realize that the discourse of antagonism we have, with Wampold and Norcross, inherited, and within which we have conducted this investigation, is a projection. We have, collectively, turned our field and the theory and practice of counseling and therapy into an imago of the tensions existing in our cognitive-behavioral and underlying neuronal processes. To bring together the two theses all that is required of us is to continue to observe and understand human development and how the developmental assistance given the client by the clinician occurs within the dialectic between goals and process informing the two *pathways for intervention and technique.*

Our quest has illuminated four primary themes in counseling and therapy:

Theme 1 The human psyche and its behaviors are the product of two distinct neural networks in the human brain and soma

Theme 2 The two neural networks are *antagonistic*: more activity in one tends to mean less activity in the other, which *translates through to our behavior*

Theme 3 Counseling-and-therapy exists as a unitary hybrid endeavor comprised of two distinct, yet inseparable strands of clinician behavior mediated through the two antagonistic networks; all clinician behaviors in counseling-and-therapy are, to infinitely varying degrees, both goals-based and process-based

Theme 4 Different clients at different times in treatment require a different mix of goals-based and process-based working; in order to satisfy client need clinicians must have sufficient developmental competencies to adjust the mix of goals and process

---

1 Clinton, H. R. (1994). *At* Whitewater news conference, 22 April

Our working hypothesis is that counseling-and-therapy is a *developmental endeavor* assisting persons to process experience and make meaning in more adaptive ways; this allows the person to "balance [entering] into a full expression of feelings as represented by Sensorimotor experience with the ability to become more concrete and analytical as the situation changes"; and this in turn permits the person to be more happy in relationship and in context. In this endeavor the therapeutic relationship plays a pivotal role; the clinician is required to *extend Self* to the client, operationalizing her *Einfühlungsvermögen* and working from her Feeling-Sensing Style in specific ways furthering under-standing, getting to the heart of the problem, uncovering the dilemma, empathizing with the exquisite reluctance to let go and sharing the pain; the clinician is also required to use her Therapist-Self to afford her client a corrective emotional experience in the transference relationship, to permit the client fully to detach from the influence of the past on present behavior and achieve personality change; concurrently the clinician works from her Doing Style to assist the client's acquisition of necessary new information, behaviors, cognitions and competencies and to maintain the focus on clinical goals including safety. Thus it is, at any rate, for the process-preferring clinician with a predominant Feeling-Sensing Aspect: for the clinician with a predominant Doing Aspect, it is the other way around.

At all times the therapist is required to maintain *intentionality*. Intentional behaviors include preparedness for a range of client response to the treatment strategy, a commitment to uphold both sides of the client's dilemma and maintaining balance between the therapist's Feeling-Sensing and Doing Aspects to allow her to give the client just the right combination of goals-based and process-based methods, theories and interventions. When done optimally and adroitly, and without the projection into the therapy of clinician need, treatment and clinician will be in flow. For all these things to happen the counselor and therapist must possess certain autotelic developmental competencies in her Feeling-Sensing Aspect and, specifically, *Dialectic-Systemic Style*—development in which competencies can, in certain specific ways, be afforded the beginning clinician during training. In pursuing this inquiry we have refined our understanding of evidence-based practice in psychology: done properly, it is done in the ways described in these pages. Intentional intervention and EBPP are synonymous.

Writing this book has taught me much, changing the way I work and giving me a new understanding and a new hope for what is achievable in counseling and therapy. It has taught me the existential basis for our theory in evolutionary science, key to forging our synthesis between magic (process) and science (goals). It has taught me that neuroinformatics corroborates established, empirical theory and facilitates clinical decision making and intentionality. Writing this book has taught me how to catch myself when I am drifting clinically and in particular when, as a process-preferring clinician, I need to switch to goals. It has taught me the full beauty of the goals-based approach, which, done properly, is both goals-based and process-based.

In augmenting our grasp of the possibilities extended us and our clients by the DCT developmental metamodel, the concept of the dialectic between goals and process provides an expanded frame allowing us better to understand and manage the dialectical tension both in our client work and within our Self. Knowledge of the dialectic confers an important new clinical tool for conceptualizing treatment: using the *goals–process decision tree* extends accountability by helping us make the vital clinical decision of when and how to change therapeutic tack. When Good Therapy is being done we now know it: it is when the client is afforded the developmental assistance she needs by the counselor and therapist who has, herself or himself, developed so far as to let go of the many misapprehensions we had when we began this path about what therapy should look like and how it is done. We also know it when Good Therapy is absent.

We also know what to do about this. Our working hypothesis suggests we should view the arduous, uncertain process by which ordinary persons are made into counselors and therapists through the same developmental lens as we view our clients and with the same intentionality. *Transformation* is the issue and goal and the process is of transition. The transformation away from the low experiencing and over-reliance on the Doing Style that has become the hallmark of our culture outside the therapy room and which, when it impinges into the therapy room and compromises autotelic components in the Therapist-Self, may trigger an eclipse of the clinician's Feeling-Sensing Aspect. The transition to the intentionality and flow that we now surely know to be the font of good outcome.

We know also that clinicians are human and imperfect. The Good Therapist is always becoming. We define the Good Therapist as the clinician who:

- Performs Good Therapy with a particular client
- Takes steps necessary to augment her/his Therapist-Self so as to perform Good Therapy with a particular client
- Decides, if such steps prove too arduous and after reflection and consultation, to refer out the particular client

The essential feature of the Good Therapist is the ability to look at the big picture of the client's and the therapist's own developmental needs and the dialectic between them.

And we know too, with Freud and Ivey, that there is no shame in it if and when we manifest maladroitness. The thing we were frightened to say, lest it be true, has now been said and it is true: our characterological differences explain why some of us are, as therapists, more adroit and some of us less. The redeeming message we take from our investigation is this: less adroit is an expectable and permissible staging post along a prescribed, accessible developmental path to augment Therapist-Self and attain flow as a clinician practicing intentional intervention. Each can be a Good Therapist as defined and demonstrated here.

We need to make changes in the way we prepare our clinicians. We need in our classrooms to teach our students to distinguish and navigate between goals and process, counseling and therapy, 'more Doing' and 'offering an expanded scope for Doing.' We need to teach them about the rider and his Doing Style, and the perils of his inclination to confabulate, and about the elephant and her Feeling-Sensing Style that can be disavowed, denied, repressed—yet remains and persists. Most of all we need to develop our students, consciously and intentionally, to meet the awesome challenge of being someone's therapist. Very likely, in the context of a culture that rewards the Doing Style, we need to develop our student clinicians in the Feeling-Sensing Style. Very likely, given what we have seen in the preceding pages, we need to pay a special attention to our students' abilities in the Dialectic-Systemic, the Style in which we best manage the antagonistic theses of a dialectic.

No citation is needed, for the evidence is all around us, of an ever greater need for *good* therapy. If we think we now know—or even that it is really quite likely—that it is by such developmental transformation that Good Therapists are made and that, if we shall not have acted on that likelihood or knowledge in the way we prepare ourselves and others to be therapists, our failure must inevitably add to people's unhappinesses in the ways described in the foregoing pages, what, then, when we look back on what we could have done, shall we say?

San Francisco, November 29th 2016

Appendix
What Is Your Preferred Style of Helping?
ALLEN E. IVEY

Purpose

This instrument is designed to help you examine your conceptual style, the way you think about relationships, and the way you make meaning in the world. It will give you some clues as to your preferred way of interacting in the counseling and therapy session. It may be helpful to you in understanding others who may approach things differently from you. Potentially, it can help you in your personal relationships as well.

Directions

This instrument uses 10 questions, each with four possible responses. Your task is to rank the four responses from most descriptive of you (1) through least descriptive of you (4). Select the response that is most typical of you first (mark it 1), the one least typical of you next (4), then select (2) and (3) as midpoints between the two anchors. As you make your choices, focus on yourself and what is typical for you. The more spontaneous and honest you are, the more helpful the instrument will be.

Example

	I	II	III	IV
When you think about yourself as a counselor or therapist, you prefer				
a. individual counseling.			a. _3_	
b. couples counseling.		b. _2_		
c. group counseling.	c. _4_			
d. family counseling.				d. _1_

Go through the instrument rapidly rather than worrying about your responses. *There are no correct answers, and there is no "best" way to respond.* Have fun and learn a little about yourself!

Rank a through d with 1 to 4, from most descriptive of you (1) through least descriptive of you (4).

	I	II	III	IV

1. Which type of learning situations do you prefer?
   a. organized, structured, with clear directions as to what is to be done   a. ___ (III)
   b. highly involving and experiential   b. ___ (I)
   c. those that enable you to apply concepts to yourself and help you understand yourself better   c. ___ (III)
   d. those that allow for multiple interpretations   d. ___ (IV)

2. Emotionally, you tend to
   a. prefer looking at patterns of feeling.   a. ___ (III)
   b. have specific feelings, which tend to remain consistent over time.   b. ___ (II)
   c. feel deeply and immediately, and feel easily in your body.   c. ___ (I)
   d. have mixed feelings that change, depending on your perspective.   d. ___ (IV)

3. Which type of counseling theories, methods, or techniques do you prefer?
   a. Rogerian and other orientations that focus on self-development   a. ___ (III)
   b. gestalt exercises, body awareness, massage   b. ___ (I)
   c. behavioral analysis, reality therapy, logical analysis of rational-emotive therapy, assertiveness training   c. ___ (II)
   d. family systems work, multicultural emphasis, examining issues of transference   d. ___ (IV)

4. In a group counseling session, you tend to
   a. participate, but just as often like to stand back and observe the group's interaction style.   a. ___ (IV)
   b. sometimes get frustrated with all that's going on, and prefer structured groups that have a specific purpose.   b. ___ (II)
   c. like group work because it helps you understand yourself and others better.   c. ___ (III)
   d. really get into it and share, as you are especially fond of here and now experiencing.   d. ___ (I)

	I	II	III	IV
5. Which of the following describes you?				
a. concrete		a. ___		
b. sensory oriented	b. ___			
c. analytical				c. ___
d. self-reflective			d. ___	
6. People describe you as				
a. intellectual, good at planning, deliberate, adept at analyzing situations from several points of view.				a. ___
b. emotional and quick to react, creative and playful, able to be with others in the here and now.	b. ___			
c. self-reflective and aware of yourself.			c. ___	
d. ordered and organized, dependable, sequential.		d. ___		
7. Stop for a minute or two, and recall your family of origin. Which of the following most closely describes what you just did?				
a. You thought about your family genogram and how intergenerational history affects the way you and other family members are now.				a. ___
b. You visualized your family members and/or noted some specific feelings in your body.	b. ___			
c. You thought about patterns of interaction within the family, particularly those that affect you.			c. ___	
d. You recalled a specific incident, thinking about what happened.		d. ___		
8. When you think about multicultural issues, which of the following most closely describes your thoughts and feelings?				
a. You believe that people are people, and that is the most central aspect we should remember.	a. ___			
b. You feel some sense of anger because of discrimination and related issues.		b. ___		
c. You find it helpful to become aware of your own multicultural heritage.			c. ___	
d. You find that all of the above dimensions can be part of your feelings and thoughts. What occurs for you seems to change with context.				d. ___

(Continued)

(Continued)

	I	II	III	IV

9. In choosing work, you would most prefer
   a. considerable opportunity for creativity and spontaneity, and a boss who takes care of the details and structures projects for you.   a. ___
   b. an opportunity to think and use your skills of analysis and deduction, and a boss who gives you an assignment and then leaves you alone to complete it.   b. ___
   c. to be with people in good relationships, and a boss who consults with you and helps you become more effective in your own way.   c. ___
   d. sufficient structure and organization with good planning, and a boss who is there to help you when needed and who provides coaching and support.   d. ___

10. When you face an important life crisis, you
    a. are able to see so many points of view and possibilities that you sometimes become confused before you act.   a. ___
    b. tend to react spontaneously in the moment; it just happens.   b. ___
    c. tend to think what the crisis means to you and your own thinking, and then you do the best you can.   c. ___
    d. find it helpful to think about or make a list of positives and negatives and then work your way deliberately through the problem.   d. ___

            COLUMN TOTALS THIS PAGE   ___   ___   ___   ___

	I	II	III	IV

Scoring

Total the four columns at the bottom of each page, transfer the totals into the spaces provided below, and add the columns to get the grand totals.

	I	II	III	IV
Questions 1–6	___	___	___	___
Questions 7–10	___	___	___	___
Grand totals	___	___	___	___

Appendix • 193

If you add your four grand totals together, the sum should be 100. If they do *not* add up to 100, go back and check your addition of the columns on each page of the questionnaire. If the column additions were not in error, add up the total rankings for each of the four responses to each question. For each question, you ranked the responses 1, 2, 3, and 4. So the total of the rankings for each question should be 10 (1 + 2 + 3 + 4). If any question total is not 10, then most likely you wrote the same number twice or forgot to rank one of the responses

Transfer your scores into the diagram below by circling in each quadrant the number closest to the grand total of each column.

Column I   = Sensorimotor (S)
Column II = Concrete (C)
Column III = Formal (F)
Column IV = Dialectic/Systemic (D/S)

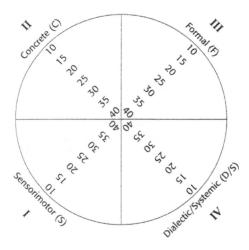

The lowest circled scores—those closest to the perimeter of the circle—indicate your preferred style areas. Connect the four circled scores. The quadrant with the tallest peak is your preferred style of helping. *Understanding your own preferences should help you work with those who interact and communicate differently from you.*

Interpretation

Every counseling and therapy student will have a different answer to the question "What is your preferred style of helping?" There is not one best way to provide help for everyone. With certain clients, the sensorimotor style is best; with others, the dialectic/systemic style might achieve better results. It is essential to be aware that each counselor typically has a preferred style. We need to be careful not to impose our cognitive/emotional style on others. Developmental counseling and therapy stresses the importance of matching interventions to the cognitive/emotional style of the client.

   I. *Sensorimotor.* Those who prefer this style area are believed to be especially good at being in the moment with clients and having access to immediate experiencing.

II. *Concrete.* Those with this preferred style tend to be good at making plans with clients, being specific, and taking action in the world.
III. *Formal.* Those with this style tend to be good at reflection and at dealing with patterns of thought and feeling. (Reflecting and experiencing feelings are not the same thing.)
IV. *Dialectic/systemic.* Those who prefer this style can take different perspectives and are adept at looking at systems of operations and dealing with complexity.

Each style has both strengths and weaknesses. The sensorimotor person at times may have difficulty organizing experiences, the concrete person may become enmeshed in detail and have difficulty in reflecting, the formal person may be good at reflecting feelings but have real difficulty in experiencing them fully at the sensorimotor level, and the dialectic/systemic person may get caught up in thinking and have difficulties in feeling or in taking action. Full development requires a counselor to be fully sensitive to each style. Rather than determining one "best" style, an effective counselor learns to access more styles at more depth.

The ordering of scores in determining areas of preference is also interesting. A few people have balanced profiles, indicating ability to work with all cognitive/emotional styles. Others show "spikes" in the diagram, strongly preferring one style. Some may be predominantly formal, for example, but also have strengths in the concrete or sensorimotor area. Each person appears to have a unique pattern.

The item stems in the instrument were designed to be positive, and all the responses were designed to be valid. The instrument should help you understand the DCT model and its implications at a more personal level. It can also help counselors diagnose preferred style in their clients, so that they can match their intervention more carefully with client needs.

Follow-up instruments

Style-Shift Inventory. The SSI presents eight case studies, and students develop treatment programs for the cases. The SSI also presents a score for preferred style of action. Available from Microtraining Associates (www.emicrotraining.com).

Gregore Style Delineator. This instrument provides very good information on cognitive style and is easy to administer and score. Available from Gabriel Systems, Maynard, MA.

Myers-Briggs Type Indicator. There are some interesting similarities between the instrument in this appendix and the Myers-Briggs Type Indicator. The sensing dimension of the Myers-Brigg seems to relate to sensorimotor experiences, the thinking dimension to concrete, feeling to formal, and intuition to dialectic/systemic.

Glossary

Antithesis Contrasted with Thesis: an argument, a linked series of Hypotheses or ideas arguing against someone else's Thesis. [*See also* Hypothesis; Thesis]

Archetype A construct advanced by Athenian philosopher Plato as a synonym for what we now call Platonic Form. Adopted by Swiss psychoanalyst C. G. Jung to describe patterns of ideation universally present in each individual's psyche and derived from the Collective Unconscious; an Archetype embodies fundamental characteristics that may or may not be manifested in the material world. For example: the King Archetype is always "kingly" but an individual king may be lacking in "kingliness." [*See also* Collective Unconscious; Platonic Form]

Aspect (*Technical usage proposed by Intentional Intervention*). A principal mode of potentiating the Therapist-Self via *either* Doing *or* Feeling-Sensing. [*See also* Doing; Feeling-Sensing; Therapist-Self]

Change, First-order Contrasted with Change, Second-order: behavioral change achieved by the client in treatment that does not take the client beyond the Dilemma; while the client may leave treatment with symptom reduction consequent upon new cognitions and strategies, these are not integrated into the client's personality—which is essentially unaltered. [*See also* Change, Second-order; Dilemma]

Change, Second-order Contrasted with Change, First-order: behavioral change achieved by the client in treatment that takes the client beyond the Dilemma; the client leaves treatment with her personality developmentally augmented. [*See also* Change, First-order; Dilemma]

Collective Unconscious "*My thesis then, is as follows: in addition to our immediate consciousness, which is of a thoroughly personal nature and which we believe to be the only empirical psyche (even if we tack on the personal unconscious as an appendix), there exists a second psychic system of a collective, universal, and impersonal nature which is identical in all individuals. This collective unconscious does not develop individually but is inherited. It consists of pre-existent forms, the archetypes, which can only become conscious secondarily and which give definite form to certain psychic contents.*"[1]

---

1 Jung, C. G., (1968.) *The Archetypes and the Collective Unconscious*. Princeton, New Jersey: Princeton University Press, p. 43

Content   What is overtly discussed in the clinical session. Content may relate in differing degrees to both Process and Goals. When more related to Goals, Content may be contrasted with Process. [*See also* Goals; Process (Technical usage—2)]

Continuum   A continuous sequence where adjacent elements are almost imperceptibly different from each other, yet the extremes (Poles) are quite distinct; imagine white paint with, progressively, one further drop of black paint added—the result is a continuum of greys on the Pole between white and black. [*See also* Pole]

Counseling   A predominantly Goals-based way of working with clients, more weighted to imparting information (e.g. psychoeducation intervention) and teaching skills (e.g. assertiveness training); the Discourse in Counseling is "I can teach or inform my client." Counseling is inseparably twinned and may also be contrasted with Psychotherapy. [*See also* Discourse; Goals-based; Psychotherapy]

Default Mode Network   (*In neuroscience*). Contrasted with Task Positive Brain: a phylogenetically older neural network that "plays a central role in emotional self-awareness, social cognition and ethical decision-making [and] is also strongly linked to creativity and openness to new ideas." [*See also* Task Positive Brain]

Dialectic   The complex, reciprocal relationship between opposing Theses or between Thesis and Antithesis. [*See also* Antithesis; Thesis]

Dilemma   The emotional conflict underlying the client's presenting problem and putting the client in an impossible situation; cognitions attached to the Dilemma are: *If I do X then A will happen, which cannot be tolerated; but if I do Y then B will happen, which is equally intolerable; X and Y are my sole choices and I am therefore condemned to misery.*

Disavowal   A defense mechanism that is neither repression nor denial and in which "the [perception] has not been eliminated but ... has been distorted, rationalized or misinterpreted in the interest of preventing anxiety."

Discourse   The conceptual frame of and cognitions informing the argument or story; "glass-half-full" is a Discourse of sufficiency, while "glass-half-empty" is a Discourse of insufficiency.

Doing   (*Technical usage proposed by Intentional Intervention*). A Discourse pertaining to interventions *directly and obviously* designed to combat the client's problem; associated with Goals and contrasted with Feeling-Sensing. [*See also* Discourse; Feeling-Sensing; Goals]

Einfühlung   [*German*] "Feeling into;" used metaphorically of the kinesthetic sense of moving to arrive at empathic understanding.

Einfühlungs-vermögen   [*German*] "Agentive capacity for feeling into;" used metaphorically of the qualities and capacities in the Therapist-Self which permit *Einfühlung*. [*See also Einfühlung*; Therapist-Self]

Feeling-Sensing   (*Technical usage proposed by Intentional Intervention*). Discourse pertaining to interventions that combat the client's problem in a *more indirect* fashion and focusing on phenomena *underlying and paralleling* the problem; associated with Process and contrasted with Doing. [*See also* Discourse; Doing; Process (Technical usage—2)]

Flow (*Technical usage proposed by Mihály Csíkszentmihályi*). "Complete immersion in an experience" to achieve a "state of effortless concentration and enjoyment" in performing the activity.[2]

Flow (*Technical usage proposed by Intentional Intervention*). Flow, as described by Csíkszentmihályi occurs in counseling-and-therapy when the clinician is able to let go of the obstructively countertransferential need for the work to go a certain way and can focus on taking the client beyond the Dilemma to Second-order Change. [*See also* Change, Second-order; Dilemma]

Goals Contrasted with Process: what stakeholders (client, clinician, environment) wish to happen as a result of treatment. [*See also* Process (Technical usage—2)]

Goals-based (*Technical usage in Intentional Intervention as in* "Goals-based methods"). Contrasted with Process-based: describing clinical work designed directly to help the client address a problem or symptom. [*See also* Process-based]

Good Therapist The Clinician who either (i) performs Good Therapy with a particular client or (ii) takes steps necessary to augment her/his Therapist-Self so as to perform Good Therapy with a particular client; and who, if such steps prove ineffective or too arduous (iii) after reflection and consultation decides to refer out the particular client. [*See also* Good Therapy; Therapist-Self]

Good Therapy Clinical work managing the Dialectic between Goals and Process in a way giving the client just what the client needs in terms of Goals-based and Process-based Theories, methods and interventions. [*See also* Dialectic; Goals; Process (Technical usage—2); Theory]

Hypothesis A lower level argument or smaller series of ideas that we can imagine and then examine its validity as in: *Let's imagine diabetes is not a standalone disease but instead part of a syndrome.* A linked series of Hypotheses combine to form a Thesis. [*See also* Thesis]

Intentionality (*Technical usage in Developmental Counseling and Therapy*). Clinical work is Intentional when clinicians choose and apply interventions within a cohesive developmental treatment plan and based on a narrow range of anticipated client response.

Intentionality (*Technical usage proposed by Intentional Intervention*). The above definition is augmented by the clinician's assessment of the client's potential developmental trajectory in relation to first-order Change and second-order Change. When the clinician lets go of any need for the work to go a certain way, intentionality brings Flow. [*See also* Change, First-order; Change, Second-order; Flow]

Main Feeling A deeper, older feeling underlying the more accessible, surface response to the presenting problem.

---

[2] Csíkszentmihályi, M. (1997). Finding Flow. New York, New York: Basic Books

Meaning-making The explanation assigned by a person to life events as in: *My parents argue about me and it is my fault…there is something faulty about me.*

Metatheory A higher level Theory that encompasses and helps us map the relationship between divergent Theories. [*See also* Theory]

Mirroring (*Technical usage in self psychology as in* "The therapist implemented Mirroring"). A widely-used and fundamental intervention (capable of being made both explicitly or implicitly) that lets the client know the clinician finds the client's behaviors completely understandable—anyone in the client's shoes would do the same. Mirroring in self psychology is similar to, but more specific than, the intervention often called "normalizing."

Personality Style (*Technical usage in Developmental Counseling and Therapy*). A person's basic way of being and relating, being an understandable reaction to environmental circumstance and serving as the person's primary defense against depression; on a Continuum from more adaptive/less symptomatic to less adaptive/more symptomatic. [*See also* Continuum]

Phenomenology The idea that observing and examining Phenomena (things that are apparently and evidently happening) is a good way to gain knowledge, by forming Hypotheses. [*See also* Hypothesis]

[Platonic] Form A construct advanced by Athenian philosopher Plato and used interchangeably with Archetype; an imago or idea: behind every thing or concept occurring in our material world is *our idea of it*, which is immaterial. There are many different kinds of table: we can only understand all of these to be tables because of our *idea* of "table" or "tableness." [*See also* Archetype]

Pole One end of a Continuum; also used metaphorically as a synonym for the Continuum. *All clinical work is somewhere on the Continuum between the Poles of Counseling and Psychotherapy/all clinical work is located somewhere on the Pole running from Counseling to Psychotherapy.* [See *also* Continuum]

Process (*Nontechnical usage as in* "Process of discovery"). Something that happens or a series of events occurring in a sequential, unfolding way.

Process (*Technical usage—1—as in* "Facilitating client Process"). A person's fundamental ongoing cognitive-emotional experience.

Process (*Technical usage—2—as in* "Process-based client work"). Contrasted with Goals: everything that is going on psychologically in the clinical encounter and related to the client's fundamental ongoing cognitive-emotional experience; in particular, everything that is going on that is *not* being talked about overtly. Also contrasted with Content when Content more related to Goals. [*See also* Content; Goals]

Process-based (*Technical usage in Intentional Intervention as in* "Process-based methods"). Contrasted with Goals-based: describing clinical work designed to help the client feel, talk about and come to terms with her Process, whether her feelings are conscious, pre-conscious or unconscious and whether or not the feelings are in relation to the clinician. [*See also* Goals-based; Process (Technical usage—1)]

Projective identification In the mechanism of Projective identification thoughts and feelings arise in the clinician that are not related to something going on in [the clinician's] personal life but nonverbal communications from the client, unconsciously projected. *Example: the clinician, a kindly man, finds himself thinking critical thoughts about his client, a woman whose father was very critical of her.*

Psychopathology Literally *story of suffering*; an explanation of how people develop psychological symptoms.

Psychotherapy A predominantly Process-based way of working with clients, more weighted to healing by augmenting development; the Discourse in Psychotherapy is "I can help my client develop to a better adaptation." Psychotherapy is inseparably twinned and may also be contrasted with Counseling. [*See also* Counseling; Discourse]

Reification (Reify, Reified) A complex human cognitive/emotional process, or series of such processes, reduced to or "made into" an abstract noun or thing; any noun ending in "-ism" or "-ness" is a Reification as well as any concept or idea; every psychological diagnosis is a Reification as are all theoretical constructs. "Table" is a noun; "tableness" is a Reification.

Self The part of us that both defines us and is simultaneously the subject and object of experience and reflection, as in: *She has a strong sense of Self.*

Self-esteem (*Technical usage in self psychology theory as in* "Mirroring builds self-structure and self-esteem"). A construct attempting to describe the attribute of not depending on the approbation of others for self-regulation.

Self-structure (*Technical usage in self psychology theory as in* "Mirroring builds self-structure and self-esteem"). A construct attempting to describe components of the Self conferring resilience and the ability to navigate toward one's own solutions.

Sensorium [*Latin*] "Apparatus for sensing." Referring to the qualities and capacities in the Therapist-Self permitting empathic understanding and awareness of Projective Identification. *Similar to Einfühlungsvermögen.* [*See also* Einfühlungsvermögen; Projective Identification; Therapist-Self]

Sichhineinversetzung [*German*] "Displacing oneself into the other"; Freud's physiological description of empathic feeling-into. *Similar to Einfühlung.* [*See also* Einfühlung]

Style—Concrete (*Technical usage in Developmental Counseling and Therapy*). The component of a person's Process (*Technical usage*—1) focusing on interest in and expression of facts and factual narratives.

Style—Dialectic-Systemic (*Technical usage in Developmental Counseling and Therapy*). The component of a person's Process (*Technical usage*—1) focusing on interest in and expression of disparate aspects and narratives, including "patterns of patterns" and giving a "big picture" perspective.

Style—Doing (*Technical usage proposed by Intentional Intervention*). The predominance in a person's Process (*Technical usage*—1) of Concrete and Formal Styles; it is hypothesized that the Doing Style is predominant in the Task Positive Brain and, in the clinician, is a cardinal Aspect of the Therapist-Self. [*See also* Aspect; Task Positive Brain; Therapist-Self]

Style—Feeling-Sensing (*Technical usage proposed by Intentional Intervention*). The predominance in a person's Process (*Technical usage*—1) of Sensorimotor and Dialectic-Systemic Styles; it is hypothesized that the Feeling-Sensing Style is predominant in the Default Mode Network and, in the clinician, is a cardinal Aspect of the Therapist-Self. [*See also* Aspect; Default Mode Network; Therapist-Self]

Style—Formal (*Technical usage in Developmental Counseling and Therapy*). The component of a person's Process (*Technical usage*—1) that focuses on interest in recognizing and drawing inferences from patterns.

Style—Personality [*See* Personality Style]

Style—Sensorimotor (*Technical usage in Developmental Counseling and Therapy*). The component of a person's Process (*Technical usage*—1) that is expression of emotion.

Synthesis A higher level argument, linked series of Hypotheses or ideas that can join together under one conceptual frame a previously conflicting Thesis and Antithesis. [*See also* Antithesis; Hypothesis; Thesis]

Task Positive Brain (*In neuroscience*). Contrasted with Default Mode Network: a phylogenetically more recent neural network which "is important for problem solving, focusing of attention, making decisions and control of action." [*See also* Default Mode Network]

Therapy Short for Psychotherapy

Therapist-Self An augmentation or developmental extension to the Self of the clinician permitting the clinician to acquire, develop and deploy qualities and characteristics necessary for clinical work. [*See also* Self]

Theory (of psychology) A way of looking at how people develop emotional problems and how they may be helped.

Thesis An argument, a linked series of Hypotheses or ideas that someone invites us to adopt; may be contrasted with Antithesis. [*See also* Antithesis; Hypothesis]

Verleugnen [*German*] "Making a liar of oneself"; usually translated as: "Disavowal." [*See also* Disavowal]

Author Index

Adler, A. 6, 79
Allen, D. M. xxxi, xxxiii
Aponte, H. xxxv, 22, 67
Argyle, M. 62

Baker, S. B. 52–3
Baldwin, M. 24–5, 81, 175
Basch, M. F. 34, 36, 38, 57, 58, 69, 148
Beck, A. 4, 16, 22, 34
Bigras, M. 88
Bischof-Köhler, D. 28
Blow, A. 7, 8, 9, 24, 35, 43, 46
Boukydis, K. 149, 151, 160
Bowen, M. xxxiv, 4, 62, 67, 166
Boyatzis, R. xvi, xvii, xxi, 168
Bridges, W. 70, 71, 76, 79, 117, 119, 120, 124, 145, 147, 150, 151, 153, 179–80
Brodley, B. 60, 78, 139
Burns, D. xvii, xviii, xxxii, 22, 42, 59

Chabon, M. 155–6, 177; *The Pleasure, Regrets of 'Manhood'* 155
Chaudhuri, H. 4, 9, 40, 51, 101
Clarkin, J. F. 16, 40, 59
Cohen, R. 29
Cooper, M. 97
Cortright, B. 39, 56, 58, 63, 69, 86, 117, 118
Correll, C. U. 16
Csíkszentmihályi, M. 178–9

Dobson, D. 96, 109–10, 156

Erikson, E. 32, 101
Erikson, J. 32, 101

Freud, S. 3–4, 6, 9, 10, 11, 16, 19, 20, 22, 29, 30, 37, 47, 57, 69, 97, 126, 127, 171, 187
Friesen, J. 6

Gass, M. A. 64, 121
Gazzaniga, M. 8

Geller, J. D. 126
Gendlin, E. T. 11, 149
Gerrard, B. ix, 6
Gillette, D. 91, 109, 110
Gladwell, M. 117, 118
Glasser, W. 21, 56, 59, 63, 68, 78–9, 112, 131, 135, 143, 159, 174, 179

Haidt, J. 8, 18, 19, 59, 169
Handal, P. xxiii
Hastings, R. 33, 35, 46, 47, 54, 56, 89, 91, 120
Hawkins, P. xii
Hess, J. 29, 39
Hilsenroth, M. xviii

Imel, Z. xii, xxxiv–v; *The Great Psychotherapy Debate* xxv
Ivey, A. E.: *Developmental Counseling and Therapy* xx, 10, 12, 13–14, 15–16, 17, 18, 19, 21, 26, 27–8, 30, 34, 35, 36, 37, 38, 40, 45, 46, 48, 49, 51, 52, 56, 57, 59, 63, 69, 70, 78, 86, 92, 93, 96, 97, 100, 110, 112, 113, 119, 121, 123, 125, 126, 127, 138, 145–7, 148, 149, 150, 151, 154, 179, 187, 189–94

Jung, C. xxiii, 48

Kahn, M. xxv, 33, 35, 39, 40, 56, 62, 69, 96, 119, 155
Kanazawa, S. 174–5, 183
Katsivelaris, N. 28, 30, 47, 120
Kelly, G. A. 15
Klein, M. 21, 171
Kohut, H. xxiii, xxv, 21, 33, 34, 39, 40–1, 43, 51, 52, 56, 63, 69, 98, 119, 155
Kramer, R. 4
Kriegman, D. H. 48
Kugler, D. J. 80

Lane, R. D. 18–19, 156–7
Lee, R. R. 33, 36, 40, 59, 80
Lévesque, M. 88
Lipps, T. 29, 126

Madanes, C.: *Sex, Love, and Violence: Strategies for Transformation* 95
Mamchur, C. 93
Meyer, J. 125–6
Molnos, A. 148–9, 160
Montag, C. 29
Moore, R. 91, 109, 110

Needleman, L. D. 108, 157
Norcross, J. C. xiii, xv, xxv, xxxi, xxxiii

Ogden, T. 25, 27, 41, 74, 119, 163, 171, 180
Owen, J. xviii, xix, xv, xxi, 185

Padesky, C. A. 107–8
Patrikiou, A. 29
Peck, M. S. 96, 111
Piaget, J. 11, 17, 19, 20
Pitner, S. 94
Plato xvi, xxiii, xxvi, 53–5
Prall, W. 30
Priest, S. 64, 121

Raichle, M. xv–xvi, xxi
Rank, O. 4, 9
Renn, P. 33, 50
Richardson, P. xxxiii, 46, 66, 81

Rogers, C. R. 4, 5–6, 7–8, 10, 21, 24, 28, 30, 35–8, 41, 52, 59, 69, 81, 113, 120, 121, 139, 148, 149, 158, 159

Saeed, S. A. 41–2, 53
Salovey, P. 125–6
Satir, V. xxxiv, xxxv, 4, 24–5, 27, 38, 39, 49, 53, 57, 71, 80, 81, 163, 175, 177, 178, 179, 183
Schlossberg, N. K. 10, 52, 71
Shohet, R. xii
Slavin, M. O. 47, 48, 56, 120
Snyder, A. Z. xv–xvi, xxi
Socrates xxxii
Stetka, B. S. 16
Strachey, J. B.: *Standard Edition of the Complete Psychological Works of Sigmund Freud* 57, 69
Sussman, M. B. 118

Titchener, E. 27, 28
Truscott, D. xix, 3, 5, 6, 7, 54, 86, 154
Turner, H. 42, 43, 44, 45, 53, 81, 176
Twenge, J. M. 40

Vitz, P. 94

Waller, G. xvii–xviii, xix, xx, xxi, xxii, 23, 42, 53, 66, 175, 176, 185
Wampold, B. xii, xxvi, xxxiv–v; *The Great Psychotherapy Debate* xxv
Winnicott, D. W. 32, 47, 120
Winter, J. xxxiv, xxxv, 22, 67

Yalom, I. 177

Subject Index

Page numbers in italics indicate figures and tables. [G] denotes Glossary entry

accountability 42, (definition) 52, (goals–process decision tree) 52–3
adroit(ness): acquiring xx; child therapy 90; client assessment 65; DCT development 18; Default Mode Network xxxii; developmental hypothesis 10; Dialectic-Systemic 45; displaying *vs.* developing xii; emotional intelligence 51; empathy 31; flow 186; goals-based and process-based methods 22; Ivey Instrument 146; key to 174; managing the dialectic xvi; outcome xxxiii; problem xiii; self-disorders and case conceptualization 41; social work training xxxv; Therapist-Self 127; timing 14; trainee 123; treating personality and symptoms xxxi; *see also* maladroit(ness)
alcoholic client *see* goals–process decision tree
Alexei, case of 151–9, ("cold-hearted") 163, (low experiencer) 163, (dilemma) 177–9 *See also* Elena
American Psychiatric Association: *Diagnostic and Statistical Manual of Mental Disorder* 15–16
American Psychological Association (APA): *Policy Statement on Evidence-Based Practice in Psychology* xviii
anxious client, trainee case 128–31, 135–7
Archetype [G]: blocked 110; cardinal 91; evidence-based practice 180; Good Therapist 111; Good Therapy xxxiii, 4, 7; Lover 96–7, (Gonzalo) 99–104; Magician 91–3, (Gonzalo) 99–102, 104, 106, (vignette) 95; Mirroring 32; projected communication 103; Ruler 93, (Gonzalo) 98–102; shadow 99, 109–10, 123, 156, 165, 166; Warrior 94–6, (Gonzalo) 98, (vignette) 95

attachment theory 48, 102, 105
autotelic personality 178–9

behavioral therapy 96
Bowenian theory, xxxiv, 4, (uproar) 62, 166

Cai, trainee therapist: case of Norah 164–70; conceptualization (eclipse of Dialectic-Systemic) 168–9, (eclipse of Doing) 165; Feeling-Sensing 164–5 (Mirroring not condoning) 167, (obstructive countertransference) 166, 168; *see also* Norah
case conceptualization xiii, 3, 16, 41, 59–63; client's failing defenses 57, (Gonzalo) 121; clinician's conceptualization group 180–3; developmental trajectory 110, 177; educator's 160; intentionality 177–8; obstructive countertransference 122, (Alexei) 151–6; priority of process 67; reified xxviii, xxx–ii, 45, 103, 107, 141, 149, 165–6, 169, (Chantal) 66, (Kevin) 71–2; symptoms *vs.* personality xxv, xxxi, 60–1; *see also* countertransference case conceptualization group
change: *vs.* transition 70, (Alexei) 153
change, first-order [G]: client satisfaction with 102, 103, 107, 110, (trainee) 118, 124; definition 64; examples of xxxii, 102; *vs.* second-order change xxxii, 64–5, 177–8, (as staging-post to) 180, 183
change, second-order [G]: annihilation of dilemma (Chantal) 78, (cognitive restructuring) 142, (Norah) 168; client preparation (Chantal) 70, 77; definition 64; developmental trajectory (foundation of first-order change) 177, (Gonzalo) 102–3, 107, 177; dialectic

203

between goals and process (Chantal) 65–6, 77; *vs.* first-order change xxxii, 64–5, 177–8; flow 180; trainee 124; treatment success xxxi

Chantal, case of 57–66, 75–80, (DCT assessment) 59, (dilemma) 64, 75–7, (disavowal) 58, (hidden emotion) 61, (horizontal development) 63, (preparedness for goals-based interventions) 61–2, 76, (presenting narrative) 57, (Style-shift to Concrete) 60

choice theory 21, 78–9, 109, 143, 179, (Norah) 174

client development (DCT): Concrete 12; Dialectic-Systemic 13; Formal 12–13; Sensorimotor 11

cognition: altering xxvii; changing *vs.* understanding xv, 135, (underlying) 137; clinician's xxx, 5, 10, 42, 53–4, 120, (distortions) 175, 182; cognitive *vs.* psychoanalytic 20–1; in DCT 14–20; encoded meaning 80; researchers' xxxi; restructuring xxix, 88, 90, 101, 142; social xvi

cognitive-behavioral therapy (CBT) efficacy xvii–iii, 42, 175–6; evidence-based hypothesis, xiv, xxix; prominence xiv–v; with psychodynamic methods xviii–xxi, xxv, 22, 41, 97–8, 172, 173–4; psychotherapy culture wars xv, 23, 176; specific treatment thesis xxvii

cognitive-emotional process: clinician's transition 127, 129, 138, 145–6; DCT schema 10–16; reification xxvii–xxviii; underlying client content xxvii

cognitive theory 4, 14, 20; guided discovery 108, 139; Socratic questioning xviii, xxxiii, 107, 163, (Norah) 169

collective unconscious [G] xxiii, 48

Concrete Style [[G—Style, Concrete] 11–14, 17; DCT assessment (client) 154–5, (trainee) 128, 131; Doing Style 19–20, 110, 121, (client) 57–8, 61, 69, 88–90, 102, 121, 129, (education) 123, 147, (less adroit clinician) 45, 143; Ivey Instrument 145–7; Style-shift from (Alexei) 158–9, (educator's) 123, 129–31, 174; Style-shift to 12, 60, 69; therapeutic communication 12, 96; vertical development 138; Warrior 96

condoning, not: educator 154; *vs.* empathizing 31–2, 34, (Mirroring) 37, 90, 154, 167; *vs.* indulgence 34; Jimmy 90; unburdening 35

confabulation 9; Chantal 66; clinician's theoretical preference 8, 23; definition 8; disavowal 59; Kevin 73; neuroscience 18; Norah 165

confrontation 148–9, 167, (of trainee) 149–59

congruence *see* Rogerian theory

continuum [G]: client change xxxii; DCT Styles 11; goals–process xv–xx, 180; meaning of empathy 28; pathology 70, 77; psychosocial development xxi

corrective emotional experience *see* self psychology

countertransference: analysis 98, 121; clinical use xxx, 25, 46, 142, 178, (Alexei) 159, (client cues) 53, (congruence) 160, (Ghislaine) 31–2, (Kevin) 26–7; clinician extension of Self 35; congruence 36; definition 25; evidence 24–5, 54, 65, (*vs.* literature) 41; Magician 93; Mirroring 33; obstructive xxxi, 25, (to client negativity—anxious client) 75, (clinician's final letting go of) 179, (colluding with client) 177, (educator) 154, (to erotic transference) 112, (in implementation of CBT) 175–6, (objectivity—depressed client) 132, (reified case conceptualization) 122, (working harder than the client) 178; theory partisanship 5; twinship 97, 168; *see also* projective identification

countertransference case conceptualization group 164–71, 174

DCT *see* developmental counseling and therapy

Default Mode Network [G]: client's 66; dialectic between goals and process 23, 41, 91, 123, 143, 146, 168; disavowal of 59; "elephant" 8; Feeling-Sensing Style 9, 20, 26, 45, 90–1, 123, 146, 176; instinctual xxxv; process 41; suppressing xxviii; *vs.* Task Positive Brain xvi, xxi–ii, xxxvi, 23

depressed client, trainee case 131

developmental counseling and therapy (DCT): assessment—client 59, 69, 128, (Chantal) 61–2, (couple communication) 177, (depressed client) 131–2, (Jimmy) 88, (predicting client adoption) 174; assessment—clinician 45 128–9,; clinician's preferred Style 193–4; introduction xx; neuroscience 18, 20; schema 11–18; "stack diagram" 17;

Subject Index • 205

Style-shifting 60, 79, 160, 174; treatment goal 13, 18, 52, 100, 123, 128; treatment planning 18, 62, 68, 70, (trainee development) 138, 143, 147, (trauma) 92; wheel diagram 19; *see also* treatment plan, DCT case hypothesis and developmental trajectory: alcoholic client 53; Gonzalo 102–3, 107–10, 177–8; trainee's 127, 149

Dialectic-Systemic Style [G—Style, Dialectic-Systemic] 11, 13–14, 17–18; accessible from Sensorimotor 19–20; client assessment 69, 99; client development 49–51, 63–4, 77–8, 92, 106; client's disavowal of 39, 57; clinician development 13, 21–3, 137–8, 143, (awareness) 80, 92, (courage) 121, (curiosity) 35, 37, 41, 137, (eclipse) 168–9, (flow) 178, 186, (Ivey Instrument) 145–7, (looking beyond) 122–3, 129, (pick out information) 163, (self-reflection) 45; Default Mode Network 20; *Einfühlungsvermögen* 126–7; Feeling-Sensing Style 20, 45, 90; key attitudes 21; Magician 92–3, 165; Style-shift to, client (Alexei) 158–9, (Norah) 174; Style-shift to, clinician 13, 122, 128, 129, 131, 132, 133; therapeutic communication 93, 101

difference between psychotherapy and counseling 51

dilemma [G] 27, 31–2, 34, 61–2, 74–5; definition 75; *Einfühlung* groups 138–42; intentionality 156, 174–8, (flow) 179–80; (Norah) 166–9; primary *vs.* secondary 98, 106; projective identification 128, 130–1, 133–4, 136; psychosomatic medicine 157; returning client to 108–9, (Alexei) 151–9, (anxious client) 130–1; second-order change 142; therapist's 48–51, 101; unfolding 46, 70, 75, 80, (therapeutic alliance) 77–8; *see also* main feeling

disavowal [G] 39, 56–60, 58, 85–6, (anxious client) 128, (depressed client) 131; assessment 65, 70; of the dialectic 110, (colluding with client's) 156, 162, 165–8; erosion 63, 174; trainee's 122, 124, 126–7, 135; *Verleugnen* 57–8

disenchantment 120–1

disengagement 120–1; client's—Chantal 61, 63, 66, (depressed client) 131, 133; trainee's 129, 134

disidentification 70–1, 120, 127

DMN *see* Default Mode Network

Doing Style [G—Style, Doing] 9; client's 53; cognitive-behavioral technique 78; counseling 54; definition 19–20, 23, 45–7, (everyday) 147; *vs.* Feeling-Sensing 91, 97, 110, 123; Warrior 96; over-reliance on 45, 120, 127, 141, 148, (anxious client) 128, (depressed client) 132, (incongruence) 149; Task Positive Brain 20, 90; under-reliance on 110, 146

drama therapy 97

Education without understanding problem (depressed client) 131–5; *see also* Elena

Einfühlung [G] 27–31, 35, 48, 59–60, 74, 125, (groups) 138–43

Einfühlungsvermögen [G] 28–30, 66, 71, 174; developing 111; emotional intelligence 126; Feeling-Sensing 127, 143; Gonzalo 100; Magician 93, 98; operationalizing 29, 39, 120, 160

Elena, trainee therapist: case of Alexei 151–4, (assessment) 155, (conditional positive regard) 163, (education without understanding) 155–6, (I can't stand the client's negativity) 156, (returning client to dilemma) 151–9, 177–9; educator's countertransference 154–5 (parallel process) 154, 157–8; low-experiencing 156, (parallel process) 159; Wellness 149–51; *see also* Alexei

emotional intelligence: client's 105, (depressed client) 131; clinician's 29, 62, (Feeling-Sensing) 143, (Magician) 93, (Therapist-Self) 125–6, 131

Empathink Association 40–1

empathy (lower case) xi, 5–6, 16–17, 27–8, 125; DCT 12, 155; DCT development 12, 16–17, 28, 125, 155; definition 27–9; developing client's 79, 90; physiology 29–30

Empathy (upper case) 28–31, 36, 126; case hypothesis 68–70, 88; curtailment in 138; operationalization 143; vulnerability 48; *see also Sichhineinversetzen*

evidence: countertransference xxx, 24–7, 41, 65, 93, (clinician's insufficiencies) 112; Default Mode Network 59; developmental hypothesis 10; Dialectic-Systemic 39, 92; Feeling-Sensing 163, 175; "follow the" xxxiii, 23, 46, 49, 54, 62; literature xxvii–i, xxxi, 41, 66,

206 · Subject Index

(reification) xxviii–x, 14; theory 21; upholding both poles of dilemma 157
evidence-based hypothesis *see* evidence-based practice in psychology
evidence-based practice in psychology (EBPP) xiv, xxix–xxxi, 45, 174–5; American Psychological Association xviii–ix; clinical expertise 41; delivery of 42, 44, 52, 176; evidence-based hypothesis xvii, xxix, 23, 54; flow 180, Good Therapy 172
evolution xix, 19; client development as 49, 51, 54; evolutionary psychology 47–8, 174; of theory 4, 6, 22
experiential training 126–8
extending Self *see* Therapist-Self

family systems theory xxiii, 13, 79–80
feedback loop 42
Feeling-Sensing Style [G—Style, Feeling-Sensing] 9; clinician's horizontal development 123, 127, 143, 146, (adroitness) 175–6; Default Mode Network 20, 90, 175; definition 19–21; Dialectic-Systemic 35, 45, 163, (eclipse of D-S) 168–9; *vs.* Doing 91, 97–8, 110, 127, 146, 173, (eclipse of Doing) 165; eclipse 123, 138, 149–4, 159, (anxious client) 128, (depressed client) 132, (educator's) 154, (educator's Style-shift to) 134; evidence 163; over-reliance on 10; "process-sensitive" 43, 45; projective identification 171; psychotherapy 54
feminist therapy 13, 93
first-order change *see* change, first-order
flow [G] 109, 121–2; definition 178–80; regaining 181
Focusing 11, 97
Formal Style [G—Style, Formal] 11–14; client assessment 69–70, 88, 154–5, (adoption of interventions) 12–14; client development 17–18, (Alexei) 159; Dialectic-Systemic 17–19, 52; Doing Style 19–20, 45, 90, 110, 121, (client) 57–8, 60, 102, (counseling) 89, (education) 147, (less adroit clinician) 143; empathy 16–17, 28, 125, 155; evaluation *vs.* feeling 147; Ivey Instrument 145–7; Ruler 93; Style-shift from (Alexei) 158–9, (Chantal) 60–4; Style-shift to 13; therapeutic communication 12–13, 93; vertical development 138

Freud, Sigmund 3–4, 69, 127; definition of mental health 10; disavowal 57; empathy 29–30; "epistemological" *vs.* "hermeneutic" 30; "first force" 10; free association 11; Freudian theory 4, 37; Good Therapy 6, 47; id 19; Love, Work and Play 10, 37; Oedipal conflict 9; projection 171; *Sichhineinversetzen* 20, 30, 47, 97

Gestalt Therapy 11–12, 97, (*Gestalten*) 21, 25, 53, 77
Ghislaine, case of 31–4, 105–6; collusion 106; confirming not condoning 31–2; countertransference 31, 105; diagnosis 32; dilemma 31; *Integrity vs. Despair* 32
goals-based [G]: CBT xiv, xxvi–i, (pioneers) xvii; client not profiting from 65–6, (Kevin) 72–3; clinician preference xxix, 19, 45, 61, (emotional intelligence) 51; definition xiv; dialectic between goals and process xvi–i, xx, xxiv, 22, 52–3, 88–90, 97, 138–9, 180; Doing Style 20, 111, 173; interventions *xiv*, xvi, (anxious client) 128, (depressed client) 132; models *xvi*; relapse prevention 53; research evidence xxxvi; theoretical stance xii; timing and preparation for 14, (educator's) 138; transference and xxv
goals–process decision tree 186; alcoholic client 53–4; Chantal 61; Jimmy 88–9; Kevin 26, 72–4; signal of the dialectic 66, 67, 174–6
Gonzalo, case of 98–107, 121; clinician's dilemma 101; first-order change 102; presenting narrative 100; preverbal wounding 104–5; transference 99
Good Therapist [G]: adroitness xi–xxii; Archetype 111; behaviors 174; conceptualization 72, (outcome implications) 9; congruence 36; countertransference management 41; definition 111–13, 187; dialectic between goals and process 107, 110; Dialectic-Systemic 176; *Einfühlungsvermögen* 66, 126; empathizing 39; Feeling-Sensing Style 43; holding position of stakeholders 79; humility 86, 122; interrupting 60; Ivey Instrument 146; Magician 92, 176; Mirroring 34; nondefensiveness 167; *Sichhineinversetzen* 47; transition to 91, 111, 129, (letting go) 144

Good Therapy [G]: Archetype xxiii, xxix–xxxi, 111, 177, (Doing *and* Feeling-Sensing) 174, 176, (essential therapist qualities) 6, (evidence-based practice) 172, (languaging) 98, (synthesizing goals and process) 7, (theory) 4; definition of xxi, 10–11, (clinician development) 187, (DCT) 36, (outcome examples) 177; developmental hypothesis 10; dialectic between goals and process 42, 110, 177; intentionality 160, (case conceptualization group) 181–3, (flow) 178–9; Mirroring 34; obstacles 23 (obstructive countertransference) 25; pain and 98; vulnerability 54

hidden emotion or problem xvii, 61, 97; depressed client 133; Kevin 71
humanistic theory 10, 37, 79, 151; Freud 10; unconditional positive regard 10
humility 39, 86–7, 91, 160; cultural 112

I can't stand the client's negativity problem: anxious client 135–7; *see also* Elena
I don't know where to go from here problem: anxious client 128–31
incongruence *see* Rogerian theory
intentionality [G] xxviii–x; clinician's transition 120–1; definition 53–4, 121–2, 177–8, (client-centeredness) 179; Dialectic-Systemic 21–2 (educator's Style-shift to) 129, 132, 134; eclipse of Feeling-Sensing 138; educator's 160; *Einfühlungsvermögen* 111; emotional intelligence 93; Empathy 143; Gonzalo 101–3, 107; guided discovery 107; Magician 93; maintaining 181–3; predictability 14, 126; *vs.* reification 123; returning client to dilemma 109, 177; therapist contributions xxxv
Ivey Instrument 19, 145–7, 189–94

Jennifer, case of: anonymously—xxvi–ii, xxix–xxxii, ("romance-seeking, shallow") xxxi, 16; case conceptualization group 181–3
Jimmy, case of 86–91, 93; goals–process decision tree 88–90; hypothesis and treatment plan 87–9; Mirroring not condoning 90; parent consultation 86–7; Ruler 93
Joty, case of: anonymously—("deeply religious") 49–51; confirming self 50; dilemma 50, (daughter's) 177; reluctance to let go 51
Jung, C. collective unconscious xxiii, 48; Archetypes 91–7; CBT and 97

Kevin, case of 24–7, 71–5; corrective emotional experience 40; DCT assessment 69; dilemma 75; goal of first session 27; goals–process decision tree 26, 72–4, (hidden problem) 71; reification of problem 56–9; Style-shift to Sensorimotor 39–40; suicide assessment 25

Love, Work and Play 10, 37, 52, 69, 131
Lover 96; Ivey Instrument 146; Magician 94, (Gonzalo) 99–104; Sensorimotor 97; shadow 109–10, (Alexei) 156, (Norah) 165–6; therapeutic communication 92, 94, 96–7; Warrior 96

Magician 91–3; confrontation 174; Dialectic-Systemic 92–3, 127; eclipsed (Alexei) 155–6, (Norah) 165–9; flow 179; Ghislaine 106; Ivey Instrument 146; Lover 94, (Gonzalo) 99–104; Ruler 93, 94, 95, 96; shadow 109–0, (Alexei) 156, (Norah) 165; therapeutic communication 92, 93, 94, 95, 96; Warrior 94, 95, (vignette 94–5)
main feeling [G] 70, (dilemma) 78, 141; change 78, 142; cognitive restructuring 142; definition 141; "dwelling in" 76–7, 98, 141–2, (countertransference to) 141, (Gonzalo) 100–4; flow 180; integration and message of 142
maladroit(ness): case conceptualization xxiv–xxxi; Chantal 66; characterological differences 187; Kevin 72–3; neediness 180; obstructive countertransference 25; *see also* adroit(ness)
Mirroring [G] 14, 26, (parental) 35; affective *vs.* explicit 34, 51; Archetype 32; assessment 65, (deficits) 33, 37, 77, (Gonzalo) 104–5 (Jimmy) 88–9; Chantal 76; confirming self 34, 47; definition 32–4; demands on clinician 182; educator's 148, (Alexei) 154, (depressed client) 132; emotional intelligence 51; evolutionary hypothesis 48; Feeling-Sensing Style 159; Gonzalo 103–7; intersubjective 46, 90, 106; Kohutian 33; letting go 77; lifelong need 155, 177; not condoning 37, 90, 154,

167; proper *vs.* improper 33–4, 46–7, (authenticity) 36, (dialectic between goals and process) 52, 54, (false self) 80; self-esteem 63; self-structure 33–4, 62, 139; vignette 108–9; withholding 154–5, 159
multicultural counseling and therapy 13

narrative therapy 14, 49, 150; Chantal 77
network therapy 93, 94
neuroscience xv–i, xix; DCT 18–19; empathy 29; neurobiology 156–0; neuroinformatics xv, 21; neuropsychology 8
nondefensiveness 39–41, 87, 96; Cai 167; Gonzalo 104
Norah, case of 164–70, 174; confabulating 165; dilemma 168; disavowal 165–6; Sensorimotor 164; *see also* Cai

object relations theory 9
Oedipal conflict 9

parallel process: Alexei 154–60; depressed client 134, 136–7
Personality Style [G—Style, Personality]: assessment 65, (Gonzalo) 99, (pathology) 69–70; change 64; conceptualization 61–2; primary defense 15–16, 26, 57, (main feeling) 78; trainee's 125, 141, 149, (Elena) 151
Platonic Form [G] xxiii, 22
pole [G]: continuum xv; dilemma 142, (Alexei) 154–9, 177, (countertransference group) 166, (Elena) 179; intentionality 101; shadow archetype 99, 109–10, 166
positron emission topography scans 18
process-based [G] xii, xiv; assessment 65; definition xiv–v; dialectic between goals and process xvi–iii, xx, xxiv, 15, 22, 53, 88, 138, 180, (clinician preference) xxix, 19, 45–6; Feeling-Sensing Style 111, 173; interventions *xiv;* models *xvi; see also* hidden emotion or problem; transference
projective identification [G]: Alexei 153, 163; anxious client 128, 130–1, 136; assessment tool 66, 138, 163; Chantal 66, 80; definition 25–6; depressed client 133–4; evidence 62, 141–2, 174; Ghislaine 31; Gonzalo 98, 100, 105; Kevin 27, 73–4; key to psychotherapy 25, 171–2, 179–80; nonverbal communication 142, 171, ("cold-hearted") 153–4, 163, ("rushed past") 71, 74, 153, 167, (somatic) 141; Norah 167; returning the projection 178; supervision/consultation 25, (Alexei) 163, (Norah) 168; vignette 94–5
psychoanalytic theory xii, xxv, xxx, 7, 21; pendulum swing to CBT 97–8
psychodynamic theory xxi–ii; adherence flexibility xviii; contemporary xxiii, xxv; discourse of supersession 5, 22; "more goals-based" intervention as vehicle for 53
psychotherapy and counseling, difference between 51

reality therapy 21
reification [G]: benefits of xxviii, 6; case conceptualization xxxii, 141, (anxious client) 128, 137, (Chantal) 66, (Kevin) 72, (Norah) 165; client disavowal 56–8, 60, 128; clinician avoidance of 108–9, (Dialectical-Systemic) 169, 176; definition xxvii; Doing Style 12, 45, 123, 137–8, 141, (mediated by Sensorimotor) 165; *vs.* evidence-based practice xxix–xxx, 27; goals and evidence xxviii–ix; risks of xxviii, 80, 103, 107–8, (in assessment) 123, (working harder than the client) 178
rider and elephant 8–9; clinician theoretical preference 8; confabulation 9, 18, (Cai) 165, 169; dialectic between goals and process 146, 173, 175; disavowal 58, 59; great debate 22; harmony 8; neuroscience and 19; signal of the dialectic 67; Therapist-Self 109–10, (eclipse of Doing) 146, (eclipse of Feeling-Sensing) 123
Rogerian theory 7, 9, 30; congruence 5–6, (Chantal) 76, (clinician at a loss) 122, (definition) 35–6, 158, (developmental goal) 36–7, 52, (Feeling-Sensing Style) 80, 113, 158–9, (Ghislaine) 31, (Jimmy) 87, (Kevin) 36, 74, (Mirroring) 33, 35–6, 46, 80, (modeling) 122; Default Mode Network 9; Empathy 5–6, 28–30, 36, (case hypothesis) 68, 70, 88, (curtailment in) 138, (*Einfühlungsvermögen*) 126, (emotional intelligence) 125, (Feeling-Sensing Style) 143, (physiological process) 31, (primary instrument) 28, 129; Formal Style 93; goal of 28; guided discovery 139, (silence) 139; incongruence 36–7, (assessment) 65, (Chantal) 60,

(client pathology) 36, (clinician's) 113, 159–60, 182, (confronting—Alexei) 163, (confronting—Norah) 167, (disavowal) 58, 69, (essential feature in dialectic) 113, (Mirroring and 14), (in the transference) 132; unconditional positive regard 5, 33, (client as agent) 37–8, 162, (client confrontation) 163, (client developmental trajectory) 110, (compromised—Alexei 163), (compromised—Norah 168), (humanistic theory) 10

Rosen method bodywork 97

Ruler (or King, Queen, Sovereign) 93; "creating environment" 93; Doing 147; eclipsed—Cai 165; Formal 93; Ivey Instrument 146; Magician 93; shadow 109–0, (educator) 166; therapeutic communication 92, 93, 94, 95, 96, 97, 107; Warrior 97, 165, (Gonzalo) 98–9

Satirian theory xxxiv–v; client base 79–80; clinician self-development xxxv; developmental *vs.* problem-solving 38, 49, 71, (intentionality) 177–9; "internal manifestations" 24–5, 27, 53

school-based family counseling and therapy 6, 79–80; assessment 89; Dialectic-Systemic 13, 93; Magician 92; Mirroring not condoning 79; parent consultation 86–7; Ruler 93; Warrior 94; *see also* Cai, trainee therapist; *Jimmy,* case of; *Norah,* case of

second-order change *see* change, second-order

self-esteem [G]: goal of Mirroring 63, 129; incongruent attempts to build (anxious client) 135–7, (Chantal) 80, (Jennifer) 181–2; "true" 80, 127

self psychology: corrective emotional experience 35, 112, (Chantal) 62, 77–8, (goal of Mirroring) 62, (Gonzalo) 104, 107, (Kevin) 40, (self disorders) 41, (trainee's) 148; Kohut xxiii; theory xvii; transference xxv, 35; *see also* Mirroring; self-esteem; self-structure

self-structure [G]: assessing 46, 65; Chantal 63; "coping skills" 21; goal of Mirroring xvii, 33, 137, ("bigger") 62, (counseling *vs.* therapy) 52; Gonzalo 104; Jimmy 90; second-order change 64; vignette 108–9

Sensorimotor Style [G—Style, Sensorimotor] 11–12; assessment—anxious client 128, (Alexei) 154–5, (Chantal) 61–2, (depressed client) 131, (Jimmy) 88–90, (Kevin) 27, 69; avoiding 27, 69; Cai 164–5, 168; client development (Norah) 174; clinician development 137–8, 143, 147–8, 172; clinician extension of Self 97; Default Mode Network 20, 90; developmental sequence 18, 100, (Chantal) 77, (Jimmy) 90; disavowal 58, (clinician) 122; Feeling-Sensing Style 19–20, 45, 90, 127, (access to Dialectic-Systemic 19–20); Ghislaine 32; horizontal development 17–18, (Chantal) 63–4; Ivey Instrument 145–7; Lover 97; main feeling 141; primacy of 14–15, 17, 100–1; shadow archetypes 110; Style-shift to 11–12, 17, (Gonzalo) 100, 106, (Kevin) 39–40; therapeutic communication 11, 97; Titchenerian empathy 27–8; transition 121, 123

Sichhineinversetzen [G] 20, 30; clinician extension of Self 97; Ghislaine 31; Gonzalo 101, 105; psychotherapy and 52

signal of the dialectic 67, 121, 174–5, 176; case examples—alcoholic client 53, Chantal 61, 66, Ghislaine 106, Kevin 73; *see also* goals–process decision tree

solution-focused therapy 93

somatic therapy 97

Style-shift *see* Concrete Style; Dialectic-Systemic Style; Feeling-Sensing Style; Formal Style; Sensorimotor Style

systems theory 79–80, 94; change, first- and second-order 64; correlated with Dialectic-Systemic 13, 93; Haley xxxiv; outcome management 41–2; Satir xxxiv; treatment planning 88

Task Positive Brain [G]: *vs.* Default Mode Network xvi, xxi–ii, xxxii, xxxvi, 23, (suppressing) xxviii; dialectic between goals and process 23, 41, 91, 123, 143, 146, 168; Doing Style 20, 45, 90; goals xxxi, 8; over-reliance 127; "rider" 8 (confabulation) 66; under-reliance 9

theory: best explanation 175; clinician preference xvi, xxvi, (rider and elephant) 8; definition 3; dialectic between goals and process *xiv, xvi,* xviii, (theory antagonism) 5; Doing *and* Feeling-Sensing 9, 172, 173–4, (cognitive-behavioral therapy) 176; evolution of 3–4, 7, (aggregation) 4–7, 21–2, 127, (supersession) 4–5; Good Therapy Archetype 7, 98, (CBT) 176; implementation xi, 46, 125; languaging

5–7; need xxxvi; neuroscience 18–20, 160; obstructive countertransference and 5, 54; phenomenological approach xxi, ("good") 5, 23, 174, ("theory on") xxi, 34, 35; proliferation xix, (metatheory xix); "therapist contributions" xiii, 24; *vs.* therapy 23; vehicle 7; work-in-progress 22, 95

therapist drift xviii, 42; definition 175–6; Lover and Magician 94; reframed 45, 53–4, (clinician horizontal development) 176–7, (vulnerable self) 54

Therapist-Self: building xxi, 46, 51, 86, ("bigger") 80, 91, (educator's "caring confrontation") 149, (transition) 124, 143; cardinal Archetypes 91–7, 110, (shadows) 109; clinician preparation xx, 22–3, 111, (*vs.* client pathology) xxii, (managing dialectic between goals and process) xxxvi, 23, (Satirian therapists) xxv, (social work training) xxxv; congruence 36; Dialectic-Systemic Style 126–7; Doing Style *and* Feeling-Sensing Style 20, 43, 45, (cardinal Aspects) 91, 110, 127, 149, (dialectic) 91, (extending Self) 51–2; *Einfühlungsvermögen* 29, 143; *vs.* everyday self 36, 97; extending Self xxiv, 35, 40, 44, 81, (counseling-and-therapy) 54, (educator) 137, 148, (Gonzalo) 105, 121, (Good Therapy) 182, (Kevin) 39–40, (Lover) 96–7, (necessity to feel) 48, (outcome) 46–7, 66–7, (preferring *Doing*) 51, (prerequisites) 111, (true caring) 178; Ivey Instrument 146; operationalizing 29, 30, 31, 44–5, 47–8, 54, 67, (emotional intelligence) 125; primary instrument xxi, 41; properties xiii, 113, 125; stress and 159; unconditional positive regard 33; variables 67, 80; vulnerability 54, 81; work-in-progress 111–12, 113; *see also* Lover; Magician; Ruler; Warrior

TPB *see* Task Positive Brain

transference xxv; assessment 65–6, 69, 76, (Chantal) 60–1, (first order change) 64, (second order change) 65; bad mother—Gonzalo 99, (reenactment) 103, 105, 107; compliant 68; definition 34–5; dilemma 78; dissatisfied—depressed client 132; erotic 112; fragile mother—Chantal 63–4, (dismantling) 77; Gestalt Therapy 21; interpreting 35, (by client—Ghislaine) 106, (depressed client) 132, (empathic break) 160, (Gonzalo) 98–9, (resistance) 141; Mirror 33; working in the xiv–xv, 35, (clinician reluctance) 137–8, (Kevin) 26, 36, 39–40, 76, (nondefensiveness) 41; *see also* self psychology, corrective emotional experience

transference focused psychotherapy 40

transference work *see* transference, working in the

transition theory 70–1; change *vs.* transition 70, (Alexei) 153; completing 65; elective 71, (Elena) 150–1; letting go 57, (Chantal) 75–7, neutral zone 71, 79, (Kevin) 75, (preparatory mourning) 76–7; (reluctance—Joty) 51

transition to clinician 117–24, 129; completing 180; Doing *and* Feeling-Sensing 122–3; flow 180; intentionality 121; letting go—author 119; neutral zone 120, (disenchantment, disengagement, disidentification, disorientation) 120–2; second-order change 123–4

transpersonal theory *see* Archetype; collective unconscious

treatment plan, DCT case hypothesis and xx, 14, 16–17, 22, 68–70; alcoholic client 53; anxious client 128–31; Chantal 60–3; client preparedness for intervention 14–15, (disengagement) 133; couple 155; dilemma 75, 177, (alliance) 77–8); Empathy 46; first pivotal point 46; goal 16, (reflective awareness) 19; Gonzalo 101, 121; Jimmy 87–90; Personality Style 69; Ruler 93; second pivotal point 75; transference xxv; trauma 92; *see also* developmental trajectory

Verleugnen 57–8; *see also* disavowal

Warrior 93–6, 156; Concrete 96; Doing 147; eclipsed (Norah) 165; Ivey Instrument 146; Lover 96; Magician 94, 95, (vignette 94–5); Ruler 97, 165, (Gonzalo) 98–9; shadow 109–0, (Alexei) 156, (educator) 166, (trainee) 166; therapeutic communication 96–7, vignette 95

Wellness theory: Alexei 149–52; neurobiology 156–7; over-reliance on 153–4, 165; Warrior 156